July 21, 1943: How shall I begin to record the things that occupied me during the last three and a half years? Why do I begin on a day that brings me particular disappointments because I have received no news about my son, who left me two days ago to go to a different place in Holland? Why begin today, when worries plague me, about my father-in-law, who now most likely will be sent to a death camp, because they want to annoy, deport, and murder not him, but simply all Jews?

ERWIN GEISMAR

The endpapers in this book replicate the paper liner from the bottom drawer of a secretary desk where the De Zoete-Geismar family Holocaust papers were found—subsequently referred to as the Holocaust drawer.

One of the many items discovered in the drawer was Erwin Geismar's memoir (overleaf), written in hiding shortly before he was murdered in Auschwitz and sixty-four years before it was found.

Narrators

Chaim de Zoete

Fifi de Zoete

Mirjam de Zoete-Geismar

Judith de Zoete-Cohen

Hadassah de Zoete-Mandel

Nathan Cohen

Erwin Geismar

David Geismar

Zigi Mandel

Historical contributions

Robert Jan van Pelt

Jennifer Magee

Translations from Dutch

Marjolijn de Jager

Judith de Zoete-Cohen

Translations from German

Robert Bjornson

Invisible Years A Family's Collected Account of Separation and Survival during the Holocaust in the Netherlands Daphne Geismar

Foreword by Robert Jan van Pelt

David R. Godine, Publisher
Boston
1970 | 50 YEARS | 2020

Contents

Narrators

Chaim and Fifi de Zoete with their daughters

Hadassah, Mirjam, and Judith de Zoete

Nathan Cohen

David Geismar with his grandfather Max

Erwin Geismar with his wife, Grete

When I first read a draft of Daphne Geismar's *Invisible Years*, I was captivated by the beautiful design for the book and the remarkable integrity of content and form. And from the moment that I opened the manuscript, I recognized a shared task. "All that your ancestors bequeathed to you, / To make it really yours, earn it anew," as Faust reminds himself at the beginning of Goethe's eponymous drama. Once her mother, Mirjam, opened the "Holocaust Drawer," Daphne did not simply accept her family's wartime legacy but began the work of making it her own—the result of which is the book that you hold in your hands. A visit to Auschwitz, made thirty years ago to trace the final journey of my great-uncle Robert Hanf, put me under a similar obligation, and like Daphne, I have tried to earn the legacy handed to me by researching and writing the history of Auschwitz and the Holocaust, and through my engagement in the battle against Holocaust denial.

The written and oral testimonies brought together in this book return me to a world that is close to me. Born, raised, and educated in the Netherlands, I know the places mentioned here. The outlook, the personalities, and the experiences of the De Zoete, Cohen, and Geismar families remind me of my own grandparents, great-uncles and great-aunts, parents, uncles, aunts, and their friends, all of whom lived in the Netherlands during the German occupation, and many of whom—including my mother—experienced a larger or smaller part of the fate of Daphne's extended family. As to the particular voice of the testimonies: even in translation they preserve a certain Dutch tone that touches my heart.

When, as a student at the University of Leiden, I began grappling with my own family's legacy, I recognized the distinct atmospheres that characterized the daily lives and outlook of Netherlandish Jews and their non-Jewish neighbors. I also realized the enormous difference between the Jewish experience in my native country and that in Eastern Europe. Yet, until then, I knew little of the profound differences between the Jewish world in the Netherlands and that of Jews in Germany, France, Great Britain, or the United States. Understanding the unique position of the Jews within the Netherlands compared to other countries of the West—and the singular perspective that came with this—helps contextualize the experiences of the De Zoete, Cohen, and Geismar families recorded in this book.

———

Until 1940, the year that the German Wehrmacht (armed forces) conquered my native country, the Netherlands seemed out of pace with its neighbors Germany, France, Belgium, and Great Britain. During the nineteenth and early twentieth centuries, while other Western European countries industrialized and modernized, each in its own way, time stagnated in the Netherlands. Then, as in the seventeenth century, remembered as the Golden Age, the Dutch economy was based on trade and a strong agricultural sector. It also depended on the wealth generated by a vast colonial empire that centered on the Dutch East Indies (since 1949, Indonesia). The Indies not only added to the Dutch bottom line but also shaped the Dutch imagination, giving a romantic, orientalist edge to an otherwise phlegmatic spirit.

Between 1914 and 1918, Europe was engulfed in total war that triggered great social changes. The Netherlands, however, remained neutral, and there was no pressure to change the conservative perspective and practices that defined Dutch life.

In the early 1930s, the Great Depression hit Europe. At that time the Netherlands was led by the orthodox Calvinist politician Hendrikus Colijn, whose worldview had been shaped not only by his horror of social change but also by his sixteen-year service as a senior military officer and colonial administrator in the Dutch East Indies. As prime minister, Colijn adopted a policy of austerity. While other governments increased the money supply to encourage investment in the economy and stimulated exports by devaluing their currency, Colijn refused to sever the Dutch guilder from the gold standard until 1936. The guilder rapidly increased in value, and Dutch exports collapsed. The small internal market could not compensate for the loss of foreign markets, particularly because the government's austerity policy had lowered wages and reduced unemployment benefits, limiting Dutch buying power. As a result, the Dutch economy went into a tail-spin, causing poverty and a general mood of despondency that lasted until the late 1930s.

Unlike in Germany or France, in the Netherlands the Great Depression did not cause a general rise in antisemitism. As an explanation for social or economic adversity, the ogre-like Jew of the antisemitic imagination had little currency in the Netherlands, and even less among Calvinists like Colijn. When, in the early seventeenth century, Jews arrived in Amsterdam from Spanish-ruled Portugal, they were welcomed with sympathy and a sense of solidarity. The Dutch had started a rebellion against Philip II, king of Spain and lord of the Netherlands, in 1568, and a peace treaty would not be concluded until 1648. Creating a clear parallel between their fate and that of the Jewish Maccabees who had resisted foreign rule more than seventeen hundred years earlier, the Dutch allegorically described their uprising as a second Maccabean revolt. In addition, John Calvin, whose theology shaped Dutch Protestantism, had broken away from centuries of Christian disregard for the Old Testament. He appreciated the continued importance of the Hebrew commandments and insisted on the necessity of a thorough understanding of the biblical sources. Following the direction set by Calvin, Dutch theologians and intellectuals valued the presence of rabbis whose knowledge of Hebrew allowed their Christian interlocutors to understand the Old Testament more profoundly, and thus to become better Christians. Significantly, Calvinist theologians were also prepared to acknowledge continuity between the Old Testament and the Talmud—a body of Jewish writings that was anathema to Roman Catholics. As a result, the members of the so-called Hebrew Nation coming from Portugal and, from the mid-seventeenth century onward, Germany and Poland were welcome.

Most Jews settled in Amsterdam, and between 1650 and 1800 Amsterdam became the Jerusalem of the West—and not only because of the rights Jews enjoyed. More than one in ten of the city's 200,000 inhabitants were Jewish, and Amsterdam had the largest and most visible Jewish community in the world (by comparison, in 1800 London counted 20,000 Jews; Lwów—now Lviv, Ukraine—12,000; and Warsaw 9,000).

In the nineteenth century, Dutch governments encouraged the integration of Jews in the Dutch state and Dutch society by forcing Jewish children to attend Dutch public schools, which led to the rapid decline of Portuguese and Yiddish as Jewish communal languages. The result of these reforms was a Jewish community that was largely emancipated within Dutch society but that quickly became isolated from, and irrelevant to, the more vibrant Jewish communities in Eastern Europe. While a new form of antisemitism became a major ingredient in French politics and inspired numerous German intellectuals, non-Jewish Netherlanders remained largely immune to it. They prided themselves on a moderate bourgeois, commonsense approach to the problems of life; blaming the Jews for the ills of modernity did not make any sense to them. Because industrialization was limited, the Dutch experienced little social change, and no social group perceived a rapid decline in its fortunes—an apprehension that fueled antisemitism in France and elsewhere. And the immigration of mostly German Jews into the Netherlands, including my great-grandparents Josef Hanf and Laura Romberg in the 1890s and Daphne's grandfather Erwin Geismar in the 1920s, was too small in scope to become a political or social issue.

This did not mean that Dutch society was without anti-Jewish prejudice. But Dutch Calvinists also had strong prejudices against Roman Catholics and vice versa, and Christians had strong prejudices against Socialists and liberals. Dutch society was marked by a plurality of distinct groups or social pillars, the largest of which, the Roman Catholics—who were primarily concentrated in the south of the country—counted only 30 percent of the population. Each pillar was characterized by its own religious and political ideas, which were also reflected in the economic, social, and cultural choices people made. In sports and leisure activities, in literature and the arts, in their choice of newspapers and radio broadcasters, individuals organized themselves according to the preferences of the pillar with which they identified. These power blocs were represented in parliament by their own political parties and in the economy and society by their own professional organizations, trade unions, and school systems. The elites of the pillars collaborated with one another—otherwise the country would have been ungovernable. But Roman Catholic priests and Protestant ministers did not hesitate to use the pulpit to incite the faithful to limit their social relations to others within their own groups, creating echo chambers that reinforced feelings of mistrust toward members of the other pillars. Thus, the true constitution of the Netherlands was a contract of mutual indifference between the major religious and political groups. By and large, the prejudice against Jewish Netherlanders was perhaps somewhat stronger in degree, but not different in kind, from the prejudices among the pillars.

In 1933, there were 115,000 self-identified Jewish Netherlanders. They composed 1.5 percent of the population and, as such, they were too small in number to constitute a social pillar. One subgroup among them, the diamond workers, formed a well-organized trade union that became the avant-garde of the workers' movement in the Netherlands. But the diamond workers did not have any influence in the official Jewish community, which was led by men who had no opportunity to engage in the intensely political negotiations that shaped the lives of the elites who ran the pillars. Thus, the Dutch Jewish establishment was avowedly apolitical, proud of its willingness to engage in beneficent work (it is safe to say that in the 1920s and 1930s it saw the primary meaning of Judaism to be in an ethic of charity), but without experience in, or an understanding of, political friction, political alliance, and political compromise. Until 1940 this did not matter much. The Netherlands was a provincial, stable, and above all quiet country in which major social issues seemed settled.

Then, in May 1940, the twentieth century invaded the corner of the world where the De Zoete, Cohen, and Geismar families—and my own Hanf family—had been so much at home.

Opening the Holocaust Drawer

Daphne Geismar

Carefully, I hold the edge of the opaque green curtain against the wall and use my finger to create a small crack, only to grow rigid with fear. On the podium below me, between the pews of the elders and deacons, at a distance of perhaps four meters, there are two Grüne Polizei walking around, searching everything. And then comes the stage of paralysis, the sense that all is lost.

My grandfather's words fill my head as I stand alone in the organ loft of the Breeplein Church in Rotterdam, pulling back the heavy curtain to look down into the nave where my grandfather saw the German police.

I wonder whether there's any point in climbing back into the hiding place. Now the super-heavy ladder still has to be raised. One slip and that's the end, for the Germans are already below me in the foyer, from which we are separated by thin slats of wood; they're coming up the stone staircase to the little storage space. I close the trapdoor.
CHAIM

I let the curtain fall and climb the ladder to see the hiding place where my grandparents Chaim and Fifi de Zoete survived the Holocaust. Below a steeply pitched roof, the attic's brick and cement walls are windowless, and there is no floor—only joists; one must step from beam to beam to avoid falling through the ceiling below. I wonder what they whispered during those long months, frigid in winter and suffocating in summer. I imagine how they worried for their eleven-, ten-, and nine-year-old daughters, Mirjam (my mother), Judith, and Hadassah, who were hidden with other families, separately, to increase their chances of survival—their long braids cut and Jewish Stars removed.

———

That moment in the church sparked a decade of research and the book you now hold. For the congregation's seventy-fifth anniversary, the Breeplein Church had invited descendants of the two Jewish families who had been hidden in the church attic during the Holocaust to meet the later generations of the Dutch families who had cared for them. They had gone to great lengths to locate us—and succeeded, thanks to an Israeli newspaper advertisement and the sharp eyes of my aunt Judith's friend. In November 2006, eleven of Chaim and Fifi's relatives traveled to Rotterdam to express our gratitude: my mother, Mirjam, from the United States; her sister Judith, from Israel; and their children and grandchildren. (Hadassah, the youngest De Zoete sister, could not make the trip.) It was the beginning of a deep and emotional dive into my family's wartime experience in the Netherlands.

The day we arrived, I stepped into the church and found it cavernous, plain, beautiful, and much larger than I had imagined. Over tea and cake, we met the children and grandchildren of Chaim and Fifi's caregivers, the Reverend Gerrit Brillenburg Wurth and his wife, Gerda, and the sexton Jacobus de Mars and his wife, Annigje. I took in a display of remnants from the hiding place: a chocolate wrapper, tins, a hair clip, and a book cover. And I stood with my teenage daughter in the church courtyard, where a resistance worker had brought my aunt

Hadassah to play in 1943 so that Chaim and Fifi, unable to reveal themselves, could see her alive and well from their hiding place.

During the formal ceremony that afternoon, my cousin Sharon thanked the Brillenburg Wurth and De Mars families for "the nobleness of spirit with which you gave your help to others without expecting anything in return." She spoke of her hope against the return of evil times but added, "If evil does return, we will know from whom to take an example." The ceremony ended with a compilation of Jewish folk songs and the Israeli national anthem, played on the organ. My grandparents could not have imagined, hiding silently in the attic, that sixty years later their children, grandchildren, and great-grandchildren would sit below in the pews, listening to the resonant sounds of a Jewish culture that was, for them, a death sentence.

On our last night in the Netherlands, Reverend Brillenburg Wurth's grandchildren invited us to dinner at their home. Mirjam and Judith told us more about the particulars of their experiences as *onderduikers* (people in hiding) and shared stories of other family members hidden throughout the Netherlands: Chaim and Fifi, Hadassah, David Geismar (Mirjam's future husband and my father), and Nathan Cohen (Judith's future husband). We observed that no person had the complete story because secrecy had been paramount. Everyone knew only his or her own experience—family members were unaware of related details, left out parts too painful to tell, or lost memories over time. More than sixty did not survive to share their own accounts. In Rotterdam, I understood that the stories I thought I knew were broader and more interconnected than I had realized—and that the story-holders were aging. At dinner that night with the Brillenburg Wurths, my relatives and I made plans to piece together the history of our families during the German occupation of the Netherlands.

Back home in Israel and the United States, respectively, Sharon and I reached out to our mothers. In Connecticut, Mirjam surprised me by leading me to an antique desk and sliding open a bottom drawer packed with journals and papers. Inside this beautifully lined drawer (see endpapers), she had put everything Holocaust related. When I called Sharon in Israel to tell her the news, she exclaimed that, amazingly, Judith had a Holocaust drawer too. The quantity of material that survived in these drawers, until then unknown to us, is remarkable. We found our grandparents' personal and official documents, created during the occupation and shortly after, and our parents', aunts', and uncles' accounts and interviews, in which they reflected back on their experiences over fifty years later. We discovered Judith's Jewish Star (see pp. 78–79), Chaim's and Fifi's journals and letters, and—a miracle—a forty-nine-page memoir written by my paternal grandfather, Erwin Geismar (see pp. 1, 166–67). He began writing on July 21, 1943, in the Amsterdam apartment where he was hidden, two days after he had sent his thirteen-year-old son, David (my father), to a safer address. Writing in his native German, Erwin meticulously documented the occupation, his work for the Jewish Council, and his distress over the fate of his family and all Jews. Six weeks later, he was captured by the Germans and, on November 19, 1943, murdered in Auschwitz. Somehow—we do not know how—his memoir was returned to the family. Decades later, when my grandmother Grete died, it went into my mother's Holocaust drawer with other Geismar family papers, concealed in an envelope from the Union Electric Company of Missouri. Neither my mother nor my father knew it lay hidden in that envelope; my father died three years before we found it.

For me, bringing Erwin's and David's voices back together is the joy and sorrow of this book.

July 21, 1943: How shall I begin to record the things that occupied me during the last three and a half years? Why do I begin just on the 21st of July? On a day that brings me particular disappointments because I have received no news about my son, who left me two days ago to go to a different place in Holland? There, he will wait for the end of this awful situation.

Why begin today, when worries plague me, worries about family and human life? Worries about my father-in-law, whom I've been able to keep in the Westerbork transit camp for three and a half months, who now most likely will be sent on the next transport day to a death camp, because they want to annoy, deport, and murder not him, but simply all Jews.
ERWIN

My father met a man on the street who had connections to the underground. This man said he could arrange for me to go to Friesland, to the northern part of Holland, to farm country. I was with my father for three weeks while this man made arrangements. I remember very distinctly when I left my father because it was the last I ever saw of him. This was the only time in my life that I saw my father emotional. He said to me, "I hope God is with you." That's the only time I ever heard him say something like that. I think he knew how this was going to end, or he had the feeling.
DAVID

As Sharon and I orchestrated the slow process of translating Dutch and German documents from our mothers' Holocaust drawers, our now-focused search turned up other treasures. My mother's friend gave her a book, *The Path of the Righteous: Gentile Rescuers of Jews during the Holocaust*. Astounded by the book's detailed section on the De Zoetes and information about the families who hid and helped them, I wrote to the author, Mordecai Paldiel, to ask where he had gotten the information. Paldiel shared that in the early 1960s, he was the first director of the Righteous Among the Nations Department at Yad Vashem, the World Holocaust Remembrance Center in Israel, which commemorates non-Jews who took great risks to save Jews during the Holocaust. My grandfather Chaim, I learned, was one of the first Jews to ask for commemorations for those who helped his family. At my request, Yad Vashem sent copies of Chaim's twelve original letters. Each is a story of its own, with specifics of hiding addresses and circumstances, and the names, occupations, and motivations of those who helped. With this information, I was able to create a map of my family members' hiding locations across the Netherlands (see pp. 110–11).

Opening the Holocaust Drawer

Piecing together the narrative was anything but linear. Each newly found and freshly translated document illuminated something we had missed or overlooked, spurring a return to Judith's and Mirjam's Holocaust drawers to sift again for answers. In my aunt Judith's drawer, Sharon found our grandmother Fifi's diary, written before the family went into hiding. Fifi wrote anxiously of Hitler and the possibility of war, of Chaim's discharge from his job because of anti-Jewish restrictions, of fleeing their house when Rotterdam was bombed, and how all this affected her daughters. Findings in Judith's drawer reminded Mirjam that she had more papers in her bedroom. There, I found Chaim's handwritten diary describing the April 1945 raid on the Breeplein Church. Although we had read Mirjam's translation of his account, Chaim's original included a careful diagram of his hiding place, showing the ladder and trapdoor to the attic and the peephole that looked out onto the nave where the Grüne Polizei searched (see p. 119). In another stack, I discovered a thin sheet of paper, written on both sides in Fifi's handwriting and dated April 23, 1943—the day that all Jews in the Netherlands living outside of Amsterdam had to report to the Vught concentration camp (see p. 94). My mother translated it on the spot:

April 23, 1943: Today is the last day that the Germans are tolerating Jews in the Netherlands. Does everyone have to go to Vught? My husband and I won't go. We're staying with Jewish friends who until today had an official stamp. Tonight we have no prospect of a roof over our heads.
FIFI

In her diary, Fifi goes on to tell of meeting Reverend Brillenburg Wurth, who arranged for them to hide with one of his parishioners. This was Chaim and Fifi's eighth hiding address. After six weeks, rumors of a neighborhood raid forced them to leave once again. Reverend Brillenburg Wurth then asked his sexton to prepare the church's attic for them; to his surprise, the sexton informed him that another Jewish family had already been hiding there for a year. They prepared a second place, on the other side of the organ pipes, for my grandparents. They stayed there—separated from their three girls—for two years.

When I found notes and a poem that Mirjam wrote in hiding to be delivered to her parents (see pp. 125–26), I learned about Riek Dekkers, a resistance worker who took it upon herself to keep Chaim and Fifi informed about their daughters—until it became too dangerous to deliver letters and information between hiding addresses.

———

Our family story was a puzzle that we were piecing together. Sharon and I entered every document into a physical and digital archive. I became a tenacious researcher undeterred by obstacles, of which there were many. To start, I don't speak Dutch. Like so many immigrants, my parents silenced their native language when they came to the United States in an effort to blend in, and my siblings and I did not grow up bilingual. My husband, Rob, translated Erwin's German text, and my mother and Judith helped with the Dutch; we also engaged professional translators, learning the hard way how subjective that process can be. My grandfather Chaim's seventy pages of postwar writing didn't sound true to his voice until they were translated a second time. I desperately wished I could read the letters, diaries, and documents written in Dutch and German that filled the drawers.

More disheartening, my mother was diagnosed with dementia, and her symptoms progressed as we worked on this project. With Hadassah's death in 2009, Judith became the only remaining De Zoete sister with a clear memory. Despite the ocean between us, I grew closer to Judith and Sharon, galvanized by the need to finish this project, which had gathered so much weight and urgency.

As our archive turned into a book, Judith revealed that she had left out a part of her story that was too difficult to talk about. She had written about it but kept it sealed in an envelope for her daughters to read after her death. When we realized that our book might be published, Judith decided that it was important to share the painful truth of her complete story with the world. She sent me her full account of the two years that she was hidden with a large family, together with a photograph of the parents. On the back of the photograph, Judith wrote, "He is the one!" (see p. 142); other handwritten notes describe the crimes committed against her by the father and his two sons.

After Hadassah's death, her husband, Zigi Mandel, gave Sharon a box full of Holocaust-related documents, including his own testimony. At age thirteen, Zigi fled Poland on foot. His odyssey took him to the Ural Mountains in Russia, a Polish orphanage in Uzbekistan, then through Afghanistan and India on his way to Palestine. Zigi's story is a counterpoint to the experiences of the rest of the family, who were all in the Netherlands during World War II. A reminder of the enormity of the battle between the Axis and Allied powers, Zigi's separate yet simultaneous experience is presented as an addendum to this volume.

Ten years after the visit to the Breeplein Church, we decided we had almost all that we needed to bring the stories together into a book. In what would be the final phase of our research, Sharon and I united to collect the missing pieces and to visit some of the locations on our map of family hiding addresses.

In April 2016, I went to Israel. We visited Hans Goldberg (now called Zvi), who had been in hiding with Mirjam, to borrow a photograph of Mirjam, Hans, and two other Jewish children who were hidden for two years at the home of Nel van Vliet. In Israel, I also met with the current director of the Righteous at Yad Vashem to ask about my grandfather's letters and, having learned Judith's full story, to ask them to remove a name from the Righteous.

Sharon and I next flew to the Netherlands. We returned to the Breeplein Church, where we exchanged information with historians and educators who consult for the church. We also rendezvoused with the granddaughter of Gerrit and Gerda Brillenburg Wurth to obtain a photograph of her grandparents (see p. 115). We visited a historical society in the Dutch town of Gendt to pick up a photograph of Theo van Dalen, a police officer dedicated to sabotaging the German war effort (see p. 149). Theo and his wife, Betsy, hid Sharon's father, Nathan, with his entire family, as well as Allied pilots whose planes had been shot down by the Germans. Nathan, twelve years old at the time, was delighted with the captive audience of pilots—he practiced English, played chess, and discussed the war news with the crew members.

In Amsterdam, we visited the apartment where Nathan was first hidden, and then the row house where Erwin was hidden and captured. Just one year earlier, in 2015—eight years after I found Erwin's memoir—we had found out who hid Erwin, where he was hidden, and how and when he was captured. On that day in 2016, we stood in front of what had been Nathan's and Erwin's hiding addresses and read excerpts from their writings.

Sharon and I now held a complete story of our family in the occupied Netherlands, who, when faced with imminent deportation and death, had split up and gone underground. In reading and rereading their letters, diaries, interviews, and documents, I understood that my relatives—the Geismar, De Zoete, and Cohen families—offered distinct perspectives on a shared story.

As I ruminated on how to construct the book, I experimented by printing out, cutting up and then sequencing all the text in the archive, arranging it so that my family members were speaking to one another. I could see that, when woven together, their separate voices formed a single narrative. It was then, while sitting at the kitchen table to read their interwoven accounts, that the heartbreaking horror of their collective experiences hit me, and I put my head on the table to weep.

———

The Holocaust survivors in my family, like many, didn't discuss their wartime experiences for fifty years. When my parents finally started telling the outlines of their stories, they spoke in classrooms—though not in mine. In fact, I first read my father's general account when our town newspaper covered his lecture at a local Kiwanis Club. However, once my parents began talking about what they had endured and witnessed, they continued to do so regularly. My parents hoped that people who listened to them would recognize that fascism's inherent hate makes large groups of persecuted individuals anonymous and expendable, stripping them of their humanity. Their wish—as well as mine—was that their stories will help people understand what it is like for each person who is treated unjustly as part of a persecuted mass.

In the end, I hope that my lines will be read by people who will see how we struggled under terrible circumstances, and that the reader will want to take up this struggle that we have fought and experienced from the front lines for the construction of a worthwhile human society.
ERWIN

Primary Source Documents and Language

More than fifty sources compose the narrative mosaic of *Invisible Years*: letters, interviews, memoirs, diaries, and reports. Below is an overview of the primary documents used in the making of this book. For a complete list of sources, see Primary Sources on pages 226–27. Unless otherwise noted, all documents and interviews originated in English, which was not the native language of any of the story's central voices.

CHAIM DE ZOETE

Excerpts of Chaim's writing were taken from a summary of his wartime experience and from twelve reports he wrote in 1963–64 to pay tribute to individuals who helped his family during the Holocaust. Chaim's narrative also draws from his account of the raid on the Breeplein Church (1947, in Dutch), and a seventy-page letter to his three daughters, Mirjam, Judith, and Hadassah, that delivers a philosophical guide for living in the aftermath of the Holocaust (1950, in Dutch).

FIFI DE ZOETE

All of Fifi's text was excerpted from her diaries (1937–63, in Dutch).

MIRJAM DE ZOETE

Mirjam's passages were taken primarily from her 1979 and 1990 written accounts, a 1980 interview by the Fortunoff Video Archive for Holocaust Testimonies at Yale University, a 1997 interview by the USC Shoah Foundation, a 2000 interview by Diane L. Wolf, and a 2007 interview by Sharon Cohen-Strauss.

JUDITH DE ZOETE

Judith's selections came from two accounts she wrote in 2004 and 2005, a 2007 interview by Sharon Cohen-Strauss, and correspondence with her daughters and niece in 2015.

HADASSAH DE ZOETE

Hadassah's source material included a 2006 speech, an account written in 2007, and an interview by Sharon Cohen-Strauss in 2007.

DAVID GEISMAR

The majority of David's passages were taken from an account he wrote in the 1990s, a 1980 interview by the Fortunoff Video Archive for Holocaust Testimonies at Yale University, and a 2000 interview by Diane L. Wolf.

ERWIN GEISMAR

The entirety of Erwin's narrative was excerpted from the memoir he wrote while in hiding (July 21–September 1943, in German).

NATHAN COHEN

Nathan wrote two accounts of his wartime experience, in 2004 and 2007; all of his passages were taken from these documents.

ZIGI MANDEL

Zigi's narrative was derived from an unpublished memoir he authored in 2007.

Supporting Narrators

Nine supporting narrators make cameo appearances in the main narrative, where they are identified by first and last name. These family members, helpers, and fellow hiders provide information that supplements the primary narrators' stories. For a complete list of sources for supporting narrators, consult the Primary Sources.

Editing

The majority of passages used to construct this book's collective narrative are excerpts from lengthier accounts. At times, this fragmentation necessitated the addition or replacement of a word to transition from one source to another. Portions of original text were sometimes cut and selections rearranged to create a linear narrative from multiple firsthand accounts; in these instances, ellipses were not used to note deletions. Similarly, pull quotes condensed from the narrative do not use ellipses to note deletions. Because English was not the native language of any of the book's narrators, and because some of the original texts were written in Dutch or German, efforts were made to retain individual intonations while editing to improve clarity; spelling and punctuation were refined. On occasion, non-English words or acronyms were retained and defined. Non-English proper nouns are not italicized so as not to place too much emphasis on these words. For the sake of consistency, post-1947 Dutch spelling is used throughout the text. Words that were underlined for emphasis in primary documents are italicized.

Dates and Estimated Figures

In certain instances, dates varied slightly between sources. Every effort was made to confirm correct dates by consulting reputable historical sources (see Further Reading, pp. 240–43). Concerning the figures presented in this book, it was common during the research process to find different published estimates relating to World War II events, especially with regard to fatalities. Although estimates presented in *Invisible Years* are taken from publications with high research standards, these numbers are only as accurate as the information on which they are based, which is often incomplete.

Decrees and Restrictions

The anti-Jewish decrees and restrictions noted in this book are not comprehensive. For a more complete list, see *Ashes in the Wind: The Destruction of Dutch Jewry*, by Jacob Presser.

History Briefs and Annotations

Historical context for the primary narratives is provided by a chronological series of history briefs (pp. 228–39) cross-referenced in the margins of the narratives. Additional marginal notes identify individuals mentioned in the narratives and clarify details.

Postcard sent to Erwin Geismar
in the Netherlands from Max
Heinsheimer, his father-in-law,
in Germany, February 2, 1934

Front: German stormtroopers and
SS parading through the Brandenburg
Gate on January 30, 1933, the day
Hitler was appointed chancellor of
Germany; captioned, "Germany,
Germany above all else!"

Extract from note on the back:
Will have to make a decision now.
MAX HEINSHEIMER

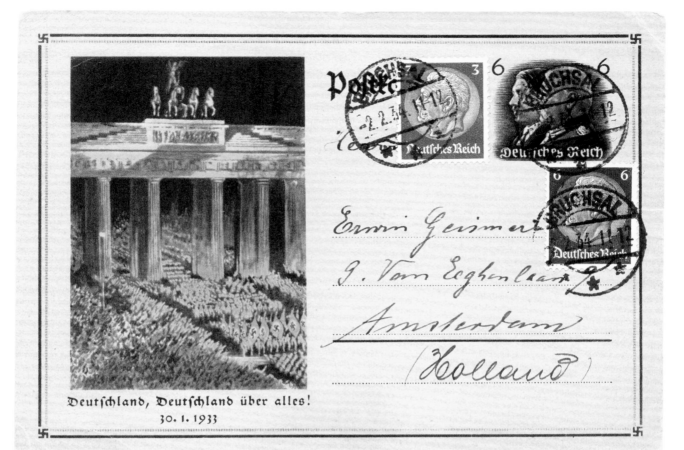

Deutschland, Deutschland über alles!
30. 1. 1933

Before

On January 30, 1933, Adolf Hitler became chancellor of the German Reich. A February 27 arson attack on the federal parliament building allowed him to claim emergency powers just before the March parliamentary elections. The elections were held in the wake of mass arrests, and the new parliament gave Hitler the power to rule by decree. Many German Jews were engaged with the left and fled the country. On April 1, the government initiated a boycott of Jewish businesses, followed by the dismissal of Jewish civil servants. As a result, Jews who had been politically inactive left the country as well. By January 1934, some 60,000 Germans, including 48,000 Jews, had found a haven abroad. The Netherlands had admitted 6,000 without requiring compliance with the usual passport regulations, but in response to rapidly rising unemployment, the Dutch government passed legislation making it impossible for refugees to obtain a wage-earning job in 1934. The leadership of the Jewish community was hesitant to challenge the government's decision, preferring to deal with the fallout by means of philanthropy alone.

In late 1938, the refugee problem in the Netherlands turned into a full-blown crisis when the German government initiated a clear policy of expulsion supported by arson, looting, and mass arrests. In the wake of Kristallnacht, or the Night of Broken Glass, over 120,000 Jews left Germany during the winter of 1938–39. Thousands, including 1,800 unaccompanied children brought by the so-called Kindertransport rescue effort, crossed into the Netherlands, many of them illegally. The Dutch government realized it could not send these refugees back to Germany. In agreement with the Dutch Jewish leadership, government officials decided to create a closed refugee camp for Jews near Westerbork, a small village in a thinly populated area close to the German border. Westerbork was to serve as a semi-extraterritorial waiting room until passage to a country of final settlement could be secured.

1921–1940

1921
Erwin Geismar leaves Freiburg, Germany, to live and work in Amsterdam.

December 18, 1928
Erwin marries Grete Heinsheimer, of Bruchsal, Germany; Grete joins Erwin in Amsterdam.

August 14, 1929
Chaim and Fifi (née Polak) de Zoete wed in The Hague, South Holland.

Chaim and Fifi move from Rotterdam to the Dutch East Indies, where Chaim is required to work as a military pharmacist in return for the military financing his education.

February 7, 1930
David Geismar is born in Freiburg, where Erwin and Grete have traveled for his birth.

August 1930
Erwin and Grete return to Amsterdam with David.

May 13, 1931
Nathan Cohen is born in Heiloo, North Holland.

July 23, 1931
Mirjam de Zoete is born in Celebes, the Dutch East Indies.

December 14, 1931
The NSB, the Dutch Nazi party, is established.

September 22, 1932
Judith de Zoete is born in Celebes.

January 30, 1933
Adolf Hitler, leader of the National Socialist German Workers' Party, is appointed chancellor of Germany.

February 27, 1933
Berlin's Reichstag, home of the German parliament, burns down; the Nazis baselessly declare the fire a communist plot and suspend civil liberties, purge political opponents, and suppress the free press.

March 1933
Dachau, the first Nazi concentration camp, opens in Germany.

The Committee for Jewish Refugees is established in the Netherlands to help Jews fleeing Germany.

October 17, 1933
Hadassah de Zoete is born in Banjarmasin, the Dutch East Indies.

September 15, 1935
The Nazis establish the Nuremberg Laws, denying German Jews citizenship and forbidding marriage and sexual relations between Jews and "Aryan" Germans.

1936
Chaim and Fifi return to Rotterdam with Mirjam, Judith, and Hadassah after Chaim completes five years of work for the military in the Dutch East Indies.

David has a final summer visit with his grandparents in Germany.

1937
David's grandfather Max Heinsheimer is arrested in Germany; upon his release, he agrees to immigrate to the Netherlands.

1938
Nathan's family welcomes Gertrude, a five-year-old German Jewish refugee, into their home.

March 12, 1938
German troops enter Austria; an *Anschluss* (union) is proclaimed on March 13, and Austria becomes a province of the German Reich. Anti-Jewish violence follows.

October 1938
The NSB bans Jews from becoming members, marking the beginning of the Dutch Nazi Party's embrace of antisemitism.

November 9–10, 1938
Kristallnacht (Night of Broken Glass) pogroms take place throughout Germany: Nazis burn over 900 synagogues; destroy 7,000 Jewish businesses, schools, and homes; kill 91 Jews; and send 30,000 Jewish men to concentration camps.

1939
The De Zoete family takes Ingrid, a ten-year-old German Jewish refugee, into their care.

September 1, 1939
Germany invades Poland, beginning World War II.

September 3, 1939
Great Britain, Australia, New Zealand, and France declare war on Germany.

October 1939
Westerbork admits its first internees—Jewish refugees from Germany who have crossed into the Netherlands illegally.

1940
Erwin, Grete, and David welcome German Jewish refugees into their Amsterdam home.

March 1940
Erwin becomes a social worker for the Committee for Jewish Refugees.

De Zoete Family

HISTORY BRIEF, PAGE 228
The Dutch East Indies

MIRJAM

First, I would like to tell you how my family's life was before the war, before Germany captured Holland. I was born in Indonesia, where my father was a pharmacist in the Dutch army. My middle sister is Judith, and she is one year younger. The next is two years younger, Hadassah. My mother's name is Sophia; she is called Fifi. My father is Hendrick Edward, and he is called Chaim.

My grandfather Moses de Zoete wanted his son to be an engineer, but my father wanted to be a pharmacist. Moses refused to pay for his studies. In Holland at that time, you could get your complete studies paid for if you agreed to go to Indonesia. My parents went on a boat, through the Suez, in 1930.

JUDITH

My parents married in 1929. Their first baby was stillborn. Then, Mirjam was born in 1931. Mirjam and I were born in Makassar, the capital of Celebes. Our Pappie was sent to the Dutch East Indies, and he did his work in an army uniform.

HADASSAH

We were all born in Indonesia. I was born in Banjarmasin.

MIRJAM

My sisters were closer to each other, and I was more on my own. Judith was the typical middle child. She felt that she wasn't paid as much attention as me, the oldest, or Hadassah, the youngest. She was actually the prettiest and the smartest of the three of us. Even today she thinks she gets the raw end of the deal, which might be partly true. Hadassah was the clown—made everyone laugh and always got her way.

HADASSAH

We left Indonesia in 1936. I was three years old, Judith four, and Mirjam five. When we returned to Holland, we first lived in a boardinghouse in Scheveningen, then we moved to a four-story house in Blijdorp, Rotterdam, and after that to Kralingen (a suburb of Rotterdam). We moved because our parents wanted us to go to a school with the Montessori method, of which there was only one in Rotterdam. I can remember the first-grade teacher, an old lady. All the time she used to say, "Hadassah can do better, Hadassah can do better." Something I heard my whole life.

MIRJAM

When my father's tour of duty was over, he got a job as chief pharmacist for the city of Rotterdam. We moved into a very nice house on the outskirts of that city—my parents, we three girls, and a maid. My school was far away, and my father brought me there sitting on the handlebars of his bicycle. I loved that. Some days, on the way home, he took me to a farm. He bought me ice cream, and we looked at the animals. It made me feel special because I was the only one who had that time, alone, with my father. When my sisters and I were in

Fifi and Chaim, 1929

Judith and Mirjam, ca. 1934

*We were truly quite innocent. We lived
on a very nice street near a park and
a lake, called Kralingse Plas. We all ate
dinner together at 6:00, and we went
to bed at 7:00. We had a very nice life,
really, before the war.*
MIRJAM

Hadassah, Mirjam, and Judith, 1935

the same school, it was too far for my father to bring more than one child, so we moved close to the school so we could walk.

JUDITH
Our living room was very cozy with a round dining table, and Mammie waited there for us to come back from school with a snack and a hot drink. We knew that this was home. The three of us girls slept in one room. On the third floor we had a storeroom and our playroom. We had domestic help day and night.

MIRJAM
We went to play outside with each other or with neighborhood friends—roller skates, hopscotch, stilts, and marbles were our favorites. We were allowed to listen to the radio for a half hour when there were children's songs. There was obviously no television. We had a record player, and we were only allowed to listen to classical music. Till today it's my favorite music. Just before the war, I saw one movie, *Snow White*. We were truly quite innocent. We lived on a very nice street near a park and a lake, called Kralingse Plas. In winter it froze over, and we went skating. My parents didn't skate, but they took us there. They had stands that sold pea soup and French fries, which were called *petites frites*. We all ate dinner together at 6:00, and we went to bed at 7:00. We had a very nice life, really, before the war.

HADASSAH
On Sabbath, Pappie would talk about Zionism and explain the principle on the huge, beautiful historical timetable he had made of the global, Jewish, and Dutch histories: three different-colored lines that would cross each other if the histories coincided. I did not like that. I never liked learning.

JUDITH
Pappie was honest, modest, and intelligent. He also had a good sense of humor. He was a good father and gave us a feeling of safety. He didn't interfere, but rather set the rules by example. He made a historical timetable for us. It was very interesting—a pity that piece of work got lost. It was a magnificent creation. I remember my father's study, a beautiful room, very modern for that time, with modern Scandinavian furniture.

MIRJAM
My father was a philosopher. He was in an organization that brought together Christians and Jews to try to work things out. He was a very quiet man; we felt comfortable with him. In the Kralingen house, he had his own room. We were not allowed to go in there unless he asked us.

My father, in his own quiet way, made it known when something was important to him. He taught us about music with an instrument he made himself from pipes hanging on a wooden frame, each pipe a little smaller than the one before. He also taught us about the history of mankind.

HADASSAH

Our parents would tell us a story before saying good night. Sometimes we would run wild before bedtime and Mammie would say, "Chaim, *go geef ze een draai om de oren*." It means: "Go give them a slap on the head." But the literal translation is: "Go give them a turn around the ears." So Pappie would turn his finger around our ears, one after the other, instead of really being mad at us. We loved that ritual.

Before Mammie met Pappie and married him, she had not lived at home for a long time. She led a sort of bohemian life in Amsterdam, where she made friends and met many interesting people: writers, poets—some famous. She was a nurse and must have been good at it because she became the director of a children's hospital. She would participate in demonstrations, mostly for feminist causes, right at the front of all the others, which would make us feel embarrassed.

MIRJAM

My mother liked writing, she loved reading (especially poems) and classical music, and was good in languages. She had a very good sense for interior decorating. She worked in a hospital when they had the terrible 1918 flu epidemic. She worked till she was thirty-three years old—when she got married. Unusually late in those years.

She came from a big family. She had very liberal ideas. I wouldn't say we were communistic but certainly socialistic. My parents felt very close to Israel. Two of Mammie's brothers were already in Israel before the war.

JUDITH

Mammie was warmhearted, intelligent, and sometimes a little critical and hyperactive. She was a full-time mother—always there for us.

MIRJAM

My mother was quite heavy. I thought all mothers were supposed to be heavy and pitied anyone who had a skinny mother because that wouldn't be someone you could cuddle up with. At that young age, I thought she was the best mother I could have. When I became a teenager, it was another story. She was bossy. What she said was what was done by all of us: the maid, my father, and the three of us girls.

HADASSAH

Mammie would start the day by giving instructions to everyone.

FIFI

September 20, 1938: We had a very long summer vacation this year. School was supposed to start on September 8, so everyone would be free for the government jubilee, the fortieth anniversary of the Queen. But during the vacation, there were more cases of poliomyelitis than in former years, and the medical service decided it was better to keep the schools closed.

August we were in Scheveningen. The girls like the sea, year after year. They invent new games, make holes and mountains and cakes in the sand, repeating the games each day but never getting bored.

Standing, third from left, in plaid shirt: Fifi, Utrecht, June 1927

(Fifi) led a sort of bohemian life in Amsterdam, where she made friends and met many interesting people: writers, poets—some famous. She would participate in demonstrations, mostly for feminist causes, right at the front of all the others.
HADASSAH

Before we went to Scheveningen, we spent an entire day at the zoo. That was a delightful day for the three darlings. Later, we went to a milk farm for the whole afternoon. I couldn't get them away. Only the promise made by the farmer's wife that the girls could visit again made them change their minds.

During the vacation, Mirjam had her birthday—we gave her a new bicycle!

Judith is struggling with herself and the world around her more than ever. It is hard to find the right tact and the right tone in her conflict. The funny thing, looking back, I see myself in her—how I must have felt as a child. She wants everything first. She is only happy when she succeeds, and unhappy when she fails. Judith thinks that she "gets, has, experiences" less than the other children. She always feels a kind of deficiency.

We also visited both grandmothers (Chaim's mother, Naatje, and mine, Goldine, whom the girls call Moeke), which the girls enjoyed. Given the nature of things, they preferred Moeke because she had a whole house at her disposal and also a big garden. Besides, the girls love my brother Hans, thus a lot of nice things all in one place.

Also, my niece Mirjam de Lange stayed with us for five days. The girls get along with her very well. She is a very nice girl, only unbelievably sloppy, which they appreciated more than I did. With her, Mirjam and Judith went one day to Tante (Aunt) Annie. I brought the girls to the tram, and she collected them. In the afternoon I picked them up on De Bijenkorf's rooftop garden. Again the girls had a great day. They even went sailing.

HADASSAH

Before the war, the family we visited with most was Mammie's older sister, Annie, who had four sons—Harry, Bob, Sally (Salomon), and Bernhard. Annie's husband's name was Jacques. Mammie's other sister, Jet, lived in The Hague. We did not like her husband, Karel, very much. As a matter of fact, we were a bit afraid of him.

MIRJAM

My mother's father died before I was born. As soon as he died, my grandmother Moeke was no longer religious. And neither were seven of her eight kids. We celebrated Passover with my aunt Annie Maarssen because she was the religious one. I loved going there. She had four boys, all older, who spoiled me rotten. I loved the food and the story and all the rituals that went with Passover. I also loved going to my mother's other sister, Jet, who had two girls, Mirjam (the same name as me) and Hetty. Mirjam was a year older, and she filled me in on things I didn't know about—like boys. Those are the cousins I was closest to. The four boys and the two girls.

There were just one or two kids in school who were Jewish. Only when the war started did we get this division about being Jewish and not Jewish. I started feeling different when the Germans made me feel different. Until then, I didn't know I was all that different from anyone. I never experienced any antisemitism. I was just another Dutch girl who happened to have Chanukah instead of Christmas.

HISTORY BRIEF, PAGE 229
Antisemitism in the Prewar Netherlands

40   Before

Fifi and her siblings, ca. 1929

Front, left to right: Beresh, Hans (murdered, Dachau), Annie (her four sons murdered, Auschwitz), and Jet (murdered with her husband and two daughters, Sobibor)

Back, left to right: Ben, Lolo, Fifi, and Sam (murdered, somewhere in Poland)

We never went to synagogue. We were very much assimilated—
besides the affiliation with Israel. I knew about Israel because of my
Zionist father, and my uncles—Beresh and Lolo, my mother's brothers—
lived there. I knew there was a country where Jewish people once
lived, and a lot of people wanted to go back there.

My parents weren't religious Jews, but they both belonged to
Zionist groups as students, and they always meant to go to Israel.
And, actually, in 1939, my father got the papers to go. It looked like
war was likely, and he didn't feel it was right to leave Holland. So,
he just deferred the papers to go to Israel. In case of a war, he had to
supply the city of Rotterdam with medication and bandages, and he
had organized a whole way of moving the medication and the first
aid to wherever it was needed. At that point, he didn't know how bad
it was going to get.

HADASSAH

I remember that on Saturday (we never really kept Sabbath as a
day off) Pappie would take us for walks in the woods, and he
would teach us the difference between poisonous and edible mushrooms, and also the names of birds. I just wanted to go home
and read my books or look at journals and cut out pictures of film
stars. I was not interested in talks about birds and mushrooms.
I read a lot. Everywhere I was during the war, they would register
me at a library.

We didn't lead a religious life. No celebrations of Jewish holidays,
not even Pesach (Passover), Rosh Hashanah (New Year), Yom Kippur
(Day of Atonement), or lighting candles for the Sabbath. On the
Pesach holidays, we would go to Mammie's sister Annie, who led
a traditional lifestyle, and had the Seder with them.

MIRJAM

We celebrated a holiday in Holland called Sinterklaas on December
5th. A Spanish bishop comes on his white horse with his black
helper, which nowadays would be politically incorrect. You put your
shoes by the chimney, and they put candy in them—and presents.
We were told this was just a story. We were never told things that
weren't true. On Chanukah, we just lit the candles and were told
the story.

My father always had the feeling of doom just before the war; he
always thought something terrible would happen. I didn't actually
hear the words he was saying, but I knew he was a very scared man.
That was the last year before the war. I remember a dream I had
before the war where a fat guy who looked like Hitler came into a
street, and everyone was scared, and this was a dream I had several
times. I knew there was maybe going to be a war, but we were very,
very protected. Kids were supposed to be protected. We weren't
supposed to hear fairy tales with death in them—we almost never
went to the movies—we were only allowed to listen to the children's
programs on the radio. In conversation, we were told it would be
okay. My parents were very worried; we could see that. We heard
our parents arguing in bed at night.

HISTORY BRIEF, PAGE 229
Zwarte Piet

Before

FIFI

January 1, 1939: Today the girls had a conversation about the war. One of them asked if there is going to be a war.

Judith: "As long as there is Hitler there is sometimes war."

Hadassah (indignant): "Sometimes?!! Always!!"

Mirjam: "Is a war coming now?"

Judith: "If the peace lamp doesn't burn."

Later in the year, Judith looked quite exhausted. She stayed with Jet and Karel for a week. Funny how you constantly have to think about a child when she is gone. She looked a little better when she returned. Home, in the evening, back in her own little bed, she whispered in my ear, "I longed for you so much." And I said, "I longed so much for you."

CHAIM

I had a series of dreams in September 1939 that made me ponder some grave issues. In the third dream, I saw a city with buildings engulfed in flames. I was walking among the burning houses. The war in Poland had recently broken out.

HISTORY BRIEF, PAGE 229
The Invasion and Partition of Poland

MIRJAM

In late 1939, before Germany entered Holland, Ingrid, a German Jewish girl my age, came to live with us. That was the first we children knew that something was very, very wrong. Her parents sent her to Holland from Germany because they thought it would be safer for her. Many people thought that Hitler would try to capture the surrounding countries, but not Holland. Boy, were they wrong! I felt sorry for Ingrid— that she had to stay with strangers—not knowing that the same would happen to me just a few years later.

Sometimes we were nasty to her like kids can be. After this was all over, we never knew what happened to her. I feel kind of guilty. I was always so amazed how calm she could be without her parents, and that she could live a normal life with us. After it happened to me, I sometimes thought about that. You can really do just about anything if you have to.

Nathan Cohen

I was born in the small village of Heiloo, next to Alkmaar, in North Holland, in 1931. My father was a doctor, a general practitioner. I was the second child, red-haired, the eldest being my sister Henny, who was three years older than me. Two years later, we left Heiloo for Utrecht, where Father specialized as a dermatologist. There, my younger sister, Annemieke, was born.

I hardly remember anything of Utrecht, except that we lived on a wide street, with a garden next to a creek. I remember it as a continuous time of spring and summer, catching caterpillars in the shrubbery—watching them transform into cocoons and butterflies was one of my major occupations. I remember an autogiro, which was a forerunner of the helicopter—a plane with a freely rotating top rotor and a propeller and stubby wings. This autogiro landed on a small grass field not far from our house, where I, together with a crowd of children and grown-ups, watched it lift off again.

———

After specialization, my father bought a medical practice in Apeldoorn. We lived in one-half of a duplex house, opposite the Oranjepark—one of the big public parks in Apeldoorn. My parents hired Corrie, a young girl, as household help. In time, she became a part of our family. She was a confidante to my sisters, always had a joke ready for us, told us stories, and even helped us with our homework if we had problems. She was a marvelous storyteller. From her came the stories about Pipi the mouse and his friend Popi, who had hair-raising escapes from dangerous situations.

My best friend was Henk, a neighbor with a garden adjoining ours. We were part of a gang of kids—a nearby garden of an empty house was our territory. In it, we had made a small hut, built of sticks, covered by shrubbery, which we used as our clubhouse.

We played war with bows and arrows, spears and clubs, went swimming in the pond, and, in the winter, we went ice skating as a group and generally had a very good time. During the summers, I was at home only to eat, sleep, and, as little as possible, do my homework.

———

My parents were not religious but kept a kosher kitchen, and Jewish holidays were observed. In fact, I always invited Henk to Chanukah, when presents were given, and I went over to his house for Christmas. This was a wonderful arrangement for us, since this way we got twice the presents we would normally get, and had a festive meal on both Chanukah and Christmas.

———

In 1938, my parents took in Gertrude, a German girl the same age as my younger sister, Annemieke, whose parents sent her and her brother and sister to Holland because they felt they would be safer there. Gertrude came to us, and her older brother and sister were sent to a Dutch Jewish refugee center in Deventer, a city not far from Apeldoorn. Gertrude was a shy and quiet girl. Soon Annemieke and Gertrude were good friends.

Nathan Cohen with his sisters, Henny and Annemieke, in 1946, after they had returned to Apeldoorn following the war

My best friend was Henk, a neighbor with a garden adjoining ours. We were part of a gang of kids—a nearby garden of an empty house was our territory. We played war with bows and arrows, spears and clubs, went swimming in the pond, and generally had a very good time.
NATHAN

David & Erwin Geismar

HISTORY BRIEF, PAGE 229
The Committee for Jewish Refugees

HISTORY BRIEF, PAGE 229
Relations between Dutch Jews and German Jews

Erwin was a German emigrant; in 1901, he was born in Freiburg and moved to the Netherlands in 1921. This section was crossed out of his handwritten memoir.

DAVID

I was born in Freiburg, Germany, in 1930. I am an only child. I was six months old when I came to Holland. Until I was six years old, I went back every summer to Germany to visit my grandparents; 1936 was the last time we went. My grandfather (Max Heinsheimer), my mother's father, lived in Bruchsal, Germany, where he was born and owned malt factories. In 1936, my father, Erwin, begged my grandfather to come to Holland. My grandfather was a German army officer in World War I. He did not believe, as a veteran in the Kaiser's army, that anything could happen to him. Well, a half year later, the Germans arrested him. My father went back to Germany and got my grandfather released from jail after signing all his possessions over to the Germans. The man moved to Amsterdam with just the clothes on his back.

Before the war started, I lived a normal life in Amsterdam. I went to public school and played with neighborhood kids. My father owned a leather goods factory for the garment industry. He went to France several times a year to see the fashion there. My mother gave cooking classes—food is the only thing that is important to her. I got along better with my father than my mother. I had an aunt, uncle, and cousin (Luzie, Eugen, and Felix Peter Eschenheimer) in a suburb outside Rotterdam. I spent most of my vacations with them.

My parents were not very religious—they were called Reform. We observed the high holidays. I was sent to Sunday school, which I hated. I knew I was Jewish like the next kid was Protestant, Catholic, or whatever. I never felt singled out or treated differently from any of my friends.

My father gave a Seder every year. We had a lot of guests, about twenty-five to thirty people, particularly after Jews started fleeing Germany. A lot of refugees came. I became aware that there was something different between us Jews and the other people.

In early 1940, my father got involved with the Committee for Jewish Refugees, helping Jewish refugees who fled Nazi Germany. I understood that in Germany there was something wrong.

ERWIN

One generally didn't like them; one can almost say that they were hated. The emigrants, above all the Jewish emigrants....I often had to say, when making a new acquaintance and wanting to be seen in the right light, "I've been in Holland since 1921," or, "I am no emigrant," or, "Our boy only speaks broken German." Usually the response was, "So, you've been here so long, you're not an emigrant. You know, there are very nice people among the emigrants, but..."

Naturally one shouldn't generalize, and I had good and true acquaintances and friends among the emigrants that I wouldn't have wanted to miss. I met some political emigrants whom I admired, but even they had an "air of German-ness" that many Dutch and the Jews, in particular, found unappealing.

Emigrants are welcome nowhere—what they do, they do wrong, and especially with Jews, it is worth considering whether our history of wandering made us unloved.

David, Bruchsal, Germany, May 1936

Until I was six years old, I went back every summer to Germany to visit my grandparents; 1936 was the last time we went. In 1936, my father, Erwin, begged my grandfather to come to Holland. Well, a half year later, the Germans arrested him.
DAVID

Trapped

After Germany attacked Poland on September 1, 1939, France and Britain declared war on the hostile nation. The Netherlands remained on the sidelines. German forces occupied Denmark and Norway in April 1940, and on May 10, they launched a crushing assault on the Netherlands, Belgium, Luxembourg, and France. In the Netherlands, many thousands made for the North Sea ports seeking passage to England; many hundreds committed suicide. The Dutch soldiers fought tenaciously, but the bombing of Rotterdam, on May 14, led to the decision that the Dutch soldiers in the Netherlands surrender to the Germans. The kingdom of the Netherlands would continue the war as an ally of Britain, with Queen Wilhelmina and the Dutch government in London.

The Belgian army surrendered at the end of May, and the French government agreed on June 22 to a harsh armistice. The fall of France confirmed German hegemony on the continent: the Soviet Union had been neutralized as a challenger as the result of the Molotov-Ribbentrop non-aggression pact; Hungary, Romania, and Bulgaria had lined up with the Reich; and most people expected that Britain would be forced to agree to German rule over the conquered countries. The United States did not want to get involved. For the foreseeable future, Berlin was the place where the future of Europe would be decided.

In the summer of 1940, senior officials in the German Ministry of Foreign Affairs and the security police were drafting plans to ship all Jews under German control to the French colony of Madagascar. This Final Solution to the Jewish Problem in Europe appeared viable after the surrender of France, and in view of the expected defeat of Britain.

1940

May 10, 1940
Germany invades the Netherlands.

May 13, 1940
Queen Wilhelmina of the
Netherlands and her government
escape to England.

May 14, 1940
Germany carries out an aerial
bombardment of Rotterdam.

Chaim, Fifi, Mirjam, Judith, and
Hadassah leave their house in
Rotterdam to escape the bombing.

David is visiting relatives outside
of Rotterdam; Erwin and Grete
remain in Amsterdam to wait for
their son's return.

Nathan's family tries—and fails—
to escape the Netherlands
for England.

May 15, 1940
The Dutch army within
the Netherlands surrenders
to Germany.

ca. May 24, 1940
David goes home to his parents
in Amsterdam.

May 28, 1940
The occupied Netherlands is put
under the control of Reichskommissar
Arthur Seyss-Inquart, who has
been a committed Nazi since the
early 1930s.

July 28, 1940
Queen Wilhelmina makes her
first broadcast from London on
Radio Oranje.

David & Erwin Geismar

HISTORY BRIEF, PAGE 230
The Invasion of the Netherlands

HISTORY BRIEF, PAGE 230
The Bombing of Rotterdam and the Capitulation of the Dutch Army

ERWIN

On May 10, 1940, a sound that reminded me of shooting woke me at 3 a.m., as dawn began. I didn't attribute any significance to this, and imagined training exercises or shooting by English or German airplanes, which flew over Dutch airspace. This happened often. However, around 3:30 a.m., I noticed my neighbors talking loudly at their windows and on their roofs, and I went into our yard and saw a vast number of airplanes being shot at with shrapnel. Memories of the war from 1914 to '18 awoke in me. I had often seen planes being shot at in my former homeland. And now, the same image twenty-five years later. About five minutes later we realized our situation when the radio reported that German parachutists were landing in all parts of Holland. We were trapped. Trapped by the Germans.

DAVID

When the Germans attacked Holland, I was on vacation with my aunt in a little town named Hillegersberg. It was three or four miles from Rotterdam. The first things I saw were the massive planes coming in and bombing Rotterdam—the sky was darkened with so many planes. In those days, it was a rarity to see an airplane flying over, so this was a very impressive thing to me. We heard about the attack on the radio and could hear the bombing of the city. The noise was very impressive.

ERWIN

Despite all the war rumors setting the mood, which in the first two days took the form of the wildest gossip, air-raid sirens, blocking of telephone lines, and so forth, I knew it was critical not to lose my nerve. Our son was in Rotterdam, which was being bombed, and for that reason an escape to England was out of the question for my family from the beginning. Dutch authorities forbade us, as German citizens, from leaving our apartment, and we had to consider ourselves interned in our own home.

Besides, we still had a woman staying with us, a socialist who had been imprisoned for one and a half years before her emigration from Germany, and a gentleman and his wife, who had written and published a book critical of the German regime. He was also a reporter for a Swiss newspaper. These three managed, with great difficulty, to escape to England on May 14, via IJmuiden. The man, however, on the day they were to flee, was so overcome by the situation that he tried to hang himself when he realized that the conquest of Holland could not be stopped. Fortunately, I noticed his plan because I happened to be searching for a strong rope. He had already fastened it to the balcony. Only by keeping myself calm could I counteract the very nervous mood in the house. I, too, knew that we were trapped, trapped in every respect, and I was determined not to let the situation bring me down.

DAVID

The Germans put an ultimatum to Holland to capitulate or the next city to be bombed would be Utrecht. We saw the Dutch army, and it was a very sad-looking group—not well trained, not ready for war. In World War I, Holland was neutral. In World War II, Holland never expected to be attacked, and the army was never taken seriously. As a child, I really did not put the war together with me as a Jew or think that something particular would happen to me.

I remember my parents had someone living with them who went to one of the coasts to flee to England. My parents would have gone but didn't because I was not at home. A week or two after Holland capitulated, my parents sent a friend with a car from Amsterdam to get me in Hillegersberg (near Rotterdam). On the way home, we saw all kinds of dead animals from the bombing, some airplanes that were shot down, and houses that were hit. Roads were broken up, so we had to make detours. I had never seen death in my short life, so the dead animals made quite an impression because there were lots of them; plus, at the age of ten, you think you are indestructible. At once, you realize anything close to you can be taken away. This is very scary for a ten-year-old boy.

As we got near Amsterdam, there was less destruction. Animals were grazing in the fields. There were lots of soldiers with convoys of cars and trucks. I never saw so many trucks as in those first days of the war. I was only familiar with the Dutch army (which was very small), not with the tremendous mass of the German army that over-ran the whole country.

So, we got back to Amsterdam. I was glad to see my parents, understanding there was a certain amount of danger to this. Their reaction made me realize that I'm a lucky kid, that something could happen to me.

We lived on the third and fourth floors of a four-story house in a residential neighborhood. Across the street from us was a Catholic high school that was run by priests. After I was home for about three weeks, the Germans took the school as barracks for their troops. All their trucks were lined up on the street. The thing that impressed me was that they never turned off the trucks. For twenty-four hours those engines were going. Later on, I learned that the engines were run on generators, on coal, and they couldn't get them started fast enough if they turned them off. I started realizing how strong and powerful a well-organized army is (and the Germans were very organized).

Before the occupation, I idolized soldiers. I played soldier on the street with kids in the neighborhood, pretending our bicycles were motorcycles. After the occupation, we didn't play soldier anymore. I was told that people got killed and hurt in the houses that were bombed. The destruction really worried me; I didn't think a soldier was such a great thing anymore.

The Germans pulled out and left our neighborhood alone. For a year, life went on as normal, like before the war. That first year they did not go after the Jews in Holland. I heard them talk at home about the German refugees—they were the first ones the Germans were after—and how the Germans wanted them to register. There was a story on the radio about Mussert, head of the Dutch Nazis, and how he got his people together.

Anton Adriaan Mussert founded the Nationaal-Socialistische Beweging, or NSB (Dutch Nazi Party), in 1931.

ERWIN

When Holland surrendered to Germany, the consequences for the Committee for Jewish Refugees were unavoidable. The immediate impact of antisemitism meant that many people were excluded from working, especially the self-employed. These circumstances caused a huge increase in people requiring help. I believe that the committee counted 5,000 people in Amsterdam and the province of North Holland who needed relief. They were nearly all emigrants.

I soon became an expert in career counseling, and from 1940 to '41, I was running three or four businesses every day in addition to my own. Often, I was trying to find work for artists, work that required a certain amount of business education that they lacked. It was my job to help them learn how to operate their businesses.

I remember a young artist who created drawings and vignettes for well-known Dutch newspapers and magazines, a man forced to leave his profession because he was a Jew. I looked at his designs and projects and saw that his work was very original: sculptural murals made of wood and clay for a child's room, book covers made of hemp, catalog covers pasted with sand and shells, advertisements and shop windows. In short, he created a tiny, colorful world of unique ideas.

I had the idea to hire him for my factory and to show him a wide variety of materials as inspiration. Since I worked with clothing and fashion wholesalers, I suggested that he try to create brooches and pendants. In a short time, he made a very beautiful collection from the simplest materials, but so artistic that I had no doubt they would be successful. The business side of things required a lot of time on my part, but I was able to set the young man's finances in order quite quickly. He was able to get by without support and to pay back some of his debts.

Sadly, after his situation had greatly improved, this young man was captured in a raid and taken to Mauthausen concentration camp, along with a thousand other young Jews from Holland. That was around May 1941.

From the camp, he wrote two letters to his wife, which I read when I was helping her move. His handwriting in these letters made me conclude that he wasn't able to write properly, due to either extreme physical labor or weakness, while the content prepared the wife for his death. Five weeks later came the official death certificate. And still, we Jews had no inkling of the fate that awaited most of us.

The daily struggle for existence and the lack of money was an enormous strain on the nerves, especially as the noose around the necks of us Jews tightened, and many couldn't bear it. Officially, the committee couldn't take that into account, of course, and so it fell to the counselors to provide psychological support.

How quickly indeed is a person worn out, when one simply works constantly to meet one's basic needs! How can one enjoy work, without making progress or having a goal in mind? Who among us Jews can think of progress or goals in this time and place in which we are forced to live?

HISTORY BRIEF, PAGE 233
Mauthausen Concentration Camp

Trapped

I remember the start of the war as a time of excitement. Suddenly, all the children in our family did not have to go to school. Since a large part of central Holland was a natural barrier against the Germans and Hilversum was behind this barrier, we left Apeldoorn and drove to Hilversum, where we stayed in a pension. Planes were flying overhead, and all the grown-ups were nervous and did not check on us, so I was free to roam the streets and run around on a new set of roller skates I had gotten.

Father tried to get drafted (he was a captain in the medical reserves), but the army was not interested. The Germans bombed Rotterdam, not just the harbor but also the city, killing and wounding many civilians. There were rumors that German parachutists had been dropped to sabotage the Dutch war effort, some dressed as women.

Every grown-up was liable to be stopped by Dutch authorities and asked to say "Scheveningen" (the name of a Dutch town) since the Germans cannot pronounce the Dutch 'ch' and 'ng.'

The Dutch army was no match against the German army and surrendered after four days of fighting.

The day before the surrender, Father saw what was going to happen and decided to try and escape to England. We again got into the car and drove from port to port, trying to find any type of boat to get to England, but we were too late. All boats leaving were full, even fishing boats and pleasure boats. While driving around, we were stopped several times to say "Scheveningen." Once, Father did not see that soldiers were trying to stop us. After we passed, a soldier stepped in the middle of the road, kneeled on one knee, and pointed his rifle at the car. Father braked so suddenly that we all were thrown forward. Annemieke and Gertrude started to cry, Mother was berating Father for the way he drove, and Father, ignoring all the noise, drove backward to the soldiers, where we all had to get out of the car, the car was searched, and Father and Mother had to say "Scheveningen."

After two days of running around, we returned to Hilversum, where for the first time I saw German soldiers. They looked like a sorry lot, in their gray, sloppy uniforms, which were, in my eyes, much inferior to the beautiful Dutch uniforms with their shiny buttons. They drove funny cars with open tops and marched in perfect formation singing in German, which I did not understand. It was difficult for me to comprehend how they could have beaten our Dutch army. I was sure that if we—my friends and I—had been grown-up soldiers, we would have done much better. After a few days, we returned to Apeldoorn in a very subdued mood.

———

The Germans started to integrate the Dutch industry into their war effort, but this also had little influence on our lives. It was forbidden to listen to the BBC, the English radio station, which broadcast a program in Dutch called *Radio Oranje*, this being the name of the Dutch royal family. People listened anyway. Punishment was confiscation of the radio and a fine. For Jews, it meant imprisonment.

Nathan
Cohen

HISTORY BRIEF, PAGE 231
Radio Oranje and Radio Hilversum

HISTORY BRIEF, PAGE 231
The French-German Armistice

HISTORY BRIEF, PAGE 231
The Dunkirk Evacuation

The war news was all bad: the French Vichy armistice, the English retreat to Dunkirk, and the evacuation back to England through the English Channel with loss of all their equipment were all triumphantly described by the German-controlled Dutch radio and in the press, which of course published only the German version. The news on the BBC was not much different, although the English retreat from Dunkirk was depicted as a victory, saving the army to return at a later date to Europe. Even then, the BBC Dutch news—*Radio Oranje*—started to advise on how to sabotage the German war effort. But most people got their news from the heavily censored Hilversum radio station and the newspapers.

Things very quickly returned to normal. School went on until vacation, when we had our usual good time in our territory, only now we played war games, did battle with an imaginary enemy, and were always victorious, after which we swam in the pool or fished in the canal. Sometimes we went to watch German soldiers marching, singing loudly about *fahren gegen England*, which we at first translated to the Dutch "driving to England," and since we knew our geography, we did not understand how they could be so ignorant. Did they not know that they could never drive to England since there was a sea between Holland and England? Some grown-up translated the words as "going (to fight) against England." We soon were marching with the soldiers, and when they sang, we added our addition of *ploem, ploem, ploem* to theirs, the sound of stones hitting the water and sinking. We had a good time, and the Germans did not seem to mind.

In the autumn, we again went to school, and there were some small differences. The royal family, who had escaped to England, had till then been part of every schoolchild's life. On the birthdays of the princesses, we always made drawings and got sweets to celebrate the event. This was now, of course, forbidden. In fact, the royal family was not mentioned at all. There were collections for the "Winter Fund." This ostensibly was to help the poor but was really a fund for the NSB (Dutch Nazi Party) and paid for their activities. The school had to buy their pins, and every child got one to wear.

HISTORY BRIEF, PAGE 231
The Dutch Nazi Party

HISTORY BRIEF, PAGE 232
Underground Newspapers

At about this time, the first underground newspapers were starting to circulate. The Germans began to apply collective punishment. Mayors were replaced by members of the NSB. Mussert, their leader, was a kind of comic opera figure, a miniature Mussolini. The NSB strutted around in special uniforms. Antisemitic propaganda was stepped up—slogans were painted on windows of Jewish shops and synagogues.

We children had little interest in these matters since they made little difference to our routine. As a Jewish child, I had to be a little more careful with how I answered my teacher. I don't know if she was afraid to offend the Germans and therefore picked on me and another Jewish child in our class or if she was a member of the NSB. In any case, we were spending a lot of time doing *strafwerk* (Dutch for having to write one hundred times "I have to be polite to my teacher" or some such nonsense).

After school was out, and especially during the holidays, the routine remained the same for us: playing soldier in our garden, walking around on stilts (a new skill we learned that year), playing catch-me, and ice-skating whenever the ice was strong enough.

As you can see, the German occupation did not yet touch our lives very much, but this was soon to change.

De Zoete Family

CHAIM

After the German invasion of Poland and my warning dreams that followed, it was clear that what would have been done in biblical times under such circumstances needed to be done now as well: leave the endangered country. A misplaced sense of responsibility, however, kept me from doing so. At the time, I had an important task at Rotterdam's Air Defense Command. All of the material in the wartime first-aid station had been set up by me; it was systematically organized in the stockrooms of the Municipal Pharmacy in such a way that my presence was the only way to guarantee that it would be dispatched quickly. In addition, I supervised significant supplies of wartime reserve medications, which under my repeated insistence had been put in place two years earlier. Later on, I knew that my sense of duty had been misdirected. Under the Nazi threat that accompanied the "normal" war, the Jewish citizen ran a far greater risk than any other resident, much greater even than the communist.

JUDITH

Pappie declined emigration certificates to Palestine (Israel) for the whole family, explaining that in times of danger to one's country, one does not leave one's post. Had we gone then, there would be no story to tell.

MIRJAM

For us, the war started May 10th, with sirens going off and my parents telling us to run to the basement because the Germans were invading Holland. My father had to go to work because he was head of first aid in Rotterdam. We couldn't have lights on; we were scared. My parents said they would take care of us—that nothing would happen to us, and we'd stay together. We totally believed it. There were Dutch soldiers stationed in front of our house. They came in to use our bathrooms. My mother made them coffee and tea. On the fourth day of the invasion, they told us we had to get out of Rotterdam because the city would be bombed.

HADASSAH

One of my most vivid memories was the bombing of Rotterdam, which our whole family watched from the outskirts of town.

JUDITH

It was a very unnerving and scary experience to see a burning city.

MIRJAM

When we went back to our house, a lot of things had been stolen. We didn't know if it was Dutch or German soldiers who did it. I saw my father sitting on the steps crying. This was the first time I was afraid. When you see your father cry, it's very scary.

FIFI

December 11, 1940: The girls have already gone through a lot in their young lives. A big sea journey, getting adapted to different standards

December 11, 1940: The girls have
already gone through a lot in their
young lives. A big sea journey, getting adapted to different standards
of living and customs in a different
country, and now, this year, the war
and a bombardment.
FIFI

Hadassah was erg blij. Ik had
voor haar warme handschoenen
en een muts bij mij.
De he winter weer een ....plas.
Mirjam leerde goed schaaken en
Judith begint ook al aardig te
krabbelen.

11/12 En nu zijn we een jaar verder.
Vrijdag 12/11 is pappie ontheven
van de waarneming van
zijn functie als Gemeente-
Apotheker. Wij probeeren het
elkaar hoe veel prettiger te
maken nu en nog meer samen
een te zijn. Jullie begrijpt er
al een klein beetje van en kunt
soms aandoenlijk lief zijn.
Je hebt al heel wat meegemaakt
in jullie jonge leven. Zoo'n
groote hebben 't aanpassen aan
allerlei andere levenswijzen en
gewoonte's van een ander land
en nu dit jaar de oorlog en
een bombardement. Die dag
na het bombardement hebben
jullie je voorbeeldig gedragen.
Wij waren dinsdag 14 Mei hier
hier gegaan naar Dot en Lena
in Hillegersberg en hebben
daar ook geslapen. Wij hadden
geen van allen moed om
de volgende dag weer naar
den Haag terug te gaan.

Left foreground and back row, left
and far right, wearing bows: Mirjam,
Hadassah, and Judith, Montessori
classroom, 1937

*We loved school. It was a pity though
that we had such a short time to
enjoy it.*
JUDITH

of living and customs in a different country, and now, this year, the war and a bombardment. They behaved extremely well the day after the bombardment. We left our house on Tuesday, May 14, and went to Dolf and Lena in Hillegersberg, where we spent the night.

We didn't have the courage to go back and walked about in Terbregge the whole day. Pappie was especially downcast by all of it—so much so that a normal workday was not in the order of the day.

In the evening, back home on the Plaslaan, our house was a mess. In the one and a half days that we were away, our house had been broken into. Everything edible was gone, clothes were stolen, and worse—two excellent cameras and a pair of binoculars were taken.

Because our front door was left open, a man and his wife whose house had burned down entered our house and slept there. We found them when we returned home.

There was no gas, so cooking was a problem. Our next-door neighbor let us use her electric hot plate. We ate at one o'clock midday, and they at six o'clock in the evening. That's how we helped each other through the first days.

MIRJAM

I remember hearing *Hitler*, *Hitler*, *Hitler*, and that name just made us shiver. I must have been hearing about things going on.

My mother's brother Ben, who was a communist, was right away in the underground. All the communists in Holland organized after the war started. I'm sure, through him, my parents knew right away what was going on.

FIFI

December 11, 1940: School went back to normal pretty fast, which was good for the girls. But the anti-aircraft artillery, light-bullets, shooting, and bombing every night were difficult. The girls didn't sleep well and were tired and irritable during the day.

MIRJAM

We had Nazis living on our street. I don't remember the man or his wife, but his son went to school with me. His name was Wim—blond, skinny, and not very well liked in school. Before the war, his parents wouldn't have dared to come out to say they were Nazis. As soon as Germany took over, all those Nazis popped out of the woodwork. They were not known to me but must have been known to my parents. My father tried to protect us and told us to stay away from this kid. Don't say anything and don't be nasty to him because they are the ones who are against the Jews; they are called the NSBers.

Forbidden

In 1940, Hitler aimed to unite all Germanic countries—Germany, Denmark, Norway, Luxembourg, the Netherlands, Sweden, and Switzerland. Rather than place the Netherlands under military occupation, like France or Belgium, he imposed a civilian administration that would prepare the country for its absorption into the Reich. The Austrian-born Nazi Arthur Seyss-Inquart was tasked with winning the hearts and minds of the Dutch. Among his first official acts, Seyss-Inquart ordered the return of 280,000 Dutch prisoners of war to their families. The great majority of the Dutch population, and the entire civil service, settled on a course of accommodation. With one exception, a ruthlessly suppressed strike held in February 1941 in support of the Jews, the Dutch stood by as decree after decree pushed the Jewish population—now officially sorted into "Full Jews" (140,522), "Half Jews" (14,549), and "Quarter Jews" (5,719)—into an ever-smaller corner, with every act of Jewish resistance punished harshly. Throughout 1941, German officials still assumed that Madagascar might become a sultry ghetto for Western and Central European Jews; in late summer and fall 1941, open massacres of Jews occurred only in the German-occupied Soviet Union. But when Germany declared war on the United States in December 1941, Hitler decided on the genocide of all European Jews.

In Amsterdam, the Germans requisitioned a theater to serve as a collecting point for arrested Jews. They took control of the Westerbork refugee camp, transforming it into a transit point to undeclared destinations. In July 1942, the first train with deportees was dispatched from Westerbork to Auschwitz. Key to the success of the deportations was the cooperation of the Jewish Council, established a year earlier. The Germans allowed the council to issue 40,000 exemptions from deportation. By focusing the attention of the council on the exemptions, the German security police proved able to remove the rest of the Jewish population without too much fuss or bother.

1940–1942

September 6, 1940
Jews can no longer be appointed
to jobs in the civil service.

September 26, 1940
Jewish newspapers are forbidden.

October 5, 1940
Civil servants are ordered to declare
if they have Jewish grandparents.

October 22, 1940
Jewish-owned businesses must register as part of the Germans' effort
to "Aryanize" Jewish property, thus
appropriating most possessions
from the Jews.

ERWIN

It was clear to everyone that the Germans wanted the Jews and their
businesses registered in order to confiscate them. We were required
to provide every detail about the business. I was pleased to honestly
state that in the entire year of 1939 I only ordered sixty guilders of
goods from Germany. When one considers that this was for a sample,
which I then had copied in France, no one can accuse me of not supporting the boycott of Germany. I can say, despite my limited resources
and difficulties, that I expended a great deal of time and money to
avoid German products. I was the first belt producer in Holland who
didn't use any German imitation leather. The German offerings were
good and cheap, but on principle, I only used British and American
imitation leather.

    It was not only in business that every right-thinking person should
have boycotted Germany, but every Jew had to mentally oppose a
country that, for no reason, treated him as not even a second- or third-
class person.

DAVID

Our landlord was Jewish. He owned a lot of houses. He had an office
on the street—the office disappeared. Another guy came to collect
the rent from my father because our landlord wasn't allowed to own
his houses anymore.

November 21, 1940
All Jewish civil servants in the
Netherlands, which includes school-
teachers, university professors,
and municipal employees, are fired
from their jobs.

HISTORY BRIEF, PAGE 232
The Great Surrender

NATHAN

Jews in government jobs were dismissed. No Jew could hold an official position. This meant that Jewish professors were dismissed from universities, Jewish doctors from hospitals, Jewish judges dismissed, etc.

JUDITH

I don't remember exact dates and time spans. But one day, Pappie was dismissed from his rather important job in Rotterdam. He was the number-one person responsible for collecting, buying, and distributing all medical supplies for the Rotterdam district.

MIRJAM

The Germans put one of their people in as city pharmacist.

FIFI

December 11, 1940: Pappie was discharged from his function as a municipal pharmacist. We try very hard to make each other more comfortable, and to be together as one. The girls already understand the situation a little and are touchingly sweet.

ERWIN

HISTORY BRIEF, PAGE 230
Reichskommissar Arthur Seyss-Inquart

Thus, Holland's first war year came to an end. Although a civilian government had been set up under the Reichskommissar Seyss-Inquart, the German authorities had not yet gotten us Jews within their grip. The Germans tried to cast the Jews in a poor light via their usual propaganda, and all Jews were laid off from government positions, although they were given pensions.

CHAIM

"Do something," I said to myself after I was discharged because of an anti-Jewish decree, and we had to live off a small income. The landlord offered to let us live free of charge in our house until the end of the war. In full conscience, I could not accept this offer and started, with great resolution, to look for another place to live—first around Rotterdam, then in The Hague, and finally in Voorburg where I found a house on the other side of the *vliet* (a little river) so that we still belonged to the municipality of Leidschendam. This was important because, as became clear later, the raids in Voorburg started before they started in Leidschendam. And again I said to myself, "Until the last moment man has the freedom to act and to break through a seemingly unchangeable destiny."

HADASSAH

We had to move to a smaller house. We lost the house we enjoyed and our beloved Montessori school with all of our friends.

FIFI

We wanted very much to stay in the neighborhood of Rotterdam and searched for a long time. You could say we looked everywhere, in every spot we thought there was a chance to find what we were looking for, but without result.

Forbidden

Chaim (left) at his job as a pharmacist for the Municipal Public Health Service of Rotterdam, June 1940

"Do something," I said to myself after I was discharged because of an anti-Jewish decree, and we had to live off a small income. "Until the last moment man has the freedom to act and to break through a seemingly unchangeable destiny."
CHAIM

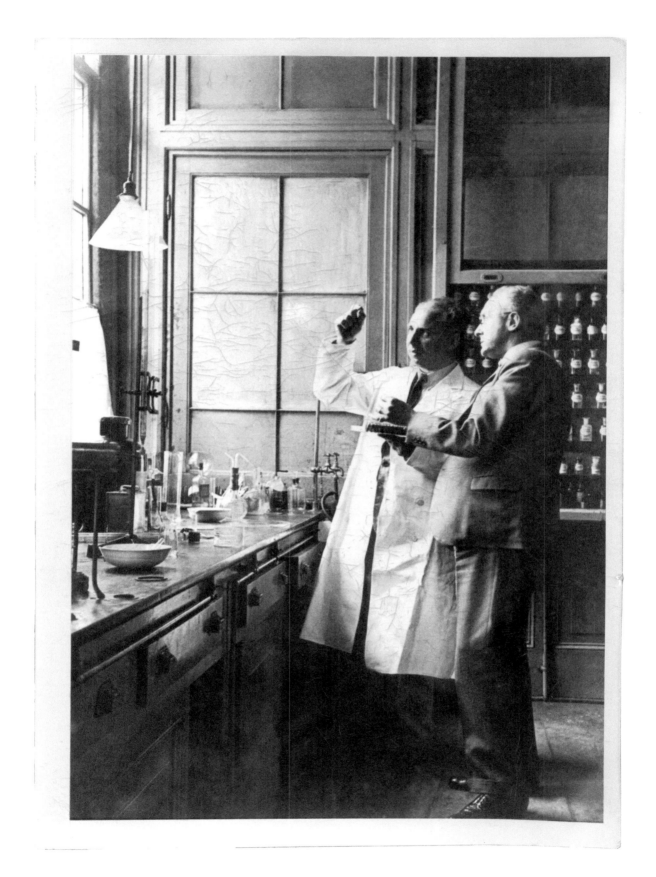

Then, we went to a real estate agent's office in Voorburg. The Montessori school there had an especially good reputation. Indeed, we found a house near a canal and the school was a dream come true. Pleasant teachers and nice, kind pupils. And very soon all three girls felt at home. Mirjam and Hadassah in particular soon made friends; with Judith it doesn't work that fast, but a few weeks before summer vacation she made a friend.

We discovered in our neighborhood, at Cia van Boord's, something really nice for them: a puppet theater. Not the usual one with Katrijn and Jan Klaassen, but a fairy-tale puppet theater with handmade puppets. The performance took place in the attic of an old farm.

MIRJAM

At our new Montessori school, there was the Willemse family: mother, father, two sons, and a daughter. They became friends of our parents, and I befriended the daughter, Barta. A very smart, beautiful, and self-assured girl. She took me under her wing since I was very shy. The family was well to do and had a beautiful house with a swimming pool.

JUDITH

In Voorburg, in a much smaller but still two-story-plus-attic house, we had Pappie's mother, Naatje, and sister, Martha, living with us. They also needed (a lot) less-expensive lodgings.

We went again to a Montessori school for a short period (at a reduced fee, since Pappie was not earning any money). The school, which was in a beautiful mansion with a big garden and lots of trees, had very nice teachers and well-educated pupils. We loved school. It was a pity though that we had such a short time to enjoy it.

HADASSAH

Naatje and Martha stayed in our guest room, and every night before bedtime we went to say good night to them. Martha died in the camps with Pappie's mother. She was nice.

JUDITH

With no job, Pappie still found himself things to do. Between reading, writing, and listening to music, he started gardening and even took up piano lessons (from a friend—no fee). Mammie kept house for the seven people.

January 10, 1941
German administration orders anyone with at least one Jewish grandparent to register with the Census Office.

HISTORY BRIEF, PAGE 232
The Census

DAVID

In 1941, all Jews or "half" Jews, 160,000 people, were registered with the Germans. The Germans now had complete control over every Jew in Holland.

Forbidden

February 13, 1941
At the Germans' behest, the Jewish
Council is established in Amsterdam
to control those living in the city's
Jewish quarter.

DAVID

The Germans made the Jews organize the Jewish Council. This organization helped the Germans tremendously, later on, to deport the Jews
from Holland. The Germans were very successful at getting Jews to
work for the Jewish Council by giving workers a special stamp in their
identity cards that exempted them from deportation. My father worked
for the Jewish Council as a social worker to help old and sick people.

HISTORY BRIEF, PAGE 233
The Jewish Council

ERWIN

The Jewish Council encompassed everything related to Jewish issues.
Because the organization had to register and manage about 140,000
Jews, which required more work than under normal circumstances,
the council had a great many employees. The council encompassed
not only the support organizations related to the Committee for
Jewish Refugees but also all public and private organizations: welfare
offices, newspapers, hospitals, private businesses, old-age homes,
etc.—everything was registered by the council.

February 22–23, 1941
German police raid Amsterdam's
Jewish quarter, seizing 427 men ages
18–35 for deportation to German
concentration camps.

ERWIN

In February 1941, a small group of Dutch Nazis entered Amsterdam's
Jewish neighborhood in a very provocative manner. They marched,
singing and playing antisemitic songs along the Jodenbreestraat. The
local residents found this new behavior hard to bear, and young Jewish
men beat the leaders. This resulted in the arrest of about 500 young
Jewish men, who were sent to the Mauthausen concentration camp.

HISTORY BRIEF, PAGE 232
The First German Raid on Jews

February 25–26, 1941
Workers in the Netherlands strike
to protest the Germans' raids and anti-
Jewish measures, resulting in a
violent crackdown by the Germans.

ERWIN

The German reaction caused a two-day strike in most of Amsterdam's
businesses as well as government offices. Sadly, the response resulted
in many deaths. For us Jews, it was an especially sublime feeling that
there remained one city in the world that would step into the breach
for us. However, six weeks later, the parents of the boys taken to
Mauthausen received official German death certificates. What exactly
happened to them never came to light. Shortly after, there was
another, similar reprisal, and our lives no longer felt safe, because anyone could be singled out by a Nazi and deported in the same way.

HISTORY BRIEF, PAGE 233
The February Strike

Arthur Seyss-Inquart, Reichskommissar of the occupied Netherlands, speaking at the Concertgebouw (concert hall) in Amsterdam.

March 12, 1941

We do not consider the Jews to be members of the Dutch nation. The Jews for us are not Dutch. They are an enemy with whom we cannot have a cease-fire nor make peace. Do not expect me to set this down as a regulation except in police measures. We will hit the Jews where we can. And those who help them will be hit just as hard.

ERWIN

Seyss-Inquart once declared in a speech, "We will strike the Jews, wherever we find them." Well, I had to take up this fight, and take it up I did. I defended myself, my family, and my fellow Jews without fail—even now, despite all the difficulties. If it should be my fate to give my life to this struggle, I will be glad, to my last breath, that I was granted the chance to fight on the front lines.

April 11, 1941

The Jewish Council publishes its first issue of the German-controlled, heavily censored *Joodsche Weekblad* (*Jewish Weekly*), a newspaper used to communicate antisemitic orders to the Jewish population. All other Jewish newspapers in the Netherlands had been forbidden since September 1940.

NATHAN

Jewish journalists were forbidden to write, except in the one Jewish publication.

April 15, 1941

Jews are given two weeks' notice to surrender their radios.

May 1, 1941

Jewish professionals such as doctors, dentists, and lawyers are forbidden from serving non-Jewish clients.

June 4, 1941

Jews are prohibited from using public beaches and swimming baths and attending public markets.

MIRJAM

We were told we had to do things and we did them. The Germans were the people who could take you away and put you in prison. You did what you were told.

ERWIN

After radios were confiscated in spring 1941, and we were prohibited from cafés and bars in the summer, Jews could no longer travel

Forbidden

without a special travel permit. Soon we were excluded from butchers and produce markets, and even barbers. We were forced to shop in special Jewish stores.

DAVID

Until 1941, life was not very different. In 1941 and 1942, measures against the Jews constantly increased. For us children, the war started hitting home. We wondered, Why are we losing everything? Why are we discriminated against, when we are no different from our friends who aren't Jewish?

NATHAN

Signs saying ENTRANCE IS FORBIDDEN FOR DOGS AND JEWS were placed in public places (dogs were put before Jews, being more important).

Since Father was forbidden to receive Gentile patients, his practice was gone, and he looked for other work. My parents started a pension for Jews from the big cities, mostly Amsterdam. Apeldoorn is situated in the countryside, and my parents were soon booked full for the whole summer vacation.

Corrie, our household help, had to be dismissed. As a Gentile, she could not work for Jews. We were very sorry to see her go. My parents hired a German refugee, Heinz, as help. This was of mutual benefit since this way Heinz had work, and with work, he could get a permit to stay. The Germans had started a concentration camp in Westerbork in Holland, and all young German Jewish refugees who did not have a permit had to go there. Heinz was a cheerful young man. I don't know what his profession was, but he was a great athlete—doing handstands, walking on his hands, and other impossible feats. He tried to teach us how to walk on our hands, but none of us had much success. Apart from these accomplishments, he helped my parents running the pension. Salomon Cohen and Bram Wijnberg, two of my cousins, also came to help.

One part-time job Father took was as the general practitioner at the Apeldoornse Bos, an insane asylum for Jewish children, situated about five kilometers outside Apeldoorn. This asylum was lucky in that most of its psychiatric staff were Jews so that its operation could continue in a nearly normal way.

HISTORY BRIEF, PAGE 235
Westerbork

June 1941
The letter *J* is added to Jewish identification cards.

ERWIN

Every person in Holland received an identification card, and Jews were "favored" with an extra *J* on their card. In addition, we were required to carry an identification card from the Jewish Council, declaring each as a "full" Jew or "half" Jew.

NATHAN

You were a Jew if one of your grandparents was a Jew.

June 22, 1941
German forces invade the Soviet
Union.

HISTORY BRIEF, PAGE 234
Germany Invades the Soviet Union

NATHAN

That summer, the Germans attacked Russia, and we were sure that
this would be the bite on which they would choke. But the Germans
seemed to run through Russia and seemed to be invincible.

August 1941
Jews must deposit all liquid financial
assets over 1,000 guilders to Lippmann-
Rosenthal & Co., a former Jewish
bank now under German control.

ERWIN

All Jewish valuables were confiscated, and everyone was required
to deposit their assets in a special bank created for this purpose.
Each person could spend no more than 250 guilders per month, and
any excess earnings were confiscated. Business assets were exceptions from this requirement. At the same time, all foreign Jews were
required to register at the Center for Jewish Emigration. Naturally,
emigration was not an option; rather, they wanted to know, as
precisely as possible, the assets brought by Jews emigrating from
Germany (for which they had paid taxes, by the way) or earned
here in the Netherlands. An exact list of collections, art, jewelry,
gold and silver, antiques, etc. was also required. Even luggage had
to be surrendered.

HISTORY BRIEF, PAGE 233
The Central Office for Jewish Emigration

August 25, 1941
Decree forbids Jewish children from
attending public schools; the
Jewish Council sets up a segregated
education system.

FIFI

September 22, 1941: At the beginning of September, when the three
girls were supposed to start school again, it was forbidden for
Jewish children to attend all schools. The Blik-Kalker family and
a few other people organized and managed to set up a small,
private Montessori school. Now the girls go three mornings and one
afternoon to school. We were happy to have them in the school
system again, but not with the solution of Mrs. Cohen ter Vaert. We
got to know her in Rotterdam as head of the girls' school. She was
theoretically very good, but in practice absolutely couldn't manage
it at all. Children perceive that immediately. She has no sense of
humor. Maybe she is too old. In any case, she acts old and causes too
many problems. So now the girls just have to bite the bullet. They
miss their former school a lot; it is very noticeable.

MIRJAM

We were about to be murdered by the Nazis, and our parents were
still worried about our education. Small schools were set up all

over Holland just for Jewish teachers and pupils. My parents came together with the other Jewish parents and started a Jewish Montessori school. My mother's sister Jet, together with the head of the Montessori school in Rotterdam, were the teachers for five or six classes.

JUDITH

For a short time, we went to an improvised Jewish school in The Hague, which was about an hour away by scooter. I say "improvised" because it wasn't a real school. It was two rooms in an empty mansion that had been relinquished by its Jewish owners. A few Jewish teachers, including Mammie's sister Jet, somehow taught a bunch of kids of all different age groups together. How they did that with all the pressure they were under, I don't know. We kids still had fun, though not for long.

NATHAN

After the summer vacation was over, my father took a second job as a teacher at the Jewish school. He had gone to a teacher's college and become a schoolmaster before deciding that teaching was not for him and deciding to study medicine instead. This Jewish school was in a building about five kilometers from our house. (Maybe less, but in my memory, it was a very long walk.) There were two classes, one for children in first to fourth grade, and the second from fourth grade till high school, where Father was the teacher. I was in the second class and did not enjoy the experience of being the teacher's son. Father took his job seriously, and we had to do much homework.

DAVID

At the Jewish school, we had to have all Jewish teachers. The Dutch started realizing what a danger it was to have all Jews in one place. At that time the Germans started arresting young Jewish boys, supposedly for work camps in Germany.

At the Jewish school, I played the same handball as in the not-Jewish school. We were the only people who were Jewish on our street, but I kept on playing with friends from my neighborhood after school. They didn't care that I had a star. For some reason, we didn't have to move (to the Jewish Ghetto). I could still play at my friends' houses. They didn't shut me out because I was Jewish. Their parents probably explained to them what was going on—that it was a bad situation for the Jews and not to make it worse for me.

September 15, 1941
Jews are barred from public parks, cafés, restaurants, hotels, theaters, museums, and zoos.

Registration with Lippmann-Rosenthal & Co. bank is required for Jewish-owned land and real estate; once registered, Jewish property became the target of expropriation.

Second row, fourth from right:
Mirjam, class photo, ca. 1938

We were about to be murdered by
the Nazis, and our parents were still
worried about our education.
MIRJAM

October 1941

German authorities order employers to dismiss Jewish employees. Workers are given three months' notice and significantly reduced pensions; many lose their work permits.

The NSB (Dutch Nazi Party) establishes a bureau to take over Jewish businesses. Within the month, 1,400 Jewish textile dealers lose their businesses.

ERWIN

Our situation as Jews became ever more dangerous. Gradually, all of the large businesses passed into German hands. In October 1941, about 400 of the largest fashion houses were forced to close, and from one day to the next, I lost all of my customers. My employees remained loyal, and I devoted all my energy to keeping the business afloat via the production of paper bags and belts.

I knew that one day I, too, would have my company taken from me, and I had to arrange to get cash to keep my family and myself alive. Therefore, unofficial sales, unofficial resources. I saved and set aside as much stock as possible with the hope that this troublesome war would end someday, and my family and I would still be here. I began providing false numbers in my monthly reports and thereby saved a few hundred meters of leather and imitation leather and spirited them out the door, in the hopes of using them after the war. My conscience was completely clear. Sewing machines were exchanged too. The good ones left and bad ones replaced them. Hopefully, I'll see them again.

DAVID

My father had a leather goods factory for the garment industry. The factory was taken away. He had about thirty-five, forty employees. The Germans put a woman in charge as administrator. My father was not allowed to enter his own factory.

ERWIN

A reader who doesn't know me should not assume that I am a person who is always calm and composed, melting with sympathy out of pure benevolence. Nothing could be further from the truth. Many of my clients can attest that I can say the most unpleasant truths in a booming voice directly to your face and that my words are not unpacked, silk-wrapped, from Knigge's book *On Human Relations*. Raw and never lacking in naturalness, I can throw a rude expression right in someone's face.

November 16, 1941

The Jewish Symphony Orchestra, comprising the seventy-five best Jewish players dismissed from the Netherlands' professional orchestras, performs its first concert, playing a Mendelssohn program at the Hollandse Schouwburg (Dutch Theater).

Erwin (in white coat) in his
Amsterdam leather goods factory,
ca. late 1930s

*Our situation as Jews became ever
more dangerous. Gradually, all
of the large businesses passed into
German hands. In October 1941,
about 400 of the largest fashion
houses were forced to close, and
from one day to the next, I lost all
of my customers.*
ERWIN

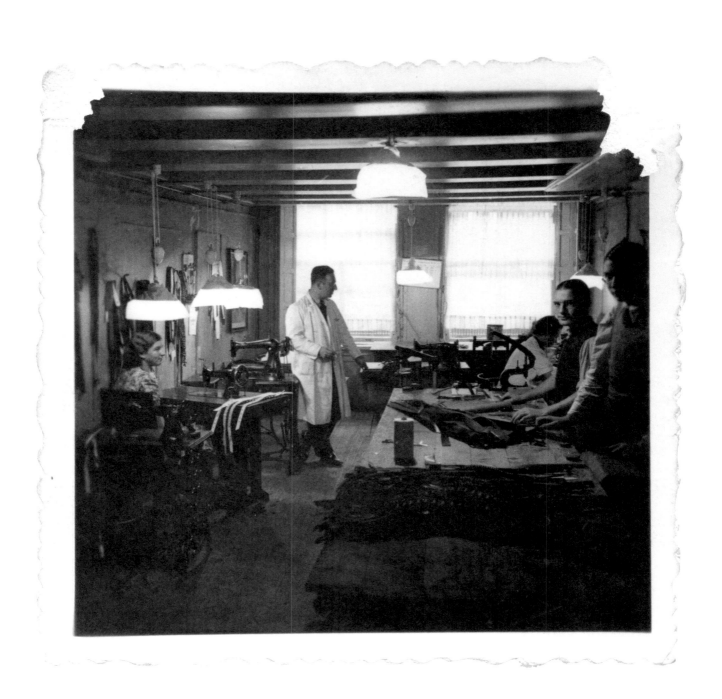

HISTORY BRIEF, PAGE 234
Jewish Symphony Orchestra

ERWIN

In spite of the ever-worsening circumstances, we did all we could to maintain a cultural life. Two theaters for Jews opened their doors. An unforgettable experience was attending the opening concert of the Jewish Symphony Orchestra in November 1941. It was a superb Mendelssohn program, with the best Dutch musicians. I think it will be rare, in the future, to attend a concert with such famous musicians. I also continued to hold chamber music evenings, and I enjoyed playing the flute more than ever before. I remember with pleasure the four house concerts we gave, in which I was the soloist in the Haydn concerto for flute and orchestra. Until June, we had weekly music evenings without interruption, which took place in our apartment since we had the space (we cleared a big area after the removal of our antique furniture), and we couldn't have wished for better acoustics. We always invited listeners, who were very thankful to hear good music.

How painful it is to remember these pleasant evenings. I am constantly pursued by the terrible thought that most of the friends and acquaintances who either played or listened had the awful fate of being deported to Poland. That I write "most" has terrible significance because those who weren't captured and deported took their own lives. Only very few were lucky enough to remain in Westerbork.

December 7, 1941
Japan bombs the US naval base in
Pearl Harbor, killing over 2,400
Americans.

December 8, 1941
The United States enters World War II,
declaring war on Japan.

December 11, 1941
Germany and Italy declare war on
the United States; the United
States immediately returns the
proclamation.

NATHAN

In Russia, freezing temperatures slowed the Germans' advance outside of Moscow. *Radio Oranje* sent reports of the terribly cold weather in Russia and the difficulties for the Germans. We totally believed that the BBC was always telling the true story, and I think that this was usually the case. The Dutch (German-controlled) radio started to send requests that people should prepare packages with balaclavas, scarves, gloves, and other warm clothing for our brave soldiers defending the West against the Bolsheviks.

In December 1941, Japan raided Pearl Harbor and declared war on all colonizing countries. The United States declared war on Germany after Pearl Harbor. This again was good news, since everyone (at least all of our acquaintances) was sure the Germans would be defeated very soon as they could not fight the whole world.

HISTORY BRIEF, PAGE 234
Japan Attacks the United States

January 1942
The Jewish Council reveals the names
and addresses of unemployed Jews
for deportation to forced labor camps.

De Vonk, a Dutch underground newspaper, calls upon all Dutch people
to sabotage the "thousand fears in
which the Jews are forced to live,"
indicating the long list of antisemitic
orders, the deportations of over
900 mostly young Jewish men to
Germany, and their deaths.

January 17, 1942
The first group of provincial Jews
is removed to Amsterdam. Evacuees
are required to give police their
house keys and a list of the possessions they are bringing with them.

DAVID

Jews from all over Holland were forced to move to the Jewish section
in Amsterdam that the Germans had developed. We lived in a neighborhood where very few Jews lived—we never got an order to move.
My aunt, uncle, and cousin—the Eschenheimers—had to move to
the Jewish section in Amsterdam. My cousin, Felix, was six years old
at the time. He lost his toys, friends, and school.

    The Germans only allowed the people to take clothes, bedding,
kitchen utensils, and one room of furniture with them. My aunt, uncle,
and cousin moved in with my grandfather Max—four people in two
rooms. Living conditions became very crowded in the ghetto: more
than one family to one room, six families to one toilet and one kitchen,
no shower or bathtub. After six o'clock, Jews were not allowed on
the street. With all those regulations, it was very easy for the Germans
to round up the Jews and deport them.

HISTORY BRIEF, PAGE 234
The "Ghetto"

January 20, 1942
Nazi leaders meet to discuss the Final
Solution—their plan to round up
all European Jews and send them east
to extermination camps—at the
Wannsee Conference in Germany.

March 20, 1942
Jews are forbidden from owning and
driving vehicles.

NATHAN

Our car, a 1936 Willys, was put on jacks in the garage in our garden.
Sometime later, if I remember rightly, it was confiscated.

March 26, 1942
Jews are forbidden from marrying
non-Jews.

The citizens and royal family of Denmark protected its Jewish community from persecution and death; however, the people and king of Denmark did not wear the Jewish Star. In fact, Jews in Denmark were not required to wear the star.

April 29, 1942
Jews are ordered to wear an identifying Jewish Star on their clothing as of May 3.

DAVID

We were marked. Jews had to wear a yellow Star of David with the word *Jood* (Jew) in imitation Hebrew letters on their clothing—these we had to buy. The Germans tried marking the Jews in all the occupied countries in the West of Europe. Overall, the Dutch did not like it but didn't make a big fuss. In Denmark, the whole Danish population started to wear the stars, including the Danish royal family, and the Germans revoked the order.

NATHAN

One day I was playing outside, and coming home saw a German car in front of our house. I ran away, took off my coat with the yellow star, and went and sat in the Oranjepark, from where I could watch the house. How long I sat there, I don't know, but in the end the car drove off, and I went home, fearing that my family had been transported. My parents in the meantime had missed me and were phoning friends to see if I was playing there and had forgotten to come home (which was apt to happen).

Pesach that year was not a festive occasion. Both sets of parents of my cousins Salomon and Bram were sent to Westerbork, also another aunt and uncle.

MIRJAM

Every Jew over the age of six had to wear a big yellow Star of David on whatever clothing she or he was wearing. One day it was said in the newspapers that at such-and-such place you could buy the star outside of a building. We all did exactly as we were told. That's how people were those days. I remember how awful I felt whenever I was outside. I knew I wasn't bad, but I felt ashamed. You were a non-person, a person people didn't want to associate with; you were different. Maybe you are bad because the Germans said Jews are bad? It's terrible when you are told, "There goes this person with the star, don't associate with her." It makes you feel like you are nothing.

My parents explained that there are people in the world who hate Jews. There was no reason; they just hate Jews. How do you explain this? We were so little aware that we were different. We were just Dutch, but people were afraid to socialize with us.

HADASSAH

I understood that being Jewish was walking around with a yellow Star of David. Before that, we had no awareness of Jewishness.

May 21, 1942
Jews must turn in art, jewelry, precious metals, and funds above 250 guilders to the Germans, with the exception of wedding rings, gold teeth, and one set of silver flatware per person.

DAVID

Jewish belongings were stolen and taken to Germany. The Germans were told these things were gifts from the Dutch. After the people were forced to leave their houses, a moving van from Puls (a Dutch Nazi moving company) came in front of the Jewish homes and emptied out all the belongings, even items that had been in the family for years.

ERWIN

Because my goal was always to stay one step ahead of the authorities, I took care to remove all of our valuables from the apartment: antiques, silver, linen, carpets, electronic devices, porcelain, even extra clothing and food. Sure enough, we were soon forbidden to remove anything from our apartments. To enforce this, the Germans inventoried all Jewish apartments, and anything the officials found, they immediately took. Especially objects that fit comfortably in their pockets.

DAVID

We had an attic, and my father cut a hole in the ceiling. He put some thin mattresses down and said if the Germans come, we will hide in the attic. Non-Jewish friends hid my parents' silver, jewelry, and everything of value.

June 15, 1942
The Dutch press reports an affirmation from Nazi leadership that Germany is devoted to the annihilation of the Jews.

June 24, 1942
Bicycles belonging to Jews outside of Amsterdam are confiscated. Failure to hand over bikes results in arrest or fines.

NATHAN

Jews had to turn in their bicycles, and there was a fast exchange of good bicycles for old and unusable ones. We were glad to give the Germans only the worst, and our neighbors were probably glad to get new, or nearly new, bicycles for the wrecked ones they gave us. For me, it was no great loss, since I went around on my roller skates, which the Germans did not forbid us to use.

MIRJAM

Jews were not allowed to own cars or bicycles, and we weren't allowed to go on the tram anymore. Since our school was quite far away, the three of us left every morning on our little scooters, with a little backpack, for an arduous one-hour trip each way.

June 30, 1942
A new order institutes a curfew between 8 p.m. and 6 a.m. for Jews, restricts the hours when Jews can shop, and prohibits Jews from visiting the homes of Gentiles.

HISTORY BRIEF, PAGE 235
Looting and the Abraham Puls & Sons Moving Company

Judith's Jewish Star and book, 1942

At that moment, I didn't realize the danger of keeping the star (in hiding). Afterward, I kept it a secret, realizing I had disobeyed my father. After the war, I put it in a book I loved to read.
JUDITH

RIEKES GROENHOUT

Gijsje

*Roman over kinderen
voor kleine en . . . . grote mensen*

A. J. G. Strengholt's Uitgevers Maatschappij. N.V.
Aan de Leidschegracht 11 te Amsterdam

NATHAN

Gentiles were forbidden to offer hospitality to Jews. This meant that a Jew could not visit a Gentile (Aryan) friend at his house. Henk and I did remain friends, though it was now less fun since there were a lot of activities I could no longer participate in. Every year there was a fair in Apeldoorn, and 1942 was no exception. Since it was in the marketplace, it was open all around. Signs forbidding entry for dogs and Jews were also prominently displayed. I once took off my yellow Star of David and went anyway but did not enjoy it, since I felt like a fugitive, even while riding the merry-go-round, which usually was one of my favorite attractions with its loud oom-pah-pah music.

Henk and I still went to each other's houses, though this was forbidden. I only went through the connecting garden and only after making sure that no strangers were at their house. We still could go to our garden and play and swim there, but it seemed to become smaller than before, probably because we were growing up. I was afraid of the Germans and would go to the other side of the road when meeting them.

July 5, 1942
Summons are sent to 4,000 Jews to report for transports to the east between July 15 and 18; when fewer than one-third of those summoned show up, Jews from Westerbork are added to fill trains headed for Auschwitz, where most are murdered.

Telephone service is disconnected for Jews living in Dutch provinces. In Amsterdam, phone companies require subscribers to declare their race; those who identify as Jewish receive notice that their service is terminated.

July 20, 1942
Bicycles belonging to Jews in Amsterdam are confiscated.

ERWIN

Now, reader of these lines, we have reached the point where the worst time has to be described. A time of fear and danger, despair, calamity, suffering, and persecution. It lasted exactly one year, from July 1942 to July 1943.

August 6, 1942
Black Thursday raid rounds up 2,000 Jews to fill the Germans' deportation quota; raids increase as Jews go into hiding rather than show up for transport.

NATHAN

The Germans stepped up their anti-Jewish measures. Dutch Jewish families had to report for transport to Westerbork or were woken in the middle of the night to be sent there. The Hanff family (an elderly German couple who were staying at our pension) had to report to be transported, but Father gave Mr. Hanff an injection, which made him very ill (on purpose), and he could stay with us under medical attention. But after a few weeks, the Hanff family had to go to the Westerbork concentration camp.

The Germans said that the Jews would be sent to the east, to work there, and most Jews believed them. The general opinion was that the Germans, even though they behaved atrociously, were still a civilized people, with a rich heritage of Bach, Handel, Mozart, Heine, etc., and would not murder whole groups of people, even if they did not like them. Maybe the Jews would have a difficult time, but this had happened before, and after some time it would probably blow over. Also, the war could not last forever, and surely the Allies would shortly win the war.

The Dutch underground started to do some sabotage acts, and the Germans picked Dutchmen randomly from the street. If a German soldier was killed or wounded by a "terrorist act," or a train was derailed, or some other sabotage was done, some ten persons would be chosen randomly and killed as a reprisal. The Germans made no secret about it; in fact, they put up big signs with the names of the people killed.

MIRJAM
Tante Jet didn't show up at the Montessori school. When I asked my parents what happened to her, they said Jet and her family were hauled off to a concentration camp.

JUDITH
Day by day, fewer kids came to school. They either were caught by the Germans, or had gone to the train station as they were told to do by the Dutch authorities (very Dutch to do exactly as you are told to do), or had gone into hiding with the help of the underground movement.

NATHAN
After vacation, we again went to school, but pupils disappeared at an alarming rate: their families either were sent to Westerbork or went into hiding. We could tell they were hiding when the Germans published "wanted as runaway criminals" with their pictures in the local paper. Empty chairs in the class became just another part of our routine.

The teacher of the lower-grade class also went into hiding or was sent to Westerbork. I don't know which, and Father was left with a class of children aged six to thirteen.

DAVID
The Germans took people from old-age homes and orphanages.

MIRJAM
We heard about people committing suicide—a man and wife had jumped off a building. I remember thinking, How can people kill themselves? It seemed so strange to me.

DAVID

Our doctor was Jewish and a very good friend of the family. He had about six or seven kids, and his sister lived about two houses down from the Jewish school I attended. She and her husband had four kids. One day, a lot of police were in front of their house. Her whole family went into the kitchen, she turned on the gas, and they committed suicide—or she committed suicide for the family. I thought, Why would somebody take their own life? I played with the doctor's kids, and his sister's kids were sometimes at the house, so these were people that I knew. As an eleven-year-old kid, I couldn't understand why people from my circle would kill themselves. I think people heard what happened in some of the camps and started realizing what was going to happen to the Jews. Maybe the family talked about it and decided that rather than grieving and suffering, this was the best way out. I knew my parents would not do this to me.

NATHAN

All war news was bad. The Germans were again advancing in Russia, this time to the south, in the direction of the oil fields of Baku in the Ural Mountains. The Germans also went to help the Italians in North Africa and were advancing there too. The Japanese army conquered the Dutch East Indies. Singapore fell to the Japanese.

HISTORY BRIEF, PAGE 234
Japanese Occupation of the Dutch East Indies

DAVID

I was playing with a bunch of kids in front of the school. A German came up to me and said, "Hey, you Jew, start crawling on the street." Well, I was scared to death of him, and I started crawling on the street. He said, "Very good, start jumping up and run back and lie on the street again and lick the road." This was degrading, someone ordering me around in front of my friends. Friends who saw it happen right away ran to a teacher in the school and told him what was going on. They were afraid that the guy would take me. Not too far away from there was the German SS command in Amsterdam. But then, the German guy said, "You did very well, go back to your friends," and let me go.

HISTORY BRIEF, PAGE 231
The SS

I knew people who were taken away—hauled out of their houses in the night. I was afraid the Germans would take me. I'd heard of Westerbork, a camp for Jews who would then be taken to Germany. I realized this could happen to me. When I came home, I told my parents about this.

NATHAN

Salomon and Bram again were helping my parents out with the guesthouse. They were known as the refuse bins since at dinner any leftovers would disappear in their mouths. Bram and Salomon would take me on long walks, and a lot of heads would turn at the unusual sight of three red-haired boys. My cousins must have been in their early twenties, and I was very flattered that they consented in letting me go with them on these walks.

Salomon and Bram were picked up that autumn after they returned to Groningen.

Salomon Cohen, Nathan's cousin (murdered, Sobibor, June 11, 1943, 23 years old); Abraham (Bram) Wijnberg, Nathan's cousin (murdered, Auschwitz, September 30, 1942, 19 years old).

October 2, 1942

The German and Dutch police receive orders to seize over 5,000 Jewish men and send them to forced-labor camps along with their family members; approximately 13,000 are sent first to Westerbork and then to Auschwitz.

DAVID

My father decided that I should have a bar mitzvah. I was supposed to be bar mitzvahed at the end of '43, but my father thought, "Well, everyone is still there." He wanted to speed it up because he didn't know what would happen to us. I was bar mitzvahed at the end of '42. The feeling among the grown-ups was that this was the last time that everyone would be together. A lot of people who were already in hiding could not come.

NATHAN

My father had a special *Ausweiss*, a kind of work permit, as a doctor of the Apeldoornse Bos hospital for Jewish children, and therefore we were not on the lists of families to be transported.

Winter came early in 1942. I enjoyed it since I could go ice-skating with my friends. They went with me to the canal, which was not closed for Jews, or to our garden, or even to the official skating rink, where you had to pay an entrance fee. Since it was far from our house, and I did not look typically Jewish with my red hair and blue eyes, we (in reality I) chanced it, and I took off my star to skate there.

For Chanukah that year, Father made ice cream with an ice-cream machine he built by having a tinsmith fit a double-walled drum in an old washing machine. The outer drum he filled with ice from the small pond in our garden, to which some salt was added to lower the temperature. The inner drum was filled with cream, some whites of eggs, vanilla, and sugar. I think we were the only family in Apeldoorn who had ice cream that winter. As usual, Henk celebrated Chanukah with us, and I went to him for Christmas.

ERWIN

Perhaps, and maybe most likely, the non-Jewish world never fully comprehended the cruelty toward citizens by the Nazi regime. In the last few years, I often noticed that non-Jews found the German solution for the Dutch "Jewish question" horrible, but solely out of compassion for the victims, rather than their soul being gripped by the horror of it. Only when they and their families are victims of German cruelty and abduction, when their bicycle or radio is confiscated, when a son or brother is arrested on the street and deported, only then are people conscious of these inhuman methods. But to us Jews, the theft of our bicycles and radios was nothing— they took everything, even the last penny and our houses and homes, then they deported us, from fourteen-day-old infants to ninety-year-old men.

HISTORY BRIEF, PAGE 233
Dutch Accommodation

Separated

When the deportations began, Jews had few options for escape. German E-boats (fast attack craft) made a sea crossing to England impossible; journeys to neutral Switzerland or Spain were very difficult. By the late summer of 1942, knowing that they would not receive an exemption from deportation, some 40,000 Jews sought hiding places—though only 28,000 would secure them. Going into hiding meant one of two things: either one assumed a different, non-Jewish identity, or one quite literally hid—or, as the Dutch called it, lived *ondergedoken* (literally, "submerged").

The first option meant that one had to fabricate a family history and access forged documents. Dutch identity documents were notoriously fake-proof, and the Netherlands had the best population registries in the world. In addition, Dutch society, with its pillars and idiosyncratic local communities, was essentially a collection of villages in which it was difficult for a new arrival to pass as a local.

Those who "submerged" had to surrender whatever remained of an independent life, accept the severance of all ties with society and family, and consent to a life in a very small and often very uncomfortable place, invisible to the world, for an indeterminate period. In many cases, hiders were also expected to contribute financially to their sustenance. It was a difficult decision to make. Many of the helpers were people who felt the need to act and who were willing to risk their freedom. Thousands of these helpers worked alone, thousands had the support of their immediate families, and thousands were part of grassroots networks that became quite experienced in finding hiding places, escorting the hunted to safe havens, and meeting needs once there.

1942–1943

August 19, 1942
Mirjam begins her time in hiding with the Willemse family in Voorburg.

Judith and Hadassah first hide with Kees and Tine Hos in Rijswijk.

August–September 1942
The four sons of Fifi's sister Annie Maarssen—Harry, Bob, Sally, and Bernhard—are murdered in Auschwitz.

September 1942
Hadassah changes addresses, moving to Franciscus and Petronella Lafontaine's home in Wassenaar.

Judith moves to Alida Wouters-van der Lely's home in Wassenaar.

September 2, 1942
Mirjam moves to Jan and Nan van Gelder's home in Wassenaar.

Autumn 1942
Chaim and Fifi go into hiding with Johanna Leepel-Labotz in The Hague.

Winter 1942
Chaim and Fifi go to the Hos family in The Hague, followed by stays at two undocumented locations.

December 17, 1942
The Allied powers release a joint statement acknowledging "the bestial policy of cold-blooded extermination," detailing how the Germans are "carrying into effect Hitler's often repeated intention to exterminate the Jewish people in Europe. From all the occupied countries Jews are being transported, in conditions of appalling horror and brutality, to Eastern Europe."

January 1943
Chaim and Fifi move to a new hiding address with Tjeerde and Antje Miedema in Ede, a city in the central Netherlands.

ca. January 1943
David's aunt, uncle, and cousin, the Eschenheimers, whom David vacationed with, are forced to move to the Amsterdam ghetto.

January 16, 1943
The first Jewish prisoners arrive at Vught, a transit camp in southern Holland run by the SS, the Nazis' paramilitary unit.

January 21, 1943
Nathan goes into hiding with the Zoon family in Utrecht.

Nathan's parents begin hiding with a doctor friend in Velp, in the east-central Netherlands.

January 28, 1943
Nathan moves to Amsterdam, where he stays with Johan and Mop Hunningher.

ca. February 1943
Nathan's parents go to hide in Anne and Jo Bakker's home in Velp.

March 1943
David begins hiding in a superintendent's apartment at an Amsterdam wallpaper factory.

March 2, 1943
The first transport leaves Westerbork for the Sobibor extermination camp.

March 9, 1943
David's aunt, uncle, and cousin—Luzie, Eugen, and Felix Peter Eschenheimer—are murdered in Auschwitz.

March 30, 1943
The Germans order all Jews from eight of the eleven Dutch provinces to the Vught concentration camp by April 10.

Mid-April 1943
David returns home to his parents after a close call with the Dutch and German police while attempting to switch hiding addresses.

April 13–23, 1943
On April 13, all Jews remaining in the Netherlands, with the exception of those living in Amsterdam and those with temporary exemptions, are ordered to go to Vught before April 23.

Chaim and Fifi go to the Groeneveld family in Rotterdam.

April 29, 1943
Growing public pressure about the need to save Jews in Europe forces the American and British governments to meet at the Bermuda Conference. Fearing a refugee crisis would distract from winning the war, the delegates evade addressing the Nazis' plan to annihilate the Jews. The Americans refuse to take more Jewish refugees; the British avoid discussion of permitting Jewish refugees into Palestine.

June 1943
Fifi's sister Jet de Lange and nieces Hetty and Mirjam are murdered in Sobibor.

Early July 1943
The Geismars split up: David and Erwin go into hiding with Erika Heymann in Amsterdam; David's mother hides as a non-Jewish maid for the Hoyer family in the Amsterdam suburb of Amstelveen.

July 16, 1943
Chaim's mother and sister, Naatje and Martha de Zoete, are murdered in Sobibor.

July 19, 1943
David leaves his father to hide in Friesland, a rural area in the North.

De Zoete Family

HISTORY BRIEF, PAGE 235
Flight Options

Jet Polak-de Lange, Fifi's older sister (murdered, Sobibor, June 11, 1943, 49 years old); Karel de Lange (murdered, Sobibor, July 23, 1943, 42 years old); Hetty and Mirjam de Lange, Fifi's nieces (both murdered, Sobibor, Hetty on June 11, 1943, 8 years old; and Mirjam on June 14, 1943, 13 years old).

Hans Polak, Fifi's younger brother (murdered, Dachau, February 20, 1945, 28 years old).

HISTORY BRIEF, PAGE 235
The Dutch Theater

CHAIM

As the situation grew more difficult by the day, schools grew emptier and razzias to round up Jews were held in the nearby village of Voorburg. We decided to go into hiding—with the children separate in order to enhance their possibility of survival.

MIRJAM

We were kept in the dark because you weren't supposed to worry kids. My parents were very much aware of what was going on. We would hear them whispering and crying. They must have been planning to hide all of us for quite a while. About two weeks before we went into hiding, I asked my father if we would ever be separated. And he said no, we would always be together.

It was just the night before we went into hiding that our parents told us it was no longer safe for us to stay home. Any day now the Germans and the Dutch Nazis could burst into our house, load us on a truck, and put us on transport trains to the concentration camps. Many Jews had already been transported to the camps.

My father was amazing. He planned and insisted that we hide. He just totally saw that the whole thing was very dark, and he was obviously right. There were two groups of people: the ones, like my father, who saw it—that it was going to be terrible and we had to do anything we could not to get transported; and then there were my mother's sister Jet and her husband, who thought that as long as we did exactly what the Germans said, then we'd be okay. They went when they were told to go, for the transport. They went with their two kids, including their oldest daughter—my best friend, who had the same name as me. They went, and they never came back.

JUDITH

At this point, I would like to clarify a few things. Pappie believed that dreams could be foretelling. He had a dream about Jews being shot and thrown into graves. At that time, nobody knew about the concentration camps in that part of Europe. This dream, which he believed was a warning, made him decide to take measures, and he got in touch with the underground—I think through Mammie's brothers Ben and Hans, who were communists working for the underground movement. They subsequently were caught; Hans and his wife, Annetje, were tortured in a Dutch prison by the Dutch and the German police and sent to Auschwitz. Hans was murdered in Dachau; Annetje survived and came back to find her daughter, Chaja. Ben escaped from the Hollandse Schouwburg (Dutch Theater), where they were held before being sent to prison, and survived. All the time during the war he was active in the underground.

MIRJAM

My father thought his kids would have a better chance of surviving in hiding. It was more plausible for kids to integrate into another family than for adults. Rarely did a family hide together, because people couldn't, for practical reasons, take in entire families, and this would also increase the chance of being caught.

Fifi's nieces Hetty and Mirjam
de Lange, 1938

*My mother's sister Jet and her husband
thought that as long as we did exactly
what the Germans said, then we'd be
okay. They went when they were told
to go, for the transport. They went with
their two kids, including their oldest
daughter—my best friend, who had the
same name as me. They went, and
they never came back.*
MIRJAM

HADASSAH

Mammie told us that we could not live together for some time and that we had to go to the people where she had sent a suitcase with our clothes and favorite toys.

MIRJAM

When the time came, when we had to separate, we were told it would be for a short time. We already, gradually, had so many things we couldn't do—we couldn't go swimming, we couldn't go to the movies, we couldn't go to restaurants. So this was one more thing of the bad things that happened.

When I first went into hiding, my hair was cut, because long hair with braids makes you look more Jewish. My first name was changed to Manja. My stars were taken off all of my coats and sweaters. I remember being scared because being outside without the star was against the law.

A couple of days before, my parents brought small suitcases to the hiding places. We couldn't have luggage with us because it would be too suspicious. We were all going to different places. We were not allowed to know where in case one of us was caught by the Germans.

It was August 19, 1942. I was eleven years old. My two younger sisters, Judith and Hadassah, were ten and nine. I was the first one to leave. I was given a scooter and told to go to the home of friends of my parents. I knew the road, I knew where to go. It was a fifteen-minute ride. Their last name was Willemse; I had been to their home many times. I would be there for two weeks only. My hiding family, Jan and Nan van Gelder, could not take me till September. The Willemse family was leaving for a sailing vacation in northern Holland, but that didn't cause a problem, they would just take me with them. I think Mr. Willemse was a big shot working for the harbor of Rotterdam.

They were extremely nice to me. Nevertheless, I dreaded breakfast. Every morning, the mother of the family served hot oatmeal with pieces of burned crust in it, which we all had to eat. I guess that her kids were used to it, but I certainly wasn't!

All of us went to friends of the family, so we didn't go right away to strangers' homes. Before the war, I slept at my cousin's house sometimes, and once my parents put the three of us in a pension while they were on vacation. It was only for one week, and we were together. But this was the first time I was away and alone.

We kissed and hugged each other goodbye. Don't cry, I was told; everything had to look as normal as possible. Looking back now, I realize how much more awful it must have been for my parents to have to send their children away, not knowing how we would be treated or even if they would ever see us again.

CHAIM

On a morning in August 1942, we sent the children away on their scooters, instructing them to take off their sweaters with the yellow star on a lonely way near a canal, and then to proceed to a certain address in Rijswijk (Mr. K. Hos). From there, they were taken to the final addresses. Mirjam went to the family of Mr. Jan van Gelder, a

Mr. and Mrs. H. Willemse, the parents of Mirjam's school friend Barta, sheltered Mirjam from August 19 to September 2, 1942.

Judith and Hadassah went to Mr. K. Hos; Mirjam went first to the Willemse family, and later to the Van Gelders.

Separated

conservator at the Rijksprentenkabinet living at Oranjelaan 10. Judith first stayed at the home of Mrs. A. Wouters. And Hadassah's first hiding place was with the Lafontaine family. All were in the town of Wassenaar (near The Hague). My wife and I were first at separate addresses, which were known to be only temporary.

The Van Gelder family was the center from which the saving of our three daughters took place. It was Mrs. van Gelder who found the initial addresses for Judith and Hadassah, and Mirjam, then aged eleven, remained with them. At the time we decided to go into hiding, the Van Gelders were not at home, and so other friends of ours, the Willemses (Mr. H. Willemse was the director of a shipping agency) took Mirjam on a two-week sailing trip on the lakes in the north of the country. Thereafter, she stayed at the Van Gelders and was entirely taken up in the family life. Mrs. van Gelder also took care to remain informed about the other two daughters and helped us by selling some trinkets in order to enable us to pay our own board. She also gave Mirjam lessons so that afterward she would not lag too far behind at school.

JUDITH

We, Hadassah and me, regarded this as some kind of adventure, but for our parents it probably was one of the hardest things they ever did in their whole life—telling your children "Go," not knowing if you would ever see them again, see them back alive, is really unacceptably cruel. As a mother with children, I often remember that day. Imagine telling your children to go someplace (even to somebody you know), not knowing if you'll ever see them again. That must have been so hard.

After arrangements were made, our parents told Hadassah and me, "Go to Uncle Kees (a friend of our uncle Hans, who had already taken our cousin Chaja in his care). But before you reach his house, make a stop and go under one of the bridges on the way, and take off your jacket and leave it there." (My Jewish Star was sewn onto a jacket, which we put on top of whatever we were wearing.) "Once you reach his house, he will take care of everything."

Why did we wait to take off our jackets? Because Pappie told us! Pappie educated us by being an example, usually NOT by telling us what to do (or not). But IF he did, we never argued. Also, we didn't take off our jackets before leaving the house because Pappie probably thought there might be a chance neighbors might see us. Where we took them off under the bridge, nobody saw us doing it, and coming out of there without it wouldn't raise suspicion; it was quite some distance from our neighborhood, and it wasn't an unusual sight to see kids coming and going from under a bridge.

Under the bridge on our way to Kees Hos I took off my jacket and put it in the bag I had with me and really forgot about it. At that moment, I didn't realize the danger of keeping the star. Afterward, I kept it a secret, realizing I had disobeyed my father. After the war, I put it in a book I loved to read. I still have that book (see pp. 78–79).

I remember Kees Hos as a very nice man (I don't remember his wife, Tine) and also that Chaja (still a baby) was there. Hadassah and

Jan and Nan van Gelder, friends of the De Zoetes, hid Mirjam from September 2, 1942, to January 1943 in their house at Oranjelaan 4 in Utrecht. Nan had a PhD in the history of art, and Jan was the director of The Hague's Rijksprentenkabinet, one of the most important collections of prints, drawings, photographs, and illuminated manuscripts in Europe.

Kees and Tine Hos hid Judith and Hadassah from August 19 to September 1942 at Prins-Hendrikstraat, The Hague.

I were there for a very short time, after which we went to our first long-term hiding places, both of us to Wassenaar. Every time, thinking of the people who did what they did during the war (hiding Jewish people and working in the underground movement), I am so full of admiration. It took a lot of courage; they were in constant danger of being betrayed and caught. Did you know that most of those people were either left-wing oriented or religious? And also did you know that in Holland 75 percent of the Jews were killed during the war?

HISTORY BRIEF, PAGE 238
The Fate of Dutch Jews

Chaja Polak is Fifi's niece and the De Zoete girls' first cousin.

HISTORY BRIEF, PAGE 237
Resistance Organizations and Workers

CHAJA POLAK

Shortly after the German occupation, my parents, Hans Polak and Annetje Kupferschmidt-Polak, met with Kees Hos and his wife, Tine de Leede-Hos, in The Hague. Kees told them: "Anytime you are in trouble, you can count on Tine and me."

Kees and Hans met in high school and became friends. Kees went on to study and then teach at the Royal Dutch Academy of Art in The Hague. Hans studied electrical engineering at Delft University, where he secretly took his final exams at the homes of his professors because the Germans prohibited Jews from entering the university.

Hans had to go into hiding at several addresses after the communist resistance group that he belonged to was betrayed. Annetje—pregnant with me—remained behind with her brother Albert, Hans's mother, Goldine, his brother Sam, and Sam's wife, Fietje. They lived in a flat on the Thorbeckelaan in The Hague.

In July of 1942, when I was eight months old, we were ordered to report to Westerbork for deportation. Immediately I was brought to the home of Kees and Tine Hos, and the adults went into hiding at other addresses. About a year later, my mother joined me. Later, my father joined us as well.

On April 22, 1944, Johannes Krom from the Boetzelaer Brigade (named for Willem Baron van Boetzelaer, a member of the Waffen SS and collaborator with the security police, who arrested members of the Dutch resistance and Jews in hiding) led the Dutch police to arrest my parents, Hans and Annetje. Tine took me in her arms and said, "Doesn't she look like me?" In doing so, Tine saved my life, helped by three facts: I was blond, the Germans thought Hans and Annetje had a little boy, and my father didn't say farewell to me because he feared showing his emotions. That same evening, the collaborators came back to arrest me as well, but my father's resistance group had brought me to safety already.

After Hans and Annetje were taken to a prison in Scheveningen and before they were tortured by Johannes Krom, police reports state that my father, that same afternoon, returned to Kees Hos's house to get his coat. With the help of Tine Hos, he stood for a while at my bedside as I was sleeping, then was brought back to prison.

Until he died aged ninety-eight, Kees Hos would mourn Hans Polak's death in the Dachau concentration camp.

CHAIM

Johanna Leepel-Labotz hid Chaim and Fifi in the autumn of 1942.

After my wife and I had been for some weeks at separate addresses, Mrs. Johanna Leepel-Labotz took us in (Valkensboslaan, The Hague).

Fifi's brother Hans with his wife,
Annetje, 1940

*Hans and Annetje were tortured in a
Dutch prison by the Dutch and the
German police and sent to Auschwitz.
Hans was murdered in Dachau;
Annetje survived and came back to
find her daughter, Chaja.*
JUDITH

One day, unexpectedly, a policeman, together with two officials, entered the home. The German authorities decided to evacuate all unmarried persons in that part of The Hague to districts in the east of the country, in order to give their dwellings to people from the coastal sector of The Hague, which became entirely militarized. By acting normally, we avoided raising suspicion, but it was clear that a change of address was urgent, and we relocated to the Hos family. After several weeks, word came that neighbors who were not to be trusted had become suspicious. So we moved on again, to two other temporary addresses.

Kees and Tine Hos hid Chaim and Fifi in the winter of 1942 at their home in The Hague; they are the same couple who hid Judith and Hadassah through September 1942.

HADASSAH

Pappie had two sisters. The elder, called Grentje, was married to Gus Hartog Klop, a non-Jew, no children. There was no real connection between them and us. They really were very much estranged. So much so that when at a certain time in the war, when Fifi and Chaim had nowhere to go while in hiding, one evening they asked Grentje and her husband if they could stay with them for one night (at the time, the Germans weren't prosecuting Jews in mixed marriages), and they refused. After that, Chaim never talked to them again.

CHAIM

After having been at several hiding addresses during the first half year of our hiding, we met, in Rotterdam, a Jewish woman married to an Italian non-Jew, who gave her the nickname "de Italiaanse." Her position gave her a freedom of movement other Jews did not possess anymore, and she used it to help others. She brought us, via Amsterdam, to the Central Station in Utrecht, where she entrusted us to the leader of an underground resistance group working in the center of the country. We took the train to Ede (Gelderland), and he brought us to the home of the Miedema family, where we were cordially received.

Tjeerde and Antje Miedema hid Chaim and Fifi at Op den Berg, Ede, from January to April 1943.

We stayed there for about the first three months of 1943. We nearly never left the house. One night, our host was warned about house-to-house searching, and he took us to the building of the furniture store where he worked and hid us in the attic under heaps of packing material until the next day.

After about three months, alarming information reached our hosts: the leader of the underground group who had brought us into contact with the Miedemas was wanted by the Gestapo. He was not in Ede at the time, but his wife was told that if her husband did not report within three days, she and her children would be imprisoned instead.

After a brief consultation with our host, we decided, because of the impending danger to both sides, to depart at once, though we did not have a new hiding place. As the only possibility for the night, we thought of a childhood friend of my wife in Nijmegen, but we did not mention the address to our host. Mr. Miedema went ahead of us to see if everything was safe at the station and to buy tickets, after we had said goodbye at home, in order to avoid unnecessary speaking at the station. We could not stay with the friend in Nijmegen, and after some dangerous traveling—as our identity cards were only primitively falsified—we were back in Rotterdam.

Sometime later, we heard that the whole illegal group in Ede was rolled up. The Gestapo came to the house of the Miedema family with a list of names, including our real names (until then unknown to our hosts, making it possible to deny knowledge of our identity). Mr. Miedema and all other men of the group were sent to the concentration camp of Vught. What happened to all the Jews caught need not be mentioned. My wife and I were the only ones who escaped this ill-fated rescue attempt.

All non-Jewish men were set free after several months in the concentration camp. The leader of the group went on with illegal work, was arrested again, and was executed.

HISTORY BRIEF, PAGE 236
Vught Concentration Camp

FIFI

April 23, 1943: Today is the last day that the Germans are tolerating Jews in the Netherlands. Does everyone have to go to Vught? My husband and I won't go. We're staying with Jewish friends who until today had an official stamp. Tonight we have no prospect of a roof over our heads. Then, the doorbell rings and two reverends come in to say goodbye to our Jewish friends, who are lucky enough to have an address where they can go.

We talk a bit, and the two reverends become aware of our uncertainty. One of them remains silent for a while and then takes his leave, giving us an encouraging nod saying: you'll see me again later today. The other stays in his seat and talks, talks, talks. Finally, he tells us that we, too, are Nazis because we are Zionists. Visibly pleased that he told us this, he also leaves.

At three o'clock, the first reverend returns, radiant, to give us an address for a month or six weeks. Then, when evening falls, we're sleeping in a quiet room in a bed with fresh linens. We really do sleep because we know that each of our three little daughters has a good home.

HISTORY BRIEF, PAGE 236
April 23, 1943: All Jews Must Leave

Fifi's diary entry dated April 23 describes events that took place on April 22, when she and Chaim secured last-minute accommodations through the intervention of Reverend Gerrit Brillenburg Wurth.

CHAIM

In Rotterdam, we contacted a Jewish colleague, Mr. Jacques Wolf, who had a private pharmacy at Breeplein 6, and whom we expected to go into hiding soon. At his home, we met two Protestant clergymen, the Reverend Bakker and Gerrit Brillenburg Wurth. Reverend Bakker, a leader of the mission among Jews, entered upon a debate on Zionism, which he placed on the same line as fascism. Reverend Brillenburg Wurth, however, understood our peril, as the next day was the day on which every Jew who, until then, by some privilege or other had escaped deportation had to disappear. They were ordered to present themselves voluntarily at the concentration camp of Vught. Reverend Wurth left us quietly and did not come back until he had found a hiding place for us at the end of the day. It was with the Groeneveld family, Dordtsestraatweg 741a, Rotterdam. It consisted of a brother, Jacob, an office clerk, and his four sisters, Riek, Bets, Jans, and Anna, who had a grocery in the same building.

Jacques Wolf hosted Chaim and Fifi on April 22, 1943.

The Groenevelds hid Chaim and Fifi from April 22 to May 22, 1943.

23 april 1943. Vandaag de laatste dag dat de Duitschers Joden dulden in Nederland. Allemaal naar Vught moeten? Mijn man en ik gaan niet. We hidden bij Joodse vrienden die ook vandaag een stempel hadden. We hebben geen uitzicht vannacht een dak boven ons hoofd te hebben. Dan wordt er gebeld en er komen twee dominée's op visite om afscheid te nemen van onze Joodse vrienden die zo gelukkig zijn een adres te hebben.

Er wordt wat gepraat en dan weten beide dominée's onze onzekerheid. De een krijgt een poosje neemt afscheid nadat hij ons bemoedigend toeknikt en zegt: U hiet my vandaag nog. De andere blijft zitten en praat - praat - praat. Tenslotte vertelt hij ons dat ook wy nazi's zijn nadat hij weet dat ze zionisten zijn. Zichtbaar tevreden dat hij ons dat mededeelde gaat ook hy weg.

Om drie uur komt Dominee terug van binnen uitstralend, om ons een adres ...

Fifi's diary, April 23, 1943

Today is the last day that the Germans are tolerating Jews in the Netherlands. Does everyone have to go to Vught? My husband and I won't go. Tonight we have no prospect of a roof over our heads. Then, the doorbell rings and two reverends come in …
FIFI

We remained there six weeks. Then, the area was warned about an impending house-to-house search by the German police. The house offered no opportunity for hiding or for making a hiding place. Several weeks later, Mr. Groeneveld was arrested for possession of illegal material. The last information was that they took him to a prison in Germany, but thereafter nothing more was heard.

FIFI

We're suddenly forced to leave. It's becoming too dangerous both for our hosts and for us. It is once again Reverend Wurth who finds us shelter, this time under the roof in an attic above the organ of his church. Of course, this can't be done without consent from the sexton. The reverend says to us, "It's really pretty awful, but you'll manage for around ten days, I'm sure. It's your life that's at stake."

HISTORY BRIEF, PAGE 228
The Breeplein Church

Nathan Cohen

Johan Hunningher sheltered the entire Cohen family for two nights in Apeldoorn.

Isaak Cohen is Nathan's father.

The Zoon family hid Nathan and Henny in Utrecht from January 21 to 28, 1943.

NATHAN

In mid-January 1943, a friendly policeman came to warn Father that the Germans would transport the children of the Apeldoornse Bos that night, and we were also to be transported. Father did not believe this, since it was not in their interest to send disturbed children to a work camp. The children would only need attention and could not do any work. Father warned the doctors at the Apeldoornse Bos anyway, and some doctors and nurses went into hiding that night. Father said that if they took these disturbed children, it would not be to a work camp, but probably to have them murdered.

Our family went into hiding that evening. We stayed at a garage of a Dutch Gentile friend of my parents, Dr. Hunningher, an Amsterdam dentist, who had a summer house in Apeldoorn. When, later that night, my father went back to take some money he had forgotten, he found that the policeman was right and that the house had a seal on the door saying that it was confiscated.

We stayed in the garage for two days. We had to stay inside, a new experience that we all would get used to, and since the garage didn't have heating facilities, and it was midwinter and very cold, we were dressed in as many layers of clothes as we could wear. There were no sanitary facilities. I think there was a small closet with a bucket in a corner, but that may be imagined.

The second night, Father went again to our house, which was close by, together with Henny, my eldest sister, to take some valuables and other useful stuff.

ISAAK COHEN

In 1943, after the deportations at Apeldoornse Bos, a psychiatric hospital for Jews, we fled our home: two of our children went to Amsterdam with the Hunningher family; one to Arnhem, together with our German foster daughter, whom we had welcomed into our home around 1938. We went to a doctor friend in Velp. A month later, the Bakker family accepted us.

NATHAN

I don't know where Father got the addresses, but the family was divided in three: Henny and I went to Professor Zoon, a professor at Utrecht University, where we stayed for a week; Annemieke, my younger sister, and Gertrude, my foster sister, to a family in Arnhem; and Father and Mother went to a family in Velp.

Henny and I were the first to leave. We went on our own to the railway station, for the train to Utrecht. I don't remember much about our trip there, except that I felt very naked without my Jewish Star. The journey went without any incidents, and we arrived at the professor's house, which was near the Domkerk, a big church in the center of Utrecht. We were received in a very cool manner. I think that there was some dispute between the professor and his wife about hiding us—at least, Mrs. Zoon was very cool to us, and did nothing to make us feel at home. But maybe I imagined this.

We had to stay hidden in a room in the back of the house. We had a small room with two beds where we had to stay and even ate our meals. The only one we saw during that whole week was Mrs. Zoon, and only when she brought us something to eat or came to tell us to go to bed.

One good thing was that the room had a lot of adventure books in it, so I did a lot of reading. The WC was at the end of the corridor, and we had to quietly open the door, watch through a slit, and then quickly go to the bathroom, returning in the same manner. We had to be quiet the whole day, but that was no problem since my sister and I did not share much. She was very grown up (she was fifteen and I was eleven), and she and I had little to talk about.

We stayed with Professor Zoon for about a week, and then went to the Hunningher family, the dentist in whose garage we first had hidden. Mrs. Hunningher was a school friend of my mother, and they had kept up their friendship. They had a big house in the center of Amsterdam, Weteringschans 51, and Mr. Hunningher had his practice in the house.

The trip to Amsterdam was uneventful. We went first class and had a compartment with a German officer. I got used to seeing Germans in uniform and even smiled back when he looked my way and gave me a smile. In Amsterdam, we got on the tram. It was kind of scary to see people with yellow stars walking on the street, and not wear one yourself.

———

We called them Oom (Uncle) Johan and Tante (Aunt) Mop, even though the Hunninghers were, of course, not family relations. They had no children and lived in a big house with only a maid, an old retainer, called Mies.

In the house of Tante Mop and Oom Johan, my sister Henny and I had a big room on the top floor, at the back, which was our bed and study room, but we were free to go anywhere on the top two floors, as long as there were no visitors. The lower floor was the dentist room and waiting room, and the laboratory where Oom Johan made dentures. In the hours that Oom Johan received patients, we usually stayed in our room. We had to do some homework, but I think this was more to help us pass the time than to further our education. We also kept a large map of Russia, with pins of the front line, which slowly moved west.

I think Mies, the maid, felt sorry for us and tried to keep us busy doing all kinds of household chores, such as drying the cutlery after dinner, waxing the parquet in the living room, and peeling potatoes. I especially hated the floor waxing. I remember that we had to be very careful to peel the potatoes so that the peels were as thin as possible. If we were not careful, we would get a scolding from Mies. I was pretty ungrateful for her good intentions. She was a cheerful older woman—she must have been in her late forties, unmarried, and living somewhere in north Amsterdam.

Oom Johan had binoculars, which he loaned me, and I sat for hours looking at the city from our window. One building that stood out was the Handelsmaatschappij building, and another was the Carlton Hotel. On the roof of the Handelsmaatschappij building, the Germans had anti-aircraft guns. At about that time (early 1943),

Johan and Mop Hunningher concealed Nathan and Henny in their Amsterdam home from January 28 to early July 1943.

the Americans started to bomb Germany during the daytime. The English were already bombing Germany at night on a regular basis. We would hear the sirens go and then the noise of the RAF (British Royal Air Force) planes, which was a distinctive, uneven vrooming noise. The anti-aircraft batteries would start to fire and the searchlights, making their swings, would light up the sky. It was quite a show. Usually the firing would be ineffective, and after an hour or so, everything would quiet down, and the "all safe" would sound.

In the evenings, we would go to the living room on the second floor, and Tante Mop would play the piano, at which she was very proficient. In fact, she had studied at a conservatory and had wanted to become a pianist before marrying Oom Johan. During the day, we could hear her studying at the piano—finger exercises, as she called it. Oom Johan had two quite unusual hobbies for that time. One was making animated films, and the second was making scale working models of railway locomotives. He had made a ten-minute-long Romeo and Juliet film, in which the main characters were two aspirin tablets. It ended with one tablet being used for a headache and the second tablet jumping into a glass of water and slowly dissolving. Some evenings, he took me down to his machine shop, where a working model of a big locomotive moved over a short track. It was an accurate scale model of the largest steam locomotive the Dutch railways had. I was very impressed by this. He had also combined his two hobbies and made some railway movies, one of which I remember quite well. He had filmed it from the cab of a locomotive and at some point speeded up the film so that the train seemed to tear along at fantastic speed.

HISTORY BRIEF, PAGE 236
German Forces Surrender at Stalingrad

By February 1943, the war news was finally better. At Stalingrad, the Russians achieved a big victory after very hard fighting, defeating a whole German army group. This was the first big defeat they had.

The Germans stepped up the transportations and were starting to make house-to-house searches in Amsterdam to find Jews, weapons, or other forbidden things. It was also illegal for the Dutch to have radios; they could only listen to the cable radio, which was a box with a loudspeaker connected to a central radio, just as cable TV is today.

Oom Johan made a hiding place for us by removing the ceiling of a closet in our bedroom and replacing it with a trapdoor. We could then climb a ladder, open the trapdoor, and pull the ladder up after us. The space was very limited—I think some 2 meters by 4 meters by 1½ meters high—and was suffocatingly hot on a sunny summer day. The roof was slightly sloping, covered with flat tin or lead plate. The ceiling (the floor of this hiding place) was a series of beams to which the plaster was attached. Uncle Johan had made a platform of planks on the beams. We had to crawl from the trapdoor to the platform on a narrow walkway. We had to sit or lie on the mattresses, which Oom Johan had put there, since standing up was impossible. There was a carafe of water and a bucket for our other needs. This was the space where we were supposed to stay when the house was searched. We had practice runs, and found we could get in there and close the trapdoor in a minute. The Germans did not search in our neighborhood at that time, and luckily we did not have to use the hiding place for several months.

One morning, during an air-raid alarm, one big bomber came over the city of Amsterdam at rooftop height. It passed quite close, between us and the Handelsmaatschappij building, and the Germans fired at it with some automatic weapon. The plane was firing back at the building with machine guns. I was standing at the window watching it and only afterward remembered to take Oom Johan's binoculars, but by then the excitement was over, except on the roof of the Handelsmaatschappij, where the Germans were still running about.

One night, a plane was hit above Amsterdam. It burned fiercely. After a short while, one of its wings came off, and it started to spiral down, the motors on the remaining wing making a sound like a siren, louder when close, and less loud when on the far side of its spiral. We watched it coming down from our window and saw it crashing into a building and exploding. The next morning we saw that the plane had crashed into the tower of the Carlton Hotel—the Nazis' Dutch headquarters for the *Luftwaffe* (air force) and also where many German military personnel lived—and destroyed it. We heard that it killed several high German officers staying there, but this may have been wishful thinking of the Dutch.

The route the English flew at night to northern Germany passed over or close to Amsterdam, and nearly every night we had air-raid alarms going off at least once. One Saturday, the Americans tried to bomb the Fokker airplane factory in northern Amsterdam. The Germans were using it, and it was a legitimate target. They missed, unfortunately, and bombed an area close to it, killing many Dutch families. The Dutch (German) press made a big hullabaloo over this, claiming it as a war atrocity, conveniently forgetting what the Germans had done to Rotterdam, London, and other cities. A week later, on Sunday, the Americans bombed again, this time hitting the factory.

HISTORY BRIEF, PAGE 236
Failed Bombing of the Fokker Airplane Factory

The Germans searched our street, the Weteringschans. They would close off a section of the street and make house-to-house searches. That day, we went into our hiding place under the roof, and since it was a warm sunny day, we were soon sweltering. The space was very cramped; we had to lie there trying not to make any noise and moving as little as possible. We had taken some books and magazines with us and could read, though it was dim. That evening we had to sleep there. The air-raid sirens went on as usual, but were much louder up there—some were situated in the Rijksmuseum, which was opposite the house. Then the ack-ack, the German anti-aircraft guns, were firing, and we heard spent shell fragments falling on the roof, which was quite frightening. The next morning, we got down, had a hurried wash, and had to go up again for another very uncomfortable and long day. That night Oom Johan took us to a family in the western part of the port area.

I don't remember how we went, but traveling with two kids without proper papers was probably very dangerous, especially while a search was on. Oom Johan, who I remember as a very reserved and cautious man, must have been very scared, but there were no problems.

The family we went to were laborers—very religious, devout Protestant Christians. I don't remember their name, but it must have been a big burden for them to hide Jews, since they lived in a small apartment with five people—the parents and three children approximately our age. They must have been very sure their children would not say anything, since there were plenty of Dutch informers. I don't remember much of our stay there, except that the father prayed after every evening meal for swift relief from the German oppressor, and asked for forgiveness for the sins the family committed and for the sins committed by the Germans. I remember this made a big impression on me, since I never thought that the Germans should be forgiven for anything they did, and I could not think of any sins the family or Henny and I committed.

After about a week, we went back to the Hunninghers. The house-to-house search in our area was over, and we again could stay in "our" room, which was very comfortable and roomy in comparison to the places we had to stay in during the previous days.

ISAAK COHEN

My wife, Rivka, and I could stay at the Bakkers' "as long as we wanted," but their house was in the city, and we were afraid that there were Nazis among the people passing by. We stayed about nine months. Then, a friend of the Bakkers offered us a place at a policeman's house in a remote village.

NATHAN

One day, at the end of July, Oom Johan told us that my parents would send someone to collect us early next week. We were quite ungrateful in showing how glad we were to return to our parents, given that Oom Johan, Tante Mop, and Mies had done everything to make us feel at home.

That week passed very slowly, and when the day of our departure came, we were packed and ready to leave early in the morning. It was a beautiful day, and at one o'clock we went to dine and found a stranger at the table. I hardly had any appetite and waited impatiently for the meal to end.

Hiding was a great danger to all parties involved. Parents wouldn't tell their kids a minute before they had to. Parents who wanted to hide their family told their non-Jewish friends. The people that found you the addresses brought you away after they assured themselves that it was completely safe because of the tremendous risk they were taking.

I knew people disappeared, but hiding was not talked about. The whole business was so dangerous. I was one of the last kids in my class to go into hiding. I went in March '43. We started with a class of sixty kids and were left with ten. At home, the table talk was about how many kids were in school that day. This was how parents found out about the density of the Germans' raids. If one day ten or twenty kids disappeared, parents knew it was a raid, but if three kids disappeared, they probably went into hiding.

My parents told me what was going to happen. They did not talk to me about concentration camps but said that Jews were arrested and put in jails, and going into hiding would be the best thing to do. They told me I should listen to the people where I was hiding, and we would all get together after the war. They told me about the danger of the whole thing.

I left home in March with one suitcase. I was thirteen. They said it was only for a short time. I was hidden in a wallpaper factory with the factory superintendent for about five weeks on a little island behind the central station in Amsterdam. Then some work had to be done in the factory, and I had to be moved to another place. A friend of my parents arranged this—I forget her name. She had two bicycles with her because we had to go a long distance. I wasn't wearing a star and had false papers under the name of Dirk van Leeuwen. All during the war, my name was Dirk van Leeuwen. I was registered with that name in the Blaricum town hall.

We had to go on a ferryboat back to Amsterdam. As we left the ferry and stepped on our bikes, there was a Dutch Nazi policeman who followed and stopped us, asking for our papers. The woman was from Blaricum, which was legitimate. She had papers. And the thing was, the woman looked very Jewish. She wasn't Jewish, but they thought she was and that I was bringing her away. At thirteen-years, I did not have to have papers—all I had to be was registered at the town hall. The policeman took us to the Dutch Nazi police headquarters in Amsterdam.

They separated us. They beat me to find out what my name really was; if that woman was who she said she was; if she was really a friend who took me for an outing that day. Before, it was arranged that if anybody asked, our story was that she took me on the ferryboat. They kept us there for about four hours. They beat the hell out of her. They beat me on and off with their hands, with their belts. They mainly slapped me in the face and asked, "Isn't she Jewish?" This went on for about four or five hours. They said they would turn us over to the German Grüne Polizei (Green Police), and it was too bad for me because they could let me go if I told them who she was. I said, "Well, she is who she says she is." That was the truth. They never asked me if I was the Jewish one.

The identity of the superintendent in Amsterdam who hid David in March 1943 is unknown. The wallpaper factory was behind Amsterdam's Central Station, where the river IJ meets the Amsterdam-Rijn canal, on one of a series of man-made islands originally built to hold warehouses for trade with the Dutch East Indies.

HISTORY BRIEF, PAGE 232
The Green Police and Hanns Albin Rauter

HISTORY BRIEF, PAGE 231
**The Security Service Headquarters
in Amsterdam**

David's mother and Erwin's wife, Grete
Heinsheimer-Geismar, worked for the
Hoyer family from July 1943 to May 1945.
The bulk of her wartime experience was
undocumented and is therefore unknown.

Erika Heymann hid David and Erwin in
her apartment at Argonautenstraat 19,
Amsterdam, at the beginning of July 1943;
David left on July 19, and Erwin was there
until September 5.

They transferred us to their headquarters on the Euterpestraat
where the Grüne Polizei interrogated us. They never beat us. They
called the offices in Blaricum, where I was supposed to be registered.
It was a holiday, and they got disgusted that those offices were closed
while they had to work. They said, "Look, everything is closed, we
can't do anything today. Why don't you go home, come back tomor-
row, and we'll straighten it out." I was scared—the only thing that
got me through it was that they didn't realize I was Jewish. Well, you
know we never went back, right?

We started biking, and the woman made sure nobody was following us. She said my parents were still at home, and that I should go
there because she couldn't take me anywhere then. So, I went back
home and explained to my parents what happened.

My parents were going to go into hiding a week later. They had a
place for my father and a place for my mother, but they didn't have
a place for me. And that was what held everything up. I went back to
school, and we stayed home till July of 1943. We were among the
last ones to hide.

My mother hid as a maid, working for a family in Amstelveen—
that's outside Amsterdam. Supposedly she was from Indonesia, and
she was stuck during the war in Holland, so she hired herself out
as a maid. She worked the whole war with the same family. I gather
they must have known she was Jewish.

—————

Because my parents couldn't find a hiding place for me, the woman
where my father planned to hide agreed to take me too. I went with
my father, and my mother went alone to her address. We said goodbye very fast so there wouldn't be a scene.

This was much easier for me than my first experience hiding.
I knew the woman where we went—she was often at our house. She
was a German non-Jewish woman, living in Amsterdam, whom my
father knew from Germany. Her husband was left-oriented and was
put into a camp in Germany very early on.

She had about four or five people hiding in her apartment. They
were all older people, and it was a small apartment. They thought
it was dangerous to keep me there.

My father met a man on the street with connections to the underground. He owned an apartment in the house where we used to
live. He told my father, "This is where you can reach me; if you have
problems with hiding, I can help you." The next day, my father contacted him and told him that I was with him, and he was afraid of the
situation in the woman's apartment. There were too many people,
and he didn't like it.

This man said he could arrange for me to go to Friesland, to the
northern part of Holland, to farm country. I was with my father
for three weeks while this man made arrangements. He didn't do it for
money—he said if my father had money left, he could donate to the
underground organization.

I remember very distinctly when I left my father because it was
the last I ever saw of him. This was the only time in my life that I saw
my father emotional. He said to me, "I hope God is with you." That's

the only time I ever heard him say something like that. I think he knew how this was going to end, or he had the feeling…I did not.

My father told the man what I would be wearing. I went to a particular street corner. A man said, "Follow me," and I followed him. Then he said, "You see the other man there, follow him but don't make contact." I walked about eight or nine meters behind him. The first man walked way behind us to make sure I wasn't followed. Then a woman picked me up and said, "You're going with me," and we went to the railroad station. We took the train over the Zuiderzee and then the boat to the northern part of Holland, Friesland. She dropped me off in Sneek, at a regular family's house for an overnight stay. Another woman took me on the train from Sneek to Heerenveen, also in Friesland. I arrived in the afternoon. About an hour later, a different woman picked me up and brought me to Sint Nicolaasga, a little farming community. It's a hick town—twenty or thirty houses. This was my final destination.

A few weeks later, my father was caught.

ERWIN

July 21, 1943: How shall I begin to record the things that occupied me during the last three and a half years? How timid and careful I feel today, as I begin writing my story on these pages, a task that should take maybe a few weeks. For the circumstances in the small community in which I live are such that we must reckon with a trap springing shut; a trap from which we can—hopefully—emerge free from peril. Now, I'm left to wonder about the meaning of my short life.

Why do I begin just on the 21st of July? On a day that brings me particular disappointments because I have received no news about my son, who left me two days ago to go to a different place in Holland, to stay with people on a farm, where he "should have" more freedom, "should be able" to have more fresh air to enjoy than here, where I had to keep him trapped with us inside for three weeks. There, he will wait for the end of this awful situation.

Why begin today, when worries plague me, worries about family and human life? Worries about my father-in-law, whom I've been able to keep in the Westerbork transit camp for three and a half months, who now most likely will be sent on the next transport day to a death camp, because they want to harass, deport, and murder not him specifically, but all Jews.

I have spent so much energy on my wife and child in the last weeks that I feel despondent but not defeated. One becomes numb, especially in mishap and in danger. There is so much sadness and bitter pain as I consider the fate of 100,000 fellow believers, brothers and sisters, the millions of enemies of the current regime, who all share the same fate as my family, clients, and friends. My measure of compassion is full, but I am pursued.

DAVID

Once I became a father and then a grandfather, I have thought many times about how hard it must have been for my father to say goodbye to me, his thirteen-year-old son.

This page and following: False identity card belonging to Grete Geismar (David's mother and Erwin's wife), August 22, 1941. The handwritten *V* was likely added after the war as an Allied symbol for resistance and victory.

My mother hid as a maid, working for a family in Amstelveen—that's outside Amsterdam. She worked the whole war with the same family. I gather they must have known she was Jewish.
DAVID

PERSOONSBEWIJS

TEVENS BEWIJS VAN OPNEMING IN HET BEVOLKINGSREGISTER

De tot het bezit van dit bewijs gerech-
tigde is verplicht het te allen tijde bij
zich te dragen en desgevorderd te ver-
toonen aan iederen opsporingsambtenaar,
alsmede aan alle ambtenaren of andere
personen, door wie zulks ingevolge eenig
wettelijk voorschrift wordt verlangd.

Geldig gedurende vijf jaren

MISBRUIK WORDT GESTRAFT

I

A 35   № 558020

Wiechmann———

Margaretha———

17 September 1908
Amsterdam

NEDERLANDER

Tulp, G

zonder

22 AUG. 1941
AMSTERDAM

NR. A 35   № 558020

Datum aangifte · Gemeente en adres

Bestevaerstr 4 ^{2h}

SIGNALEMENT:

XXX VROUW

Kenmerken:

AFDRUK RECHTERWIJSVINGER

A 35   № 558020

Invisible

In hiding, one had to live silently without attracting any attention. Moments of crisis were often triggered by the smallest of incidents, and one had to be ready to move without notice. While the majority of those who offered refuge proved steadfast, risking imprisonment in concentration camps to do so, there were those who exploited and abused their powerless guests. Individuals who needed a hiding place had little choice: until the fall of 1943, there were not enough available.

Dutch accommodation with the Germans ended in May 1943 after the commander of the German Wehrmacht (armed forces) in the Netherlands ordered the internment of the former Dutch army. The implied reason: the Dutch had not Nazified themselves. This decision triggered spontaneous strikes all over the country, which provoked a harsh response that included the shooting of protesters, mass arrests, and executions. Accommodation, the convenient middle road between collaboration and resistance, ceased to be an option. More than 300,000 non-Jewish Netherlanders needed hiding places, and now many people opened their houses to all who needed to "submerge." Sadly, for almost 90,000 Jews, this belated spirit of resistance came too late: they had already been shipped to the death camps.

On September 29, 1943, the Germans completed the official liquidation of the Jewish community in the Netherlands when they closed down the Jewish Council and deported its members and 5,000 Jews carrying Jewish Council exemptions to Westerbork. That day, 56,500 Jews were left in the Netherlands: those imprisoned in the Westerbork and Vught camps awaiting deportation (11,000), those whose racial status was still being investigated or who were married to non-Jews (11,500), "Half Jews" (14,000), and those in hiding who had not yet been betrayed (20,000). Of the latter group, 5,000 would be exposed and deported to Auschwitz in the year that followed.

1943–1945

January 1943
Mirjam leaves the Van Gelders' home in Wassenaar for Nel van Vliet's in Haarlem.

May 1943
Chaim and Fifi move to the Breeplein Church in Rotterdam under the care of Gerrit and Gerda Brillenburg Wurth and Jacobus and Annigje de Mars.

Early July 1943
Nathan leaves his Amsterdam address with the Hunninghers and joins his family at the home of Theo and Betsy van Dalen in Gendt.

July 21, 1943
Erwin begins to write his memoir after David departs for a new hiding address in Friesland with the Post family.

ca. August 1943
Judith has an in-between address before moving to the C. and P. H. house in Rijnsburg.

Hadassah moves from the Lafontaine residence to Riek Dekkers's home in Rotterdam.

September 5, 1943
Erwin is captured by the Germans and taken to Westerbork.

September 29, 1943
The German occupiers complete their final raid, rounding up 5,000 Jews in Amsterdam and deporting them via Westerbork; they declare the city *judenrein* (cleansed of Jews).

ca. October 1943
Hadassah moves to a new hiding address with Hendrik and Jans van der Leer in Rotterdam.

November 16, 1943
Erwin is transferred from Westerbork to Auschwitz.

November 19, 1943
Erwin is murdered in Auschwitz.

Spring 1944
David gets a new hiding address with Pieter and Corrie Kuipers in IJlst, Friesland.

Hadassah resumes living with Franciscus Lafontaine in Amsterdam.

A new ration card is introduced to further restrict people in hiding from receiving food.

June 2, 1944
The last transport of Jews leaves Vught for Auschwitz.

June 6, 1944
The Allied forces land at Normandy, France, in an operation known as D-Day.

September 3, 1944
The last trains leave Westerbork for Auschwitz.

September 17, 1944
The Allied forces attempt to land behind enemy lines near Arnhem; although the mission—known as Operation Market Garden—largely fails, the southern Dutch cities of Eindhoven and Nijmegen are liberated.

Late September 1944
Nathan and his family leave the Van Dalen house in Gendt after the town is bombed.

October 1944
Nathan and his family pose as non-Jews, and Nathan's father, Isaak, assumes the role of town doctor in Halle.

October 26, 1944
Canadian forces liberate the Vught concentration camp.

November 8, 1944
The Canadians achieve control of both banks of the Scheldt River, making the Antwerp harbor available as a point of supply for the Allied armies.

Early 1945
David changes addresses, going to the Van Kampens' home in IJlst.

Hadassah is sent to stay with Petronella Lafontaine, the first wife of Franciscus, in Wassenaar.

February 1945
David returns to hide with the Kuipers family after hiding for ten days in the fields of IJlst.

February 20, 1945
Fifi's brother Hans is murdered in Dachau.

March 1945
The Americans cross the Rhine and advance into the heart of Germany.

March 15, 1945
Fifi's brother Sam perishes in Poland.

April 1945
Chaim and Fifi are almost captured during a raid on the Breeplein Church.

Throughout April 1945
The Allies liberate towns and cities in eastern and central Dutch provinces.

Hiding Addresses

Mirjam

1
August 19–September 2, 1942
Mr. & Mrs. H. Willemse
Voorburg

2
September 2, 1942–January 1943
Jan & Nan van Gelder
Oranjelaan 4
Wassenaar

3
January 1943–May 1945
Nel & Sonja van Vliet
Wilhelminapark 39
Haarlem

Judith

4
August 19–September 1942
Kees & Tine Hos
Prins-Hendrikstraat
The Hague

5
September 1942–ca. August 1943
Alida & Corry Wouters-van der Lely
Storm van 's-Gravesandeweg
Wassenaar

ca. August 1943
Unknown address

6
ca. August 1943–May 1945
C. & P. H.
Rijnsburg

Hadassah

4
August 19–September 1942
Kees & Tine Hos
Prins-Hendrikstraat
The Hague

7
September 1942–ca. August 1943
Franciscus & Petronella Lafontaine
Van Oldenbarneveltweg
Wassenaar

8
ca. August–October 1943
Riek Dekkers
Mathenesserlaan
Rotterdam

9
October 1943–spring 1944
Henk & Jans van der Leer
Lede 72
Rotterdam

10
Spring 1944–January 1945
Franciscus & Miep Lafontaine
Beethovenstraat
Amsterdam

7
January–May 1945
Petronella Lafontaine
Van Oldenbarneveltweg
Wassenaar

Chaim & Fifi

Late summer–autumn 1942
Hidden separately at
unknown addresses

11
Autumn 1942
Johanna Leepel-Labotz
Valenboslaan
The Hague

4
Winter 1942
Kees & Tine Hos
Prins-Hendrikstraat
The Hague

Winter 1942
Two unknown addresses

12
January–April 1943
Tjeerde & Antje Miedema
Op den Berg
Ede

13
April 22, 1943
Jacques Wolf
Breeplein 6
Rotterdam

14
April 22–May 1943
Jacob, Riek, Anna, Bets,
& Jans Groeneveld
Dordtsestraatweg 741a
Rotterdam

15
May 1943–May 1945
Gerrit & Gerda Brillenburg Wurth
Jacobus & Annigje de Mars
Breeplein Church
Rotterdam

Nathan

16
January 21–23, 1943
Johan Hunningher
Summerhouse
Apeldoorn

17
January 23–30, 1943
Zoon family
Near Domkerk
Utrecht

18
January 30–July 1943
Johan & Mop Hunningher
Weteringschans 51
Amsterdam

Summer 1943
Protestant family for one week
during raids in the Hunninghers'
neighborhood
Western port area
Amsterdam

19
July 1943–September 1944
Theo & Betsy van Dalen
Dijkstraat 31
Gendt

September–October 1944
Two farms, addresses unknown
Near Gendt

20
October 1944 (one night)
Mierlo-Staring family
Het Klooster 9
Angerlo

21
October 1944 (a few days)
Cloister, unconfirmed address
Near Doetinchem

22
October 1944–April 1945
Hiding in plain sight with his
family as non-Jews
Halle

David

23
March–April 1943
Superintendent's apartment
in a wallpaper factory on an
island behind Central Station
Amsterdam

April–July 1943
Home with his parents
Pieter de Hoochstraat 76
Amsterdam

24
Early July–July 19, 1943
Erika Heymann
Argonautenstraat 19
Amsterdam

25
July 20, 1943–spring 1944
Post family
Doniaga, province of Friesland

26
Spring 1944–January 1945
Pieter & Corrie Kuipers
IJlst, province of Friesland

27
January–February 1945
Van Kampen family
IJlst, province of Friesland

26
February–May 1945
Pieter & Corrie Kuipers
IJlst, province of Friesland

Erwin

24
Early July–September 5, 1943
Erika Heymann
Argonautenstraat 19
Amsterdam

Detail of map that was distributed
in the back pocket of *Netherlands,*
one of the books in the Geographical
Handbook Series published by the
British Naval Intelligence Division,
October 1944.

The series was created to provide
extensive information to Allied
commanding officers on the history,
people, government, industry,
geography, and infrastructure of
about thirty countries.

Chaim and Fifi were hidden by Gerrit and Gerda Brillenburg Wurth in the Breeplein Church from May 1943 to May 1945; the Brillenburg Wurths had one son and two daughters.

Jacobus (Hendrik, or Pa) and Annigje (Ann, or Ma) de Mars helped hide Chaim and Fifi in the Breeplein Church; Hendrik, the church sexton, was a former ship carpenter.

Maurice and Rebecca Kool-Andriesse and Maurice's parents, Meyer Kool and Ida Gruentemean, were the other family hiding in the church; Rebecca gave birth to a baby while hiding there.

Chaim & Fifi

CHAIM

When a warning came about house-to-house razzias after about six weeks of hiding with the Groeneveld family, Reverend Brillenburg Wurth again came to our aid by offering Fifi and me a hiding place in his church.

The place between the ceiling and the roof of the church was so gloomy that he thought we could stay no longer than several weeks, but we remained there until the end of the war. The sexton of the church, Mr. de Mars, was taken into confidence by Reverend Brillenburg Wurth, and it came out that Mr. de Mars was already hiding four Jewish people—the Kools—under the church roof. In fact, it was Mr. de Mars who knew the technical possibilities of the church building for a hiding place, and at once he set out to make the technical improvisations. Another hiding place was constructed on the opposite side of the church at the height of the organ's wind work. A bed was placed on the joisting, and a plank bridge of about 60 by 150 centimeters provided the only possibility of standing or walking, as the other planks between the joisting were too thin to support a person.

For about a year, Reverend Brillenburg Wurth or his wife, Gerda, brought us meals by going through a little garden from their home to the church and passing them through a hatch in the ceiling of a little storeroom beneath us. And it was not even too much for the reverend to empty, daily, a pail with excrement. After a year, Reverend Brillenburg Wurth was taken as a hostage to a special camp, with other prominent people opposed to the German occupation. After he was freed, the daily walk with the meals through the garden, enclosed by other buildings, became too dangerous; then, the attention to our needs was entirely assumed by the sexton and his wife.

Though for the food problem we were under the care of the Brillenburg Wurths for the first year, the other technical problems were the responsibility of Pa and Ma de Mars. A high degree of vigilance was necessary at times when we were not in our hiding places, since this was a church building with many gatherings—not only on Sundays—such as catechism for the youngsters, the church council of elders and deacons, frequent visits of the organist, etc.

Then there was the care for our "recreation." From time to time, we came together in the home of the sexton (also on the church grounds) in the evening, on which occasions he taught us handicrafts, or we exchanged thoughts about Christianity and Judaism in the presence of Reverend Brillenburg Wurth. It was in the home of the sexton, too, that a baby was born to the other Jewish family, with the help of an ophthalmic surgeon who was taken in confidence and of a nurse, Miss Riek Dekkers (who hid Hadassah).

Most of the time, we were in or near our hiding place, where we felt safer, and we urged the other Jewish family to do the same—with little success, however. This carelessness nearly led to a catastrophe, when about a month before the end of the war the Gestapo and the Grüne Polizei made a blitz-raid on the church and the sexton's house.

Invisible

MIRJAM

My parents' last address was in the attic of a church where they were the last two years of the war. The minister and the custodian made hiding places there for two families. They were told that in the daytime everyone had to stay in bed so no one down in the church could hear them. Late evening they could get out of bed and walk around a little. Imagine, they lay in bed for almost two years.

CHAIM

It is a Saturday afternoon in April 1945. A warm meal is brought to us in the organ loft. Fifi and I open our hiding place's trapdoor and come down with a retractable ladder to the loft.

It's *chicken soup*, a rare treat in times like these, but that's not the reason for mentioning it. The reason why is that from that moment on every detail and action attains an incredibly huge significance. The lives of seven Jewish people, certainly, and probably those of several non-Jewish helpers as well, are going to depend on every move, every sound.

So, chicken soup. But because even during times of war I'm not fond of it, I'm waiting for Fifi to finish. As I wait, I'm thinking: I really ought to take the key out, which is *on the inside of the organ loft door*, as a precaution. Should anything happen, it would be extremely suspicious if a key was to be discovered on the inside.

I take the key out. The meal is over, and Fifi immediately goes to bed in the hiding place. Before going to read in the organ loft, I first clean up the plates and pots (a normal safety measure); that is to say, I take them into the hiding place and put them on the little stone wall we step over to get to the attic floor. I very consciously put everything extra far in the back so I won't stumble over anything should I have to come back in very quickly. Then I sit down in the organ loft to read.

A short while later, I hear some noise in the church foyer on the side of the sexton's house. I listen briefly but then remember that the boys' catechism class was to begin again that Saturday afternoon, and so I continue reading. But then I hear someone walking through the church. Boys wouldn't do that, but it could be an organist or the glazier, and they aren't supposed to discover me either. So I go over to the window from where the organist has a full view of the church, and it's in those few seconds that my suspicion intensifies, for there's the sound of multiple footsteps. Carefully, I hold the edge of the opaque green curtain against the wall and use my finger to create a small crack, only to grow rigid with fear at that very moment. On the podium below me, between the pews of the elders and deacons, at a distance of perhaps four meters, there are two Grüne Polizei walking around, searching everything, and then farther down in the church, I see two more of them between the pews.

The next few seconds—even the smallest details of which are still vividly in my mind—were terrifying. My terror was followed half a second later by an odd sense of familiarity with the scene. What large visors their caps have, I note in a businesslike manner. My brain allows me the association with Austrian Alpine hunters. And then comes the stage of paralysis, the sense that all is lost.

Chaim was against all forms of violence and bloodshed, and thus aspired to a vegetarian lifestyle.

Chaim and Fifi's rescuers, Gerda
and Gerrit Brillenburg Wurth,
ca. early 1930s

*Reverend Brillenburg Wurth or his
wife, Gerda, brought us meals by going
through a little garden from their
home to the church and passing them
through a hatch in the ceiling of a
little storeroom beneath us. And it was
not even too much for the reverend
to empty, daily, a pail with excrement.*

*From time to time, we came together
in the home of the sexton (also on the
church grounds) in the evening, on
which occasions he taught us handicrafts, or we exchanged thoughts about
Christianity and Judaism in the presence of Reverend Brillenburg Wurth.*
CHAIM

For another few seconds, three or five (five is a whole lot under such circumstances), I wonder whether there's any point in climbing back into the hiding place. The other four Jewish individuals who have a hiding place on the other side of the organ symmetrically opposed to us—the Kools—are in the sexton's home during the day and so have likely long been picked up because it is through that house that the Grüne Polizei must have come in. And even if the Kools hadn't said a word, their ladder was still out, and their hiding place would lead the Grüne Polizei to ours. It's *useless*, I thought. But, because of years of practice and discipline, I started to climb, stiff kneed, the route to our hiding place. It felt like being in a nightmare. In terror, and with great difficulty, I put one foot in front of the other. A few more seconds… now the last stiff leg over the little stone wall. Oh yes, the plates. Too late! With a clatter, a spoon or a fork drops on the stone edge. There isn't even any time left to grow rigid with fear. "Germans! Germans!" I suddenly hear in a whispered scream. It's the Kool family—they actually reached their hiding place and now, because of the clatter, believe that we don't yet know. It means there's still a small chance! Now the super-heavy ladder still has to be raised. It can't be done hand over hand because that would make the ladder sway and bump. Throw it up, let it go, and catch it again, ten centimeters at a time. One slip and that's the end, for the Germans are already below me in the foyer, from which we are separated by thin slats of wood; they're coming up the stone staircase to the little storage space. I close the trapdoor and cover the cracks with a cloth. And a German hand is already at the door of the storage space. The door is locked, but they'll be back, of course.

I remain standing on the trapdoor, completely motionless. Fifi has taken something to help her sleep. Thankfully, the hoarsely whispered "Quiet, don't move, Germans" has barely registered with her. There they are again, coming back, whistling as they come up the same stairs. Are they that certain of their prey? They're inside, below me, with their heads not half a meter from my feet. They search a bit, then walk straight through to the organ loft. I hear them stumbling around. Then they're climbing a ladder, at about my level, searching right into the uppermost pipes of the organ. It's taking a long time; the seconds are starting to lose some of their span. But just when you imagine you're growing somewhat familiar with the danger, they come back into the small storage room below me, now systematically searching that. The seconds turn into eternities again. They're rummaging through the school materials and the crates that are there. No, not that systematically after all. They're not knocking on any walls or ceiling. Might they not be looking for people after all? Otherwise, why rummage through that school material and those little crates?

Time is now completely askew. I don't know whether they've been here ten minutes or half an hour. They leave, but run into the door from which the key was removed while we were eating! They have to go back the same way they came, right below me for the last time. Silence inside. The din outside is all the more noticeable now. Murmuring of the public that's being held back. I hear many boots in the square, and from time to time a German snarls at a citizen who wants

While in hiding, Fifi became addicted to sleeping pills.

Chaim and Fifi's hiding place,
Breeplein Church, ca. 1940s

I go over to the window from where the organist has a full view of the church, and it's in those few seconds that my suspicion intensifies, for there's the sound of multiple foot-steps. Carefully, I hold the edge of the opaque green curtain against the wall and use my finger to create a *small crack, only to grow rigid with fear at that very moment. On the podium below me, between the pews of the elders and deacons, at a dis-tance of perhaps four meters, there are two Grüne Polizei walking around, searching everything.*
CHAIM

Geref. Kerk Breeplein, Rotterdam (Zuid)

Chaim's diary, second of seven
pages describing the Breeplein
Church raid, December 29, 1947

Translation of diagram notations
Top illustration, from top to bottom:
– hatch
– floor of hiding place, and also the
  ceiling of the foyer
– ladder

Bottom illustration, from top to bottom:
– peephole for organist
– pews for the elders

Key at right:
cross section
a. organ pipe room
b. organ loft
c. work room
d. storage space
e. storage space
f. foyer
g. foyer
h. connecting space between church roof
   and pipe room roof, via which the two
   families could call out to each other
i. vestry

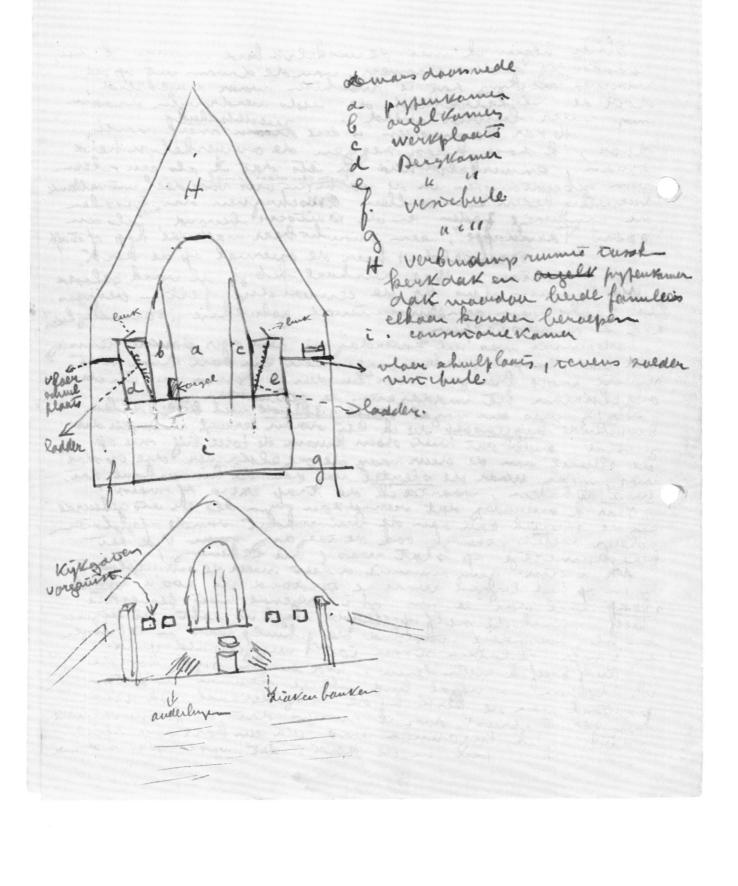

dwars doorsnede

a. pijpenkamer
b. engel kamer
c. werkplaats
d. Bergkamer
  "   "
e.
f. vestibule
  "   "
g.

H verbindings ruimte tussch
kerk dak en engelk pijpenkamer
dak waardoor beide families
elkaan konden beroepen

i. commissariekamer

vloer schuilplaats, tevens zolder
vestibule

ladder.

luik

luik

vloer
schuil
plaats

ladder

Korzel

Kijkgaten
vergruist

diaken banken

ouderlingen

to get into or out of the cordoned-off area. The entire church must be surrounded. More than an hour must have gone by; I'm still motionless above the trapdoor.

Footsteps approach, a woman's. A soft call: "Just open up." It's the sexton's wife, Ma. I turn on the light. And see a spoon, *right on the edge of the stone wall!* Just a few more millimeters and it would have clattered to the floor of our hiding space, which is the thin attic ceiling of the hollow-sounding foyer to which the Germans were so close.

The ladder is lowered, and a head appears through the trapdoor. "They've taken Pa (the sexton) away." And then she can't control herself any longer. She's been in such control.

It had been a blitz-raid. The entire block of residences, Breeplein, Randweg, and Van Malsenstraat-Jannebouwstraat had been cordoned off. The sexton's house was besieged. They'd come in over the rooftops, through the front door, and from the courtyard via the second-floor windows by standing on each other's shoulders. Though unnecessary, because next to them the *church door was open*, unlocked, this was fortunate. Had they gone that way into the sexton's home, they would have run right into the *fleeing Kool family*. For they were, indeed, at the sexton's house during those infinitely long and significant seconds described above.

For the sexton's family, those seconds were experienced as follows: Annie, the sexton's married daughter, had been on the verge of going shopping, and normally she always used a buzzer to open the door from the top of the stairs, even when she was going out herself. It had been her habit throughout the years she lived there. This time, however, she went down the stairs first, something she never did, and in the second she wanted to open the door, the Germans began to kick it with their boots. She immediately recognized the danger and ran back inside to alert the Kool family. Fortunately, the racket grew louder so now the Germans couldn't hear the escapees, who had to pass right by the front door via the catechism classroom and the second church foyer to reach their hiding place.

During those same seconds, Ma ran up to the third floor to warn the sexton, who was sick in bed. As she went up the stairs to the third floor, she saw *Maurice Kool looking down* to find out what was going on, while the Germans were already coming up the first staircase. She was just barely able to signal him to rush into the bedroom of her sick husband. However, in his desperation, he didn't know what to do and sat down on the sexton's bed. Once again, fractions of seconds on which each one of our lives depended. The sexton's wife surveyed the situation. She was just barely able to indicate to Maurice to crawl behind the bed between headboard and wall, and at the very moment that she saw the top of his black hair vanish, one of the Germans reached her and dragged her out of the room by her arm.

Then more Germans entered the bedroom. Sick as he was, the sexton was forced to get up and get dressed. Then one of them started to search the room.

They began with a wall closet below the window. They found empty preserving jars and made some comment about that but *didn't continue the search!* Just a single cursory look and they would have seen Maurice's feet under the bed. In the next room, they turned everything upside down. Including the crib with baby Kool, whom they put on the floor, but *about whom no questions were asked.* Mattresses were thrown off the beds, closets emptied, etc.

Next came the search of the living room. There, still standing *on the sideboard, were the two purses of the Kool ladies containing their false identification papers.*

"Who are they?" the Germans asked Ma. "A cousin with her daughter who went downtown to go shopping." One of the Germans, who turned out to understand a little Dutch, brought his finger to his head as a sign that he didn't believe a word of it.

The sexton was being interrogated in the vestry. It concerned weapons, and the sexton admitted that at one point weapons had been hidden in the organ loft but that they'd recently been removed, and he didn't know where to. Suddenly one of the men took out the photograph of the two Kool ladies and shoved them under his nose. "And who are they?" "A cousin with her daughter who went downtown," the sexton answered calmly. *As they were taking him downstairs, he had been made to wait on the landing for a few moments at the very moment they had posed the same question to his wife.*

They then dropped the question of the photograph. The sexton was taken away in the paddy wagon. We feared, until the end of the war, that he had been shot.

The situation was saved only because of the remarkable presence of mind of both Pa and Ma de Mars. For the last month, the whole responsibility rested on the shoulders of Ma de Mars, additionally burdened by the constant fear for the life of her husband.

Mr. de Mars was brought to the notorious prison in Scheveningen, nicknamed Oranjehotel, where, in the last weeks of the war, nearly every night prisoners were shot to make a place for newcomers. So, Mr. de Mars (and other prisoners) did not sleep at night and remained awake praying, in order that if his turn came, he could meet death in full Christian consciousness. Only if they had heard the sound of keys and the opening of doors, or if dawn came without having heard this, did they take a little sleep. Mr. de Mars was lucky to be freed at the end of the war, but his health, which was already not the best (chronic bronchiolitis), got a severe shock, and his case worsened gradually. He died about five years later, after a prolonged illness.

HISTORY BRIEF, PAGE 237
The Oranjehotel

Nel van Vliet cared for Mirjam from
January 1943 to May 1945 at her
home, located at Wilhelminapark 39
in Haarlem.

Mirjam

MIRJAM

After two weeks with the Willemse family, I moved to the home of
Tante Nan and Oom Jan van Gelder. I liked it best at their house.
I knew them very well. Their two children, Lietje and Enno, came to
our house for lunch during school because their house was too far
away. Lietje was a year older than me.

The story went that I was a niece visiting from Indonesia; my parents couldn't come to get me, so I was just staying with them until my
parents could make it back. Tante Nan sat every morning with me to
do schoolwork. She had a weaving machine and a piano in her house.
Oom Jan was head of a museum. I helped in the kitchen, played outside, and read. They had so many books. I played with the kids when
they came home from school. I could go on a bicycle and do things
I couldn't do before because I wasn't a Jewish child in their home. I had
a wonderful time there.

My sisters were hidden in that same town. One day, Tante Nan
brought me to visit with Judith. We were both so happy to see each
other. I didn't like the people with whom she was staying and felt
sorry for her. I couldn't get that picture out of my mind, my little sister
in that dark little house with two old ladies. After the war, I was told
by her that it was a lot better there than at her last family, where she
stayed the longest.

That was the only contact that I had with my family for almost
three years.

After four months, I had to leave my adopted family, who had
been so good to me. The father of Tante Nan was Jewish. He was
a psychiatrist in Amsterdam. They were afraid that if he were picked
up, he would be forced to tell about people in hiding, so it was too
dangerous for me to stay.

I was scared and wondered what kind of house and people I would
be moved to. In January 1943, on a windy and very cold day, a young
woman from the underground came for me. I said goodbye for the
third time, sad and fearful. After a train ride, which seemed to last
forever, she dropped me off at the house of Tante Nel van Vliet, a lady
who was about sixty years old (she looked very old to me), and her
twenty-two-year-old daughter, Sonja. There were also two men who
were boarders. Tante Nel's oldest daughter, Pim, was married and
lived in Switzerland. And her son, Max, worked in a German work
camp (not a concentration camp).

Tante Nel was divorced, which was unusual at that time. She was
risking her life, but it was also a way for her to support herself. There
were already three Jewish children there hiding from the Germans—
a boy my age, Dolf; his sister, Ans; and a little boy, Hans—and I became
number four. Tante Nel could not have afforded to keep four children
without payment.

I don't know how we paid for the hiding. I do know that Mammie
said, "Thank God for the diamonds we bought in Indonesia because
they managed to pay for the four years that Pappie did not earn
a living." I think, in my case, the Willemse and Van Gelder families
were not paid anything, but Tante Nel van Vliet was. Every host of
an *onderduiker* (person in hiding) was different. Some did it mainly

because of the goodness of their heart, some for religious reasons, some for money, and maybe some for more sinister reasons.

HANS (ZWI) GOLDBERG

We were five Jewish children of different ages. I was the youngest—three years old—when I came. The other children were Mirjam de Zoete, an eleven-year-old girl we called Manja because it sounded less Jewish; Dolf and Ans Vromen, a brother and a sister—he was ten, she was nine; and a girl who came later on for a short time. Her name was Fanny, but we called her Loesje—that also sounded less Jewish. She was eight, the daughter of a cousin of my father.

Tante Nel's son was, in the summer of 1942, twenty-one years old (when I arrived). The Germans sent all the strong young Dutch men to work in Germany. Some of them tried to escape, but Tante Nel told her son that he must go or the Germans would come to look for him and they would find the hiding children. He worked in Germany during the whole war.

Her daughter, Sonja, stayed at home and helped Tante Nel take care of us. She was like a stepmother to us.

MIRJAM

We stayed there for the remaining two years and five months of the war. I was eleven years old when I came and almost fourteen when the war ended. We were told that none of us were to go outside since the neighbors could betray us. Nobody was supposed to know about us. Mainly we were upstairs, not outside—never outside.

There were all kinds of rules we had to obey. We had to go to bed at seven. We had to peel potatoes very thin because food was scarce. Every peel was checked to make sure it wasn't too thick. We had to help with the dishes. We had to darn socks and underwear because you couldn't buy anything anymore. It kept us busy. I never did this at home because we had a maid. I had to help with the four-year-old boy—wash him in the morning, get him dressed, and play with him when he was bored because he had to be kept quiet, which is not that easy for a four-year-old.

Once a week, we took a bath in the living room, where a tub was filled with warm water. We had to talk very quietly because the neighbors weren't supposed to hear children in the house. We weren't allowed to go to the front rooms, only the windows in the back.

The other kids were more like brothers and sisters to me than friends because we fought like brothers and sisters, we teased each other like brothers and sisters, and we all tried to win over the lady of the house, Tante Nel. I was kind of scared of Tante Nel and her daughter. The women were the authority, but we children belonged to each other. We were dependent on each other. I felt a big kinship with the three children, more than with my sisters before the war.

I tried to be sweet to Tante Nel and somehow make her like me more than the other ones. I openly said, "I'm not going to be Jewish anymore, and I'm going to become a Protestant," because I wanted to please her. When I hear stories from people who are kidnapped today, I can very well see how they go over to their captor's side, because you

Hans Goldberg was the youngest child hiding with Mirjam at Nel van Vliet's home.

come to a point where it's the only life you have left, and you may as well please that person. Otherwise, you don't have a good life.

———

When I was moved to Tante Nel's house, I was told that it would be for a couple of weeks. I could not go back to Tante Nan, which upset me quite a bit. But Tante Nan came to visit—she sometimes had letters for me from my parents or sisters and always brought some candy for me to share. It made me feel special. She was like another mother, and her visits were the best part of hiding. It was better than a birthday party when she came. I think she came about three or four times a year, except the last half year of the war because there was no more transportation in Holland. I had gotten one or two letters from my parents over the years. I really had no knowledge of what was happening with them.

I was told if I wrote a letter, maybe my parents would get it. This is a poem I made for my father's birthday while we were in hiding. It must have been in 1943 (his birthday is February 21st), before things were so bad in Holland that the underground had no means of delivering letters from one hiding place to the other.

Dear Pappie,
It's difficult to shop,
I would not know how.
So I'll make something myself.
I will write a little poem,
because it's nice to give something homemade.
Because I can't be with you right now,
I am sending you this little flower.
I so hope that next year,
we will all be together again.
We would all love that,
because that would mean the war is over
and we will all be happy.
I am counting the days,
I can't wait.
A big kiss from me.
    Manja

For a while, a teacher came to teach us so that we wouldn't fall too far behind. We were convinced that everything would go back to normal again. We never thought that they would find us and we would have to go to the camps. We wouldn't let ourselves think about it.

I remember wanting to see the difference between night and day, sitting and watching when it would change. It was always the same. And the same and the same and the same and the same. We played lots of board games, card games, dominoes. We only had a couple of books in the house, which we read over and over again. It was illegal to own a radio. Some people had the courage to hide their radio in a closet and listen in secret to the BBC. It's from those people that we heard the truth about the war efforts. At night, we could hear the German planes flying over to bomb London. And later on, it was the

Mirjam's poem, written in hiding
for Chaim's fortieth birthday,
ca. February 1943; translation
on facing page

Mirjam's note, written in hiding
to Chaim and Fifi, spring 1943;
translation on facing page

geven I heb Wat was de
zuurstok lekker. Ik scheel nog m
fier centiemeter. met Juultje Ik
veel Ik vind zoo vein dat ik
keer een brief kryg. Weet je hoe
mij kamer er uit ziet er staat
bet in een twee genzeleg bruine zorg
een stoel het be hang is haast het
zelfden als bij ons een kast en
cebee poobretten er in ik ga mij
ver lang lysje tekken Ik maak
mijn dietjes iederen dag schoon.

other way around, with the British planes flying to Germany and the added sound of anti-aircraft guns.

Once or twice in the early evening when it was dark, around five o'clock, in the winter, before the curfews, Tante Nel and Sonja let us—as a big treat—walk outside on the street with them and then come back right away. Even today, when I walk outside in the early evening, I think about those one or two times I was allowed to be outside. Also, when I'm in a totally strange place and it starts getting dark, I feel the same homesickness that I felt at night there. When I was homesick, I thought about my parents and sisters.

I wrote to my parents sometime in the spring of 1943:
Thank you for the sweet and sour candy stick. I have four centimeters left. I had a letter from Judith. I have enough to eat. I was so happy with the letter. You know how my room looks? It has two cozy curtains, and a bed and a chair. The wallpaper looks almost the same as ours. There is also a closet. I am going to make my wish list. I clean my little [toy] animals every day.

I liked my bedroom. I did not have to share it. From my window, I could see fields of tulips, and on the wall there was a saying:

Een mens lijd meestal het meest
Voor wat nooit op komt dagen
Zo heeft hij meer te dragen
Dan God te dragen geeft.

A person suffers the most
For things that never materialize
So he has more to bear
Than God makes him carry.

Now, sixty-four years later and sixty-four more years of worrying, I have to reluctantly admit how true that is. But also how ironic, that this little poem was hanging in my temporary bedroom at a time in my life when there was actually more to worry about than at any other time in my life.

—

For a short while, we slept in regular beds in different rooms. It was a big house. Then, the Germans started to unexpectedly search homes for hidden weapons, hidden Jews, and hidden pilots from downed airplanes. It became too dangerous at night because you couldn't get to a hiding place fast enough. A friend of the family came to make a hiding place under the kitchen floor. He made a trap door and then put linoleum over it. It was about thirteen feet by twenty feet. I could sit in it without hitting my head. You could crawl in it. The four of us had to sleep there. Two mattresses were put on the dirt floor. Every night at seven, for the remaining years of the war—more than two years—we said good night, and the four of us went down into the hiding place. We were not allowed to talk out loud when we were in there—you never knew who was above your head in the kitchen.

It was quite dark. We were given one flashlight that worked with a hand pump. I remember trying to read by the little light that came in through the slit in the wall. When it got dark, I went to sleep.

For a while, I think I fell in love with Dolf. I was thirteen, then fourteen, lying right next to him, and we were both in puberty. It was just because he was the only boy there. I would never have given him a second thought otherwise.

We were not allowed to get out of the hiding place until Tante Nel or Tante Sonja opened it up for us. Sometimes the night down there seemed terribly long. Especially Sundays, when they liked to sleep a little longer. But, usually, before seven or eight, we left our little night prison, and took our blankets with us, because before we did anything else, we had to check for fleas. Everyone had fleas. There was no hot water, no soap, no disinfectant, so the only way to keep that problem under control was to try to find every last one of them and dump them one by one in a bucket of water.

During the day, we often practiced going in and out of the hiding place in the shortest amount of time. We had mirrors to see who was standing by the front door. When the doorbell rang, if we saw a guy we didn't know, we went quick, quick, quick into the hiding place. We always made sure nothing of ours was in the house. We were never told what to do in case we were picked up.

Tante Nel and Sonja were very strict with us. There was never an argument. I don't remember ever fighting with Ans or Dolf. Even the little boy, Hans, understood how dangerous our situation was and that he had to behave. I was very much afraid that if I weren't good I would be sent out on the street, although this wasn't anything Tante Nel or Sonja actually frightened me with.

HANS (ZWI) GOLDBERG
A trapdoor was cut in the floor of the living room (and later also in the kitchen). We slept under the floor, on the sand ground. The height between the ground and the floor was sixty centimeters.

During the day we could only stay in the back part of the living room, which was separated from the front part by sliding doors. In the front there was a big window where someone could see us from outside, and the neighbor across the street was the pro-Nazi mayor of Haarlem. The backyard could also be seen by neighbors, so we couldn't go out there. We went out into the garden only when we knew they were not at home.

Ans and Dolf Vromen are the brother and sister who hid with Mirjam; Dolf was Mirjam's age, and Ans was about one year younger.

ANS AND DOLF VROMEN
Although there were regular raids, the house was only searched once. Warned by a good neighbor, we children sat under the kitchen floor and, luckily, kept silent.

MIRJAM
Awful stories of what was happening in the concentration camps were told by word of mouth. From what little information we could get, we understood that the Allied forces could only slowly recapture the occupied territories from the Germans. By September 1944, they

were at the southern border of Holland. It looked as if the war was almost over. And then it stopped. The Germans regrouped; there were many casualties on both sides.

The lowest point was the end of the war. There was a lot of hunger. We didn't know it was nearing the end. Everybody was afraid it would keep going and going and going. The last year of the war for every Dutch person—not just for the Jews—was a terrible time.

The Germans stole more and more of Holland's food supply and our coal, which was the only means of heating the house. All the trees were cut down for fuel, with almost no trees left in the eastern part of Holland. Empty houses were demolished, and all the wood was stolen.

I was the oldest hidden child and least Jewish looking, so I was chosen to go with Sonja to abandoned houses where people were taking doors, windows, and staircases to get wood to make some heat. Tiny stoves were invented that used very small pieces of wood, which gave just enough heat to warm up a meal. We went to the railroad tracks with screens to sift the gravel; there were pieces of coal in there, which the firemen on the locomotives had dumped. For hours we did that, Sonja and I. You became very resourceful.

There was only an hour or two of electricity a day. Sometimes we were without water. There were no street cats; they were all eaten, sold as "roof rabbits" for food.

ANS AND DOLF VROMEN

Food was only available with coupons. Some neighbors who were in the resistance gave Tante Nel extra food vouchers occasionally, and sometimes she could buy black-market food. In the last year of the war, household linen had to be exchanged for food.

MIRJAM

To get food every day for the eight of us wasn't very easy for Tante Nel. We had ration coupons, for which every person was entitled to a certain amount of butter, sugar, flour, meat, soap, etc. Every month, rations became smaller and smaller until breakfast was one piece of dry bread. Sometimes, on Sundays, we had bread fried in oil. The people in the cities were starving, but the farmers had food. Sonja went to farms to see if she could buy food on the black market or trade it for zippers, hats, a winter coat, or gloves. It took hours, so it was decided that I should go with her.

With Sonja, I learned where to go. We had a bicycle with wooden wheels (the Dutch were allowed to have bicycles with wooden wheels because the Germans weren't interested in them). I saw German soldiers and people lying on the street, dead from hunger, not from being shot. I was thirteen and a half. I didn't want to look at them. I made believe I didn't see them.

We rode to two farmers. I followed Sonja when she went to the door to ask if they had butter or grain and showed what she had to trade. They had hundreds of people doing the same thing. The farmers had more coats, gloves, threads, and zippers than they needed, but there was never enough food. Some days, I stood in line for hours at the soup kitchen while Sonja went to the farmers to trade.

HISTORY BRIEF, PAGE 238
The Liberation of Southern Holland

HISTORY BRIEF, PAGE 238
The Hunger Winter

HISTORY BRIEF, PAGE 237
Food Rationing

One day, we heard that a sugar beet factory about eight miles away was selling leftover pulp after taking out the sugar. Before the war, the pulp was sold for animal food. We went together, Sonja and me. The sugar beet factories were in between Haarlem and Amsterdam by small red stone houses, little rivers, and lots of green, green land. We were lucky to get two big bags with pulp, which we laid over the bike for the long two-and-a-half-hour trip back home, taking turns holding the heavy bicycle. Tante Nel mixed it with a little flour and made pancakes from it.

Another day, when Sonja was sick, I had to go alone to the tulip growers. First, I was fed an extra piece of fried bread because it would be a long and very cold journey. I felt important and lucky. It rained hard, and the wind was blowing against me like a cold, wet wall. It took about two hours to reach the bulb warehouses. For hours, I went from one grower to the next. I must have stopped at twelve warehouses. Some never answered, some were sold out, and some were just plain nasty because I didn't have enough money for what they could get for a bag of tulip bulbs. Reluctantly, I turned around to go home empty handed.

The tears started to come. I felt more sorry for myself that day than at any other time in that awful war. I just couldn't pedal against all that wind, so I walked next to my bike for hours. I felt totally alone, wet, and afraid.

When I finally made it home, they couldn't see if my face was wet from the rain or from all the crying I did on the way there. I was afraid that Tante Nel would be angry with me for not bringing any food home. But I must have looked so miserable that everyone felt sorry for me. I was given a piece of bread and put to bed.

I had two close calls when I went out for food. Once, when I came with my coupons to buy something, there was an SS in the store, and he said, "What's your name?" I told him my hiding name, Manja. He said, "How did you get those coupons?" I said, "My aunt gave them to me." He didn't go any further, but I was shaking because it could have been the end for everybody.

Another time, while in the city, I saw a boy, about sixteen years old, pedaling a bread carriage. A bunch of hoodlums (they were probably just a bunch of hungry people) threw him on the floor, hit him with sticks, and took his bread. I saw it all and went to tell someone. I felt sorry for him because I thought that his boss might not believe him about being robbed. I almost offered to go with him to tell his boss what I saw. But I quickly remembered that I was not a plain Dutch citizen. I was someone that the Germans were interested in. Your whole life was one scary time. You tried to make yourself invisible.

———

Very slowly, that awful Hunger Winter passed.

Every December 5th, the Dutch celebrate Sinterklaas. Tante Nel and Sonja were determined that we should celebrate it, especially during that terrible hunger winter. Somehow they had managed to save, trade, or buy unusual little food items, like a candy stick or a piece of chocolate. We made poems for each other and drew pictures as gifts. I loved that holiday so much, I wished I wasn't Jewish. I thought

Sinterklaas, or Saint Nicholas, is the patron saint of children. The Dutch celebrate Sinterklaas on December 5, the eve of his birthday, by putting shoes in front of the fireplace to be filled with small presents and sweets, and by writing poems to family and friends.

it would be so much easier not to be. I wanted to belong. I didn't want to be this Jew person who didn't belong to the other people. Obviously, after the war, this changed. After what happened to the Jews, becoming a Christian would be like being a traitor. But at that time, I wanted to be like the people whose house I was staying at.

By the end of December 1944, we had gone through four and a half years of war, and I was a very skinny thirteen-year-old. I did not know if my parents or sisters were still alive. Neither did the other three Jewish children hiding with me.

I kept a diary in the last four months of the war. Food was very important to me (and still is).

——

Monday, January 1, 1945: Before the New Year started, Tante Sonja woke us at ten o'clock. We hurried out of our bed, put our dresses on top of our pajamas, and went downstairs. We cleaned the dining room table and played a card game called Lying. First we each got a *loempia*— a small pancake filled with noodles, cabbage, and other stuff. Then a little cup of tea with two oil-dumplings, and right after that, two apple cookies. In the meantime, we lied our hearts out. After the game, we each got some *kroepoek* (Indonesian crackers).

Midnight was getting closer; we finished the game and cleaned up the cards. We waited for the stroke of twelve on our radio. We got up and wished each other a Happy New Year. Then Hans gave Tante Nel a little plant from the four of us. After that, Ans gave Tante Son (Sonja) a four-leaf clover plant from the four of us. She always wanted one of those. We set the table and started with a delicious potato salad, cooked beets, grated carrots, and celery root. And after that, home-baked white bread, with spreadable cheese and tomato paste. Everything was delicious! Then, we went to bed. The next day, we got breakfast in bed like it was a Sunday.

Thursday, February 1, 1945: Today is Dolf's birthday. He's thirteen years old. Tante Nel went shopping for a birthday gift, but there was nothing to buy. That was a pity. But on his birthday, there were some packages anyway. He was very happy with them. Tante Nel borrowed a waffle iron and made delicious waffles. And Tante Son made tasty cookies from tulip bulbs. For dinner, we had tulip cake with syrup and sat pleasantly together.

Sunday, February 4, 1945: This morning we got breakfast in bed, as always on Sundays. Bread and *nasi goreng* (Indonesian fried rice). But it was made from sugar beets, not rice. Delicious! Also, home-cooked rye bread. Tante Nel left to see how Tante Mien (Tante Nel's sister) was. She thought she was sick. Fortunately, that was not the case. I decided to make a picture for my father. In the afternoon, I drew some more and finished it. It was a good drawing. I'll stop now because Ans is grinding some grain. With all that noise I can't write anyway.

Thursday, February 8, 1945: Tante Son and I were planning to go to Halfweg on our bikes to see if we could buy some sugar beets. But

Zondag 4 Februari

Van ochtend kregen we op bed brood wat we 's zondags altijd krijgen met nasleering van suikerbieten heerlijk! En ook eigengekookte roggebrood. Tante ging 's ochtends naar tante Ellen want we tante dacht dat ze ziek was. Gelukkig was dat niet zo. En ik ging een tekening voor Pappie maken. Van middag ben ik door gegaan en heb hem af gekregen. Ik vind hem wel leuk geworden. Ik zal nu maar uitscheiden want Ans gaat malen en zo kan ik toch niet schrijven.

Donderdag 8 Februari

Tante Son en ik zouden naar Halweg gaan voor suikerbieten. We zouden op de fiets gaan. Maar we waren de brug van het Spaarne nog niet over of pang zij mijn band en was leeg. We wisten een eindje verder een fietsemaker, maar toen we er kwamen wilde hij de band niet maken omdat hij geen solutie had. Toen gingen we maar weer naar huis. 's Middags aan tafel zei Tante Son, "zouden we maar niet lopend gaan, anders wordt het weer misschien anders. We zouden met één fiets gaan ik bij tante Son achterop en terug lopend. Toen we na een halfuur aan kwamen lieten we de zakken vullen en gingen lopend terug. Tante Son heeft van alles verteld het was dus wel gezellig maar we waren toch wel blij toen we de Amsterdamse poort zagen. Toen waren we gelukkig gauw thuis.

Mirjam's diary, January 1–February 10, 1945; see translation starting on the previous page just after we crossed the Spaarne Bridge, *bang!*, my wheel broke. We knew that there was a bicycle repair shop up the road. But when we came there, the man told us that he could not fix it because he was out of the special glue he needed for the job. So we returned home. That afternoon at lunch, Tante Sonja said we better not walk because the weather could turn worse. It was decided to go with one bicycle on the way there, and on the return, we would walk. We arrived in about a half hour. They filled our bag with the beets. On the way back, Tante Sonja told me all kinds of stories, which was entertaining. But we were glad when we finally passed the Amsterdamse Poort (Amsterdam Gate). We would soon be home.

Saturday, February 10, 1945: We were late with everything the whole day. Because of that, the candied-peel cake was baked at four-thirty in the afternoon, and then we still had to clean the kitchen. Ans and I helped Tante Son. In the meantime, the tiny stove would not get very hot so the bread would not bake, and the potatoes were only cooked by seven o'clock. By the time the soup was ready, it was eight-thirty. After finishing the cake, it was nine-thirty. Luckily, we did not have to clean the dishes. Ans went to bed, but we still got a cup of tea with ginger. And then by ten-thirty we finally went to bed!!

———

Back then, I was always worried that I got short-changed. It sounds that I liked being at Tante Nel's, but I didn't. I did not like Sonja and was unhappy about the strict discipline. And I certainly did not like being scared, hungry, worried, and locked up. But I knew that my letters would be read by my *onderduik* (hiding) parents. So, to make my life easier, I tried to please everyone. Even in my letters. That's why the few pages of my Day Book sounded more like I was in a summer camp than the young teenager who couldn't wait to get out of there.

You always thought it would be just another month in hiding. If we had known it would be almost three years, it would have been terrible for us. But we believed the English or the Americans would come, then another month went by. You lived week by week, and that's probably the only way we could stand it. You always believed it would be over soon.

JUDITH

Hadassah and I stayed for a short time with Kees and Tine Hos. Our baby cousin Chaja was also there. After a few weeks, Hadassah and I were separated.

I was sent to a family of three women. Tante Ali, a mother of two grown daughters and a son, was a widow in her fifties. Her older daughter, Corry, in her late twenties, lived at home because her husband had been sent to a German work camp. Her second daughter, Hannie, also lived at home since her fiancé was in a Japanese prisoner-of-war camp. Her son was likewise a prisoner of war. They were captured by the Japanese in Indonesia.

I felt quite alone because all three sort of lived their own private lives and kept to themselves. In the mornings, I got lessons in regular school topics, and in the afternoons, I was allowed to play outside with neighborhood kids (to them I was Tante Ali's niece; my parents in Indonesia had sent me to Holland to escape the Japanese). Once in a while, Tante Ali would take me shopping with her to very expensive stores and chic, exclusive restaurants for afternoon tea. But most of the time, I was on my own.

One of the first things they did was cut my hair (I had braids, and that made me look more Jewish).

Once in a while, I would see Hadassah, who lived with another family in the same town, but that was just by accident. We had to ignore each other since we were not supposed to know one another.

CHAIM

Our daughter Judith Ruth was placed at the care of Mrs. Wouters (Tante Ali) through the mediation of Nan van Gelder in Wassenaar. She was immediately treated as Mrs. Wouters's own daughter and got, during the whole stay there, private lessons from a qualified teacher.

After about one and a half years, police raids became more frequent. As a result of a warning, Judith went to a friend of the Wouters family to spend the night. However, the search was done just in the part of the village where that friend was living. Late in the evening, the police came. Happily, Judith was already asleep, so she did not see the policeman standing at her bedside. He was told that she was a daughter of a family member. At the moment, the man believed it, and the next day Judith was taken to another place. Let it be known that the police came back to ask for her. Now it was told that she had traveled back to her family far in the north of the country, and no further questions were asked.

JUDITH

After almost a year with Tante Ali, I had to leave. One reason was that a connection between Hadassah and me came up accidentally, which made it dangerous for the two of us to stay in the same neighborhood. We both were sent on an errand to the same butcher in town on the same day, and the butcher sent Hadassah's order to my house and my order to hers—apparently, we somehow looked alike to him. That, of course, was cause for alarm, because obviously there was not supposed to be any connection between us.

Judith

Invisible

Judith in the backyard of
Ali Wouters's house, her second
hiding address, 1943

After almost a year with Tante Ali,
I had to leave. One reason was that
a connection between Hadassah
and me came up accidentally, which
made it dangerous for the two of
us to stay in the same neighborhood.
JUDITH

The underground was notified, and I was sent to an "in-between" address, to a young couple with a baby, until a more permanent place could be found for me. I don't remember where the temporary address was, nor do I remember the names of the family or how they looked. What I remember is the Germans raided their house on one of the first days of my stay with them. This search had nothing to do with me. The Germans were looking for illegal documents, food rations, false identity papers, hidden radios, etc.—not for people. They were surprised to see me but were told that I was a guest for just one day, which they believed, surprisingly.

They looked under my blankets and under the mattress (also in the baby's bed, which was in the room with me). They did not find anything and left, but of course, after that, I had to be forwarded as soon as possible to a safer place.

CHAIM

In view of the frequent raids in Wassenaar (which might have been more frequent because nearby the V-2 was fired) and the fact that Mrs. Wouters's daughter, Corry, who could move only by means of a special cart, was involved in illegal work, it was decided to transfer Judith to another environment entirely.

———

Our daughter went to stay with the H. family. She was accepted by the family under the motto "Where so many children are, one more does not matter." Nevertheless, things weren't so simple, as it grew by the day more difficult to gather the necessary food. Father H. was a courageous, straightforward, openhearted, and energetic man.

Judith was treated as his own child. That this was more than merely a way of speaking became clear when she fell ill with severe pneumonia. Mother P. banned her husband from the conjugal closet-bedstead and slept with Judith at her side until the danger was gone. Judith remained there until the end of the war.

JUDITH

About the last address only in general lines: the place—Rijnsburg, near the town of Leiden; the people—a poor family with eight children, of which the two oldest did not live at home. First, "Pa" (the father)— he was a macho guy who scared the hell out of his little kids. Then, "Ma" (the mother)—a drudgy, overworked housewife with hysterical outbursts (sometimes ending in fainting). And then the kids, eight of them. I remember their names, even though I could have forgotten them together with the other bad memories. The girl, R., was my age, but even with her, there was not much affability.

Strangely enough, I haven't the faintest idea what I did during all that time (almost two years), besides getting up in the morning and going to bed in the evening, having meals, sometimes playing with the kids in the very narrow space between the house and the "outhouse," which was a shed with no running water, just a hole in the ground with a wooden bench on top. I remember that I liked going to church on Sundays more than the H. family's own kids. At one point, I was very sick with pneumonia.

HISTORY BRIEF, PAGE 237
V-2 Rocket Testing

C. and P. H. took Judith into their home from ca. August 1943 to May 1945.

I had no idea whatsoever what was going on with my parents, sisters, or with my more distant family. In the beginning of our hiding period, we—all three sisters—got letters from our parents, brought to us by Tante Riek, a Christian lady working for the underground (Tante Riek also took care of Hadassah for some time during the war and later became a friend of the family). I had no knowledge at all about anyone during the last year and a half of the war. No idea who was where and if still alive.

During the hunger period (mostly in the western part of Holland), we had very little to eat (bread made from beet pulp and spinach seed). But, still, we were "lucky" because Pa was involved in the slaughter of pigs on the black market. I have no idea how or where he got those pigs, but the slaughter was done in the shed. "Lucky" because with the money he made on the black market, he was able to find and pay for other food, like potatoes, which he got in the eastern part of Holland that was closed off by the Germans.

I don't know how the house was kept warm, probably partly with the cooking stove in the kitchen, and I don't know how they got the wood and the coal, but I don't remember being cold.

I remember having my teddy bear with me throughout those two and a half years.

But the rest of the time is a big blank. In hindsight, I believe I know why, but that is another story.

KEN SCOTT: NEWSPAPER CLIPPING FROM CANADA, CA. 1974

Two Monkland Grandparents Honored as Heroes by Israel

MONKLAND—Two Dutch grandparents living here, C. and P. H., have been honored as heroes by the Government of Israel for saving the life of a Jewish girl in Holland during the Nazi occupation from 1940 to 1945.

Although there were already ten in the family, [they] sheltered an eleventh, Judith de Zoete, for two years, thus putting themselves and their family in constant peril of death by firing squad or starvation.

In recognition, the sixty-nine-year-old couple was invited to Ottawa, in November, where they received a citation from the Israeli Ambassador to Canada, Ephraim Evron. The citation came from Israel, and had been awarded in October 1964, by the Commemorative Institute for Martyrs and Heroes in Jerusalem [Yad Vashem's Righteous Among the Nations].

The Jews honored this Dutch Presbyterian couple on the basis of evidence supplied to the institute after the war. How the evidence was gathered [C. and P. H.] don't know. They thought the incident was forgotten, and have never mentioned it since they arrived in Canada nineteen years ago.

Their only reminders had been several devoted letters from the girl herself, now married with two children in Arad, Israel. "I have twenty-four grandchildren and two Jewish ones," says Mr. H. proudly.

On Wednesday afternoon, [C. and P. H.] sat in the spotless green-and-white kitchen of their cozy farmhouse, about fifteen miles north of Cornwall, and reminisced about the war years.

Judith's bear, 1940s

I remember having my teddy bear
with me throughout those two
and a half years [in hiding]. But the
rest of the time is a big blank. In
hindsight, I believe I know why, but
that is another story.
JUDITH

Additional Risk

Harboring a Jew was merely an additional risk, says the couple. Mr. H. was forced to take many others [risks] to feed this family, while Mrs. H. lied more than once on his behalf to save him from being shot.

There were also two teenage boys living at home, and hiding places had to be built in the house for whenever the Nazis came looking for conscript factory hands or laborers.

One hiding place was dug out beneath the floor boards (there were no cellars) and another was atop a clothes closet. Alerts were performed by the underground resistance movement, usually within hours before the soldiers' arrival.

In order to feed ten mouths, Mr. H. bought and sold on the black market. His specialty was butchering, which was illegal and punishable by death. But it kept his family fed.

This was the situation when the [H. family was] approached by the underground movement in 1943 and asked to harbor a Jew.

"They told me it was a baby and I accepted," said Mrs. H. "When I found out it was otherwise, I didn't like it at first."

Judith arrived one day on the back of a bicycle. She had long black hair and was twelve years old. Her parents had lost track of her, nor did she know of them or her two sisters.

Barely Alive

Her parents, in fact, were hidden in a church in Rotterdam, 50 miles away—above the organ. A caretaker barely kept them alive with food from the local residents.

By contrast, Judith was plump and well fed when the war ended, said Mrs. H. Nor was she imprisoned like her parents. The [H. family] had a twelve-year-old daughter, and the two girls became like sisters, going everywhere together.

Harboring Jews was common in Rijnsburg, where the [H. family] lived, and many other villages as well. Some foster Dutch parents were paid in return, but many others like [C. and P. H.], "didn't accept one cent," said Mr. H.

German soldiers searched their property twice during the entire war, but on neither occasion were they looking for the girl, although she was hiding in the house.

JUDITH

About that report in a Canadian newspaper, I have three comments:

1. I don't remember writing devoted letters to them. (At that time, I didn't even know they had moved to Canada.)

2. Where he said, "I have twenty-four grandchildren and two Jewish ones," my first reaction was: unlikely that his sons married a Jewish girl. Then, I realized that to look good in the eyes of the Israeli ambassador, he meant the two daughters I had by 1967.

3. Here I may be wrong, but he just doesn't seem the type not to accept money.

JUDITH

May 3, 2015

Dear daughters,

You must have wondered why I, offspring of the "witty, warm Polak family," am quite different from them: I don't talk much, don't hug much, don't kiss much (more like the De Zoete side of the family), not outgoing.

But, there is also a quite different reason, about which I never talked to anyone for years and years, and then only to Mirjam and Hadassah. This occurred after an unintended response I had during a phone conversation with Mirjam. Mirjam told me about a meeting she went to about children of the Holocaust. She said, "It is unbelievable what some children went through, not a few were victims of sexual abuse." "So was I," was my spontaneous answer. Until then, I apparently had put it way back in my mind and only very seldom remembered bits and pieces of that period—Mirjam's story pushed it right back to me.

The last family I was hiding with was where it happened. The father and two of his sons, sixteen and seventeen years old, abused me. There was nothing I could do, and nobody I could go to.

In the beginning, we still had "some" contact with our parents through letters brought to us by people of the underground movement. But all that had stopped the last year and a half of the war. I am still amazed nobody in the H. family found out, given the very small living space we shared, or maybe they did and kept quiet.

The house: very, very small, just two rooms; one of which was the kitchen-living-dining space (about 2½ by 4½ meters). The other room was the "nice" room, which had a built-in sleeping space in the wall for the parents and the baby. Nobody was allowed in that room, unless for special occasions. And there was the attic used for sleeping and playing. The six children and I slept there. We also stayed there if we couldn't be told to "go outside and play" because of cold and rainy weather.

The father used to sneak me into the "nice" room. His wife was constantly busy doing housework, cleaning, cooking, taking care of the baby, yelling at the kids—in short, overworked and irritable.

The two brothers (not at the same time, though they knew about each other doing to me what they did) told me to come upstairs to the attic at times when the other kids were occupied elsewhere (playing outside, doing homework in the kitchen-living space, helping Pa in the barn).

I could have tried to tell Ma, but she probably would have gone into a hysteric fit. She used to have those now and then for many reasons, like A: a macho husband, B: impossible living conditions, C: too many children in too small a living space, D: hunger, E: being overworked, always tired, etc.

If I had told Ma, she could have decided that I had to go; that was also scary because at that time, the underground people were left with very few options for other hiding places, and lots of people were caught and put in prison (in hindsight, I suppose I wasn't really aware of that). Also, in the last year there was no contact whatsoever with people of the underground movement.

Judith's notes on the back of a photograph of C. and P. H. receiving
a commendation from Yad Vashem
for hiding her, ca. 1974

he is the one!
Righteous among the nations—
And sex abuser
(as were two of [h]is 15–16(?) year, sons
JUDITH

After telling her, she might not have believed me. Who would she be inclined to believe more: her husband and sons or me? So I kept quiet. But now, while writing this, I think that at that age I had no concept that it was something I could complain about, although in my heart, I knew it was wrong.

Thinking back, she might have believed me, knowing her husband for the man he was. Not only did I not tell anybody then, I never told anybody after the war. After all, they saved my life, so my parents would have left it at that, I suppose.

Strangely enough, I must have erased that whole period from my mind completely (not only the part of the sexual abuse). I can't even remember (till this very day) what I did daily during the last one and a half years of the war. I did not go to a school, I did not have private lessons, there were no toys or games in the house, and no friends of the children came to the house.

I DO remember having knitting contests with R. (the girl my age) and peeling potatoes or cleaning vegetables with her. Two more things I remember: I liked to go to church on Sundays and being very sick with pneumonia (no antibiotics at that time). I almost died.

Overall, the last eighteen months of the war are sort of a blackout. The part of the sexual abuse came back to me vividly after that phone conversation with Mirjam, and I thought since Mirjam now knows, I should tell Hadassah too. I never told my parents. I apparently had put it way back in my mind. And if I would have remembered, I still wouldn't have told them; they weren't really in a position to act upon it—you don't punish someone who saved your child's life.

Once, after the war—shortly after it ended—he (Pa) came to visit us. He was very polite and civil and put me on his lap, which I hated. And that was it, no more contact from me.

Years after, we got a letter from them from Canada (they moved there after the war) to tell us about the arrangements Pappie had made getting their names in the Righteous list in Yad Vashem. And sometime later, they sent us a letter with pictures of the ceremony in the Israeli Consulate, where they got a medal and a certificate, and trees planted in their name for saving a Jewish life.

Judith requested that Yad Vashem's Righteous Among the Nations—a juried list that commemorates people who saved Jews in World War II—cancel the honor C. H. received for his involvement in her rescue; in 2016, Judith's case was reviewed, and C. H. was removed from the list.

Franciscus (Frans) and Petronella Lafontaine first hid Hadassah at their home on Van Oldenbarneveltweg in Wassenaar, from September 1942 to ca. August 1943.

Hendrika (Riek) Dekkers hid Hadassah from ca. August 1943 to October 1943; she also transferred letters between the De Zoetes.

Hadassah

HADASSAH

The first family with whom I stayed was called Lafontaine—Frans and Petronella. I called them Oom and Tante. They had no children. He owned a metal furniture factory in Leiden, which in the war produced ammunition for the Germans.

It was a total change—coming from a warm, family-oriented, loving family to a pair of people not used to children, who did a lot of shouting, and where Tante Petronella (Mrs. Lafontaine) was beaten for things she'd done wrong, not to mention that she had her fair share of man-friends. And, sometimes, I would find her in bed—and not with her husband. I did not understand exactly what they were doing (not like eleven-year-olds nowadays) but knew that it was something I was not supposed to see.

I was known to friends and neighbors as Hansje Lafontaine, a niece on a visit. I went to a regular school. At that time, Judith and I were both in the same town—Judith as Juulte Wouters. We would see each other by accident sometimes but could not react because we weren't supposed to know each other, let alone be related.

About a year later, the Lafontaine couple divorced, and I had to leave. I first went to Tante Riek, the Christian lady who helped our family a lot, and stayed in touch with us as a friend of the family long after the war, till she died. I was with her in Rotterdam for three months until a new address was found. I had a happy time there, was loved and spoiled, but had to leave when a new address was found.

CHAIM

Miss Dekkers was a close friend of Reverend Brillenburg Wurth, so when he took us into hiding in his church, we came in contact with her. She became our link with the children. It was she who took Hadassah into her home when family difficulties made it necessary to take her away from the Lafontaines. Hendrika was our courier between our hiding place in the church at the Breeplein in Rotterdam and the addresses of the children; she kept visiting our children at their various addresses, and it was her reports about the children that made the difficult years of our own hiding more bearable. It was she who, through her connections with the underground movement, provided us with ration cards. As a nurse, she also assisted with the birth of a Jewish child in the church where we were hiding.

Hadassah stayed with her for about six weeks, but because Miss Dekkers had an employment agency for nursing personnel, several persons became inquisitive about her young housemate. She thought it would be safer to find a new address for Hadassah.

Once, Miss Dekkers, as a friend of the Reverend Brillenburg Wurth, took Hadassah to the home of the Brillenburg Wurths and let her play in the garden so that we, from the house of our host (the sexton De Mars), could see her unobserved. It was the only time we saw one of our three children during the nearly three years of hiding.

HADASSAH

I could not stay with Tante Riek because she was too busy doing underground work, which made it dangerous for both of us.

Invisible

Hadassah in the backyard of Hendrik (Henk) and Jans van der Leer's house, her fourth hiding address, 1944

Once in a while, Tante Riek picked me up and brought me to visit the Brillenburg Wurth family, the reverend of the church where our parents were hidden in the attic. Mrs. Brillenburg Wurth told her daughters, Mia and Hetty, to take me outside to the back garden and show me the chickens and rabbits. I never knew, till the end of the war, that while I was in the yard looking at the chickens, my father and mother were watching me through a little window in the church tower.
HADASSAH

Hendrik (Henk) and Jans van der Leer sheltered Hadassah at Lede 72 in Rotterdam from October 1943 to spring 1944.

There is conflicting information regarding Hadassah's visits to the Breeplein Church. In 1963 Chaim wrote that Hadassah visited the Breeplein Church courtyard "once," with Riek Dekkers, so he and Fifi could see her from the window; in a 2006 letter to the church, Hadassah wrote that she visited on Sunday mornings with the Van der Leer family. This excerpt is from Hadassah's 2007 account in which she wrote that she visited "once in a while" with Tante Riek.

Franciscus Lafontaine, who hid Hadassah with his first wife, Petronella, from 1942 to 1943, once again gave her shelter from spring 1944 to January 1945 with his new wife, Miep, at Beethovenstraat in Amsterdam.

My next address was at the home of Oom Henk and Tante Jans van der Leer, in Rotterdam—a couple with a little girl. The cover story was that I was a neglected child of a family of twelve children, who needed a home with better care. At that time, my name was Hansje van Borsten. This was told to everyone who asked who I was.

The Van der Leer family was a Protestant family, and very nice to me. They also kept contact after the war, and their daughter (then all grown up) visited me.

Since they had a child, the Germans provided them with special rations, such as milk (grown-ups could not buy milk). One day, I was sent to the store to get some milk but lost the vouchers. I was completely devastated, but Tante Jans accepted it as a little misfortune that could happen to anyone and was not mad at me, even though every bit of food or drink was lifesaving at the time.

Once in a while, Tante Riek picked me up and brought me to visit the Brillenburg Wurth family, the reverend of the church where our parents were hidden in the attic. I spent some time playing with their children. The reverend's children, of course, never knew about me being a Jewish *onderduiker* (person in hiding). The reverend and his wife, of course, knew who I was, but to their children I was a poor, neglected girl invited over for a good meal and some playing in the yard. Twice, I almost revealed (by saying the wrong thing) that I was not who I appeared to be. I told the reverend's children, "My sisters know how to play *quatre mains* (French for "four hands") on the piano." Not exactly something a poor neglected child would know or a thing her sisters would do. And, helping the reverend's children to set the table for dinner, I corrected them in how to place the knives, forks, and spoons in the right spot. This was also not something I was supposed to know, being who I pretended to be.

We all sat around the dining table, and afterward Mrs. Brillenburg Wurth told her daughters, Mia and Hetty, to take me outside to the back garden and show me the chickens and rabbits. I would have preferred to stay inside with them. I never knew, till the end of the war, that while I was in the yard looking at the chickens, my father and mother were watching me through a little window in the church tower. On the one hand, this must have been very special to them, to see that I was a healthy, cheerful child who was well taken care of. On the other hand, so sad, because under no circumstances could I know they were there, hidden in the church, so they could not just come out and hug me.

Altogether, it was an unbelievable, courageous act, what the reverend and the sexton and their families did for us.

———

And then, Oom Frans (Franciscus Lafontaine) asked to have me back, saying that he was very fond of me, that he was remarried, and that "Hansje" should now, again, live with him. In retrospect, it is clear that Uncle Frans used me as a cover for later, when he had to stand trial because of his connections with the Germans. And the cover worked: Pappie testified in court after the war that Mr. Lafontaine had hidden his daughter, and this served as a mitigating fact at the trial.

On our way to Amsterdam, where Oom Frans now lived, he told me that his second wife was German and hated Jews, so under no circumstance should I disclose the fact that I was Jewish. "Tante Miep," as the woman was called, was sort of nice and kind in the beginning but became less and less so with time.

One day, Tante Miep and I saw a man shot to death because he did not obey an order by a German soldier to stand still. Tante Miep's comment was, "It doesn't matter. Don't pay attention; he probably was a dirty Jew."

Also, while living there, rather traumatically, I had to stand in line to get food from the Gestapo in the Euterpestraat, a favor to Nazi sympathizers and German followers. They had the privilege of getting more food rations because Uncle Frans had good relations with the Germans because his factory produced munitions and he had a Nazi wife. I stood there in line, a little Jewish girl, mortally afraid something might go wrong.

At the time, my headaches started, but my complaints went unanswered. Then, in January 1945, Tante Miep gave birth, and I had to leave immediately. Tante Miep did not want to be bothered with a little niece of her husband. Frans brought me to his first wife, the one with the many boyfriends, Tante Petronella, in Wassenaar.

Petronella Lafontaine resumed caring for Hadassah until May 1945 at her Wassenaar home.

CHAIM

Though surely the human urge to help was there, and Mr. Lafontaine cared for Hadassah in a fatherly way—so that Hadassah, to this day, thinks of Uncle Frans with gratitude—this is the first and only rescuer who might not have offered protection purely for humanity's sake. I felt it my duty to recommend him, as a savior of one of our daughters, for distinction with Yad Vashem. On the other side, in order not to lower the worth of that distinction, I found it necessary to suggest the possibility to investigate this case more thoroughly than the other ones.

Mr. Lafontaine's factory was, during the war, working for the German occupier, and it may be that he took in a Jewish child in order to compensate for it and explain his position after the war. It may indeed be that he was forced to work for the Germans.

However, the fact that his new wife's family was decidedly on the wrong side weakens this argument. This may be confirmed by Hadassah's account that this new family got their ration cards, or extra ration cards, from the Gestapo headquarters in Amsterdam. Hadassah herself was sent to collect them in the building in the Euterpestraat, the notorious Gestapo building, feared by every true Dutchman.

Through Mr. Lafontaine's contact with the Van Gelder family in Wassenaar and Miss Dekkers in Rotterdam, he could have caused a catastrophe, but, thank God, he never did.

Franciscus Lafontaine does not appear in Yad Vashem's Righteous Among the Nations.

Theo and Betsy van Dalen hid the entire Cohen family from early July 1943 to late September 1944.

Nathan

My sister and I were introduced to Theo van Dalen, a very large man, blond, in his mid-thirties, who told us he would take us by train to our family. He had false papers for us, and we had to learn to be Hans and Henny Westerhuis from Nijmegen, who were going back home after a short stay in Amsterdam.

After saying goodbye to the Hunninghers, we went by tram to the Central Station and by train to Utrecht, where we had to wait for a connection to Nijmegen. We waited in the third-class waiting room, which was full of travelers—I had to get used to being in a room crowded with strangers, many of them German soldiers, but nobody took notice of us. Theo told us that we would be staying with him together with our parents and our sisters. We had a cup of tea (not real tea but linden tea—tea and coffee were not available, since they came from overseas) and cake. Then we took the train to Nijmegen and a taxi to Gendt, a very small farming village in a rural area between the Waal and the Rhine Rivers.

We got to Theo's house in the late evening and had a very happy reunion. He lived in a small farmhouse with two floors and a cellar. The lower floor had a *deel*, an open space in the house with a threshing floor where farmers kept their cows and pigs in winter. The *deel* had a hayloft above part of it and big double doors, which allowed a farmer's wagon to be driven in. The corridor connected the front door at one end with the *deel* at the other. The three rooms on the ground floor were the kitchen-living room in the back, a spare guest room, and the nice room in front. In rural areas, the nice room is used only for special occasions and is usually closed, with the furniture covered with sheets. On the upper floor were the bedrooms of Theo and his wife, a bedroom for his two children, and a small attic. Theo had partitioned the guest room, making a false wall of plywood and repapering the walls, so that you could not see that a small room had been added. The room could be entered through a trapdoor that Theo had made in the attic. This was our hiding place and also our bedroom. Its floor space was nearly all taken up by mattresses, and there was a small area separated by a blanket where a covered bucket served as a toilet. The radio was also kept in this hiding room, as it was forbidden to keep one.

Father and Mother came to Theo after they had to leave their first hiding address, and he suggested gathering our whole family. This was when he prepared the hiding place, or the "hole," as we called it. Theo arranged false papers for us, and we pretended we were a family staying with him during vacation. We were allowed to walk around freely in the town, play outside, and behave like normal people. After two weeks, we had to "leave," since the summer vacation was over. We stayed in the nice room. But as long as nobody was visiting, we could walk around inside the house, including the *deel* and its hayloft.

Theo also hid two young Dutch men, Jan and Wim, who got papers telling them to go work in Germany as farm help. They slept in the spare guest room and had a hiding place in the hayloft, behind the straw kept there for the pigs.

———

Invisible

Master Sergeant Theo van Dalen, who hid Nathan and his family, ca. 1930s

Theo was against dividing the Dutch into groups—Gentiles and Jews— and other restrictive laws. He was very patriotic and hated the occupation. Early in the war, he began resisting the Germans and their sympathizers, while at the same time simulating friendship with his colleagues and other policemen.
NATHAN

Theo was one of two policemen in Gendt. The other policeman was sympathetic to the Germans, or at least did not actively resist them. Theo was against dividing the Dutch into groups—Gentiles and Jews—and other restrictive laws. He was very patriotic and hated the occupation. Early in the war, he began resisting the Germans and their sympathizers, while at the same time simulating friendship with his colleagues and other policemen. His wife, Betsy, must have been an extraordinarily patient woman, since I don't remember her ever complaining about the invasion of people that they hid.

Because he was a policeman, Theo always got a list of the farms where a search was to be held, and he had to be present when the search was conducted. Since he knew the local farmers and their political views, he had a system of warning farmers he suspected of hiding Jews or Dutch fugitives from labor in Germany. Father, Wim, or Jan would phone and inform them, "In the name of group A of the underground, a razzia is to be held in the neighborhood one of the next few days." He never gave the accurate date and time, and also phoned some people that he knew were not on the list just to throw a false trail in case somebody became suspicious. Few people were caught by the Germans in his area. I am sure that Theo saved several people from being sent to concentration camps.

The way Theo arranged for our false papers was quite simple. At night, he had to guard the administration building where food stamps, identity papers, and other official stamps were kept. One night, after food stamp coupons were brought to the office for distribution, Theo was on duty. He had Father, Jan, and Wim come to the office at about three in the morning. When they were there, Theo broke open the strongbox and took all of the identity papers, food coupons, and official stamps—even those he had no use for, because it would cause confusion. They broke some furniture to make the robbery look realistic. Jan, Wim, and Father then tied Theo up on a chair in such a way that he was not too uncomfortable, and went home with their bounty. Theo sat there till the office was opened, and he was rescued by the Nijmegen police. It even made the local Nijmegen newspaper, with a description of two (fictitious) robbers, and Theo got a citation for having resisted with such force that the office was a total shambles.

———

The air raids on Germany got heavier all the time, and the Germans shot down bombers and fighters over Holland. Theo must have had good contacts with the Dutch underground, because that winter (1943–44) he had more guests—Canadian, English, and American pilots on their way back to England. The house was getting quite crowded with thirteen or fourteen people living there. The pilots had the worst of it; since they did not know any Dutch, they had to be hidden all the time. They did not stay long, but as long as they were there, they were usually in the hayloft.

I practiced my English and my chess on the poor downed aircrew members. Their preferences probably did not include teaching English grammar to a twelve-year-old Dutch boy, nor discussing the war news with him. I also started to learn English from the BBC, which had a program called "English by Radio," in which they started with simple

Invisible: Nathan

sentences and slowly expanded the vocabulary. After the war, an English soldier complimented me on my good English accent!

My father continued with our education, and we had to do some schoolwork for a few hours a day. My reading was confined to the books and journals in the house, and I must have read *Robinson Crusoe*, *Dik Trom*, and other Dutch and translated children's books dozens of times, till I nearly knew them by heart. I also read all the old prewar weeklies that Betsy van Dalen had saved up and learned a bit of recent world history through them.

I found a stack of old police journals and was soon busy checking them to find family members who had gone into hiding. The police would publish a photo with names and short descriptions of fugitives or escaped prisoners, and all Jews who went into hiding were there. We found ourselves there, and a sister of Mother, Aunt Mieke, and also the whole De Haas family. After the war, we heard that the people who were hiding the De Haas family betrayed them when their money ran out. Not all Dutch families were like the Van Dalens.

We also kept war maps and, that way, learned geography: Asia and the Pacific, where the United States was fighting the Japanese; Russia, which occupied most of our time, and where we had two different lines of pins, sometimes hundreds of kilometers apart—one where the Germans said the front was, and one where the BBC said the front was; and Africa, where the pins were moved quite rapidly after the battle of Alamein in eastern Egypt, and the landing of the Americans in French Morocco. Then, the invasion of Sicily and Italy and the Italian surrender. This was all good news, but it still seemed a long way from us. We were quite disheartened when the Germans managed to stop the advancing Allies at Monte Cassino, where the war bogged down, with the Germans having a big advantage of sitting on the high ground, and the Allies were taking very heavy casualties. This was reported by both the Germans and the BBC, so we knew that it was not the usual German propaganda.

During that winter, we could go outside on moonless nights, and we took walks in the neighborhood, up to the dike of the river, which was maybe a half kilometer away. Father taught me to find Orion and the North Star on cloudless nights, and we loved to watch the searchlights flitting all over the sky, without finding planes. The British would drop chaff, which was made from bundled strips of silver paper. This confused the direction finders of the searchlights and anti-aircraft guns. Since we lived close to the German border, there were nights that you could see the horizon in the east lit up with fires.

Theo had arranged a bell on the front gate to the garden; when the gate was opened, a buzzer would sound in the house warning all the illegal guests to go to their rooms and be quiet. Luckily for us, if the Nijmegen police or, worse, the Germans would come over, they usually phoned ahead, and Theo tried to meet them at the police station. If they were to come home with Theo to drink a glass of gin after having finished the business at hand, he would phone Betsy asking her to put the water on to boil. This was his way of saying that we should go to the hole and Jan and Wim to the hayloft.

Betje Cohen-de Haas and Julius de Haas, Nathan's paternal aunt and uncle (murdered, Auschwitz, December 7, 1942, 49 and 59 years old).

HISTORY BRIEF, PAGE 237
Italian Surrender

The new NSB (Dutch Nazi) mayor, Christoffel Becude (appointed in 1944), was a regular visitor, since Theo pretended sympathy for the NSB. We children were usually already in bed when the mayor came over. One time, the mayor arrived unexpectedly and found only Betsy and her children at home. He stayed anyway, and this developed into a dangerous situation, since Theo was out with Father, Jan, and Wim, distributing confiscated black-market products to addresses where he knew fugitives were hidden. Only Jan, Wim, and Father showed their faces to these families since they were unknown. Luckily, when they returned, Theo entered the house first, and when Betsy met him at the door, saying the mayor was visiting, Theo shouted goodbye to Father, Jan, and Wim, who got the message and waited in the apple orchard that bordered the house.

We had another close call when, one morning, a sister and brother-in-law of Betsy paid a surprise visit to the Van Dalens. Since they arrived at ten o'clock in the morning, without giving advance notice, our family went to the nice front room and the others to the hayloft, which was the drill when the warning bell sounded. Betsy entertained the guests in the kitchen, locking the connecting door to the nice room, and we locked the door from the room to the corridor. We had to be totally silent for about six hours, till the guests departed. The walls of the house were thin, and we could easily follow the conversation in the next room. At one time, Henny had a coughing attack and was nearly choking, trying to cough as quietly as possible with Mother squeezing her nose and holding her hand over her mouth. For Gertrude and Annemieke, to be silent, without moving a chair, without being able to do anything, just sitting quietly, was the toughest challenge, since they were about eight or nine years old. Those were the longest six hours of my life.

———

In early June 1944, the Dutch newspapers were full of articles ridiculing the Allies for not being able to start an invasion. The news from Italy was also not good since it had become a nearly static war. On June the sixth (D-Day), this all changed. The news broadcasts from *Radio Oranje* told of landings in northern France. We had prepared maps of the entire coast from Holland to Spain, and the map of northern France was put on the wall next to the maps of Italy and Russia. We prepared those maps ourselves, first tracing them from the world atlas, and then enlarging them by scaling, making squares on the traced map and making larger squares on a new piece of paper. This kept us occupied for a few days, since we were sure the war would quickly move east toward Germany (at least we children were).

Theo celebrated the invasion by initiating a reign of terror among the known NSB members who were farmers, setting fire to haystacks, making threats through the phone and other intimidating acts. This didn't do much to help the war effort, but it did help boost the morale of the rest of the farmers in Gendt. We now had two Allied airmen staying at the house. The German-controlled Dutch radio and newspapers ridiculed the invasion, saying that it would be thrown back in the sea in a few days, but it became clear that the invasion was a success. The names of places where fighting was taking place showed

HISTORY BRIEF, PAGE 237
D-Day

that the Allies had landed on a wide front. We listened to the news from morning till night: the Dutch station, Radio Hilversum, the German radio, and the BBC in both English and Dutch. The air attacks on German cities continued unabated, and skies full of American planes were now a near-daily sight. I think it was at this time that Hamburg was attacked for several days, and the BBC claimed that 80 percent of the city was destroyed. We were sure that the Germans would now either surrender or be quickly defeated, maybe even before Christmas. Then, the invasion bogged down. The city of Cannes in Normandy was fought over for a long period without being conquered by the British. The only moving pins on our maps were the ones in Russia, which kept moving west and getting close to the Polish border. We had to remain hidden as usual, staying indoors.

After about a month, the Americans broke through the German lines in Bretagne (the Battle for Brittany). At about this time, the Allies also landed in southern France, where there was nearly no resistance. Paris was captured without being fought over.

The British in northern France and the Americans in central France were advancing very fast, and the Americans reached the Rhine at the border of Germany. The Allies advanced through Belgium. Then, one Sunday morning, the Allies dropped an entire division of para-troopers in the neighborhood of Nijmegen (Operation Market Garden). Everybody in the village except us, it seemed, stood on the dike and watched the sky filled with parachutes. We could not go outside, and from the house we could not see anything, which, of course, was very frustrating. The landing was nearly unopposed. The first few days after that were very confused. Then it became slowly clear that the Germans were holding the line and that the Allies did not make a breakthrough. From history books, I later learned that only a minority of those brave British parachutists safely returned to the Allied lines, which in the meantime had reached the south bank of the river Waal. The German presence became more pronounced now that we were separated a mere five to seven kilometers from the English army. The problem was that we were on the wrong side of the river.

Jan's and Wim's concealment was now less necessary since the Germans were not actively looking for Dutch fugitives. So, at about this time, they left for their hometown of Arnhem.

The NSB members understood that they were in a dangerous situation. Some of the NSB went to Germany for their safety. One was the mayor, Becude, who told this to Theo in the deepest secrecy. Theo said he was going to prevent this by killing him. Father was very much against this, since this way Theo was putting himself on the same level as the Nazis. Theo decided to go anyway, and Father went with him. They came back after midnight, their faces white and withdrawn. I was sure they had killed the mayor. After sending us to bed, they told how in the end they had helped the mayor pack his things and put them in a car. Theo was in an evil mood for a few days, angry with my father that he had persuaded him to let the mayor go scot-free.

HISTORY BRIEF, PAGE 231
Radio Oranje and Radio Hilversum

HISTORY BRIEF, PAGE 237
The Battle for Brittany

HISTORY BRIEF, PAGE 238
Operation Market Garden

On September 17, 1944, Christoffel Becude fled Gendt. He was arrested in April 1945, and, in 1947, tried for his wartime actions and set free. According to Geert Visser of the Historical Society in Gendt, while detained, Becude stated, "I was a close friend of Van Dalen, he knew I didn't want to give him any trouble—I could have done that in the months before, for I knew Van Dalen lodged a Jewish family." Visser questioned the truth of this statement as Becude might have learned about the hidden Cohen family after liberation, using it to his advantage.

The mayor was caught after the war, jailed, and released after a short time. I don't think he ever knew how close he came to being killed.

Theo came home with exciting news that a whole group of Germans had arrived who seemed ready to desert. Father immediately went to talk with them and was soon discussing the war with a major, giving the impression that he was sympathizing with the Germans, but that he now thought the war was lost. The major quickly convinced Father that these were not deserters. He insisted that Father gather all the neighboring farm families at our house; the major then gave a long talk about the German war machine—how the Germans would counter-attack and throw the Allies from the continent using the Wunder Waffen, or Wonder Weapons, that the Germans would soon bring into the war. Father had to translate all this and afterward thank the major for the wonderful talk. The troops were a group of Waffen SS, fanatical Nazi soldiers. Luckily it ended without further consequences. After that, Father and Theo were a bit more circumspect in their efforts to get Germans to desert. Nobody believed the things the SS major said, but he seemed to have been well informed, for shortly afterward the Germans did counter-attack in the Ardennes (Battle of the Bulge), driving the Allies quite some distance back. The Wunder Waffen also materialized—the V-1, a pilotless flying bomb, and the V-2, the first longer-distance rocket—with which the Germans tried to terrorize the British, especially in London.

We had some drills so that we knew what to do in case of an air raid. Some German deserters strongly recommended not using the corridor, which was the refuge recommended by the Dutch civil defense, but instead the cellar or the trench outside the house. So when somebody shouted, "Air raid," we would all run to the cellar, which could barely hold us all. One time, I was standing outside when there was a dogfight between a single Allied plane and a German fighter. I was in front of the *deel*'s open doors and saw the planes careening and shooting all over the sky above me. Finally, they came directly over the house, at treetop level, and the German plane crashed some miles away. I was hauled inside by Father and got my ears boxed for unnecessarily endangering myself, which was true, since shell cases were literally raining down.

Sometime later, a German tank group was parked in the apple orchard next to the house. From the window in the nice room, they looked huge. Theo tried to send word with a sketch to the Allies showing where the tanks were stationed so that they could bomb them, without apparent results, since during the three days the tanks were standing in the orchard, no planes came near, even though the days were sunny with clear skies. The third night, the tanks left. The following morning was again a beautiful day. I was standing outside the doors of the *deel*, together with Father, when suddenly the German deserters jumped from the hayloft, not using the ladder, shouting "*Im Keller! Im Keller! Raketen Flugzeuge!*" (To the cellar! To the cellar! Rocket-firing planes!) We saw, far away, a group of double-tailed planes (lightning bombers, I found out afterward) that had a

HISTORY BRIEF, PAGE 238
The Battle of the Bulge

round protrusion in each tail section. We all ran to the cellar, as was our drill, without expecting that the planes would bomb our neighborhood. They usually followed the dike and bombed there, since the main road was on the dike. After a few seconds, there were a series of awful explosions—the floor was shaking, and I remember that I could see cracks in the wall forming and opening in slow motion. The wood shoring fell down, eggs that were stored on a rack broke, splashing yolks all over me, and the cellar was filled with dust. When things quieted down and we tried to get out, we found that the door was blocked. There was panic for a minute or two, but then someone managed to open the small window, which was in the outer wall near the ceiling of the cellar, and someone went out through it to free the door from the outside. He came back after a minute, saying that it was impossible to get to the cellar door. So we all got out through that small window—the children first, then the grown-ups. I remember that Mother and Betsy van Dalen were a tight squeeze and that it was a funny sight. I started to laugh hysterically. A cuff from one of the grown-ups brought me quickly to my senses.

Once we were all outside, we saw that the house was not hit by a bomb but that five bombs straddled it: two on the side of the cellar, three on the side of the orchard, all very close, a few meters from the walls. The outer wall looked like an accordion—depressed inward close to the bomb craters. Groundwater was rising in the craters, so the time from the falling of the bombs till we got outside must have been very short, although it seemed ages. The roof was caved in, and the first things we saw were German rifles sticking through the collapsed roof. This was, of course, very dangerous, so one British pilot climbed up and pushed them out of sight. None of us was even scratched, which was a miracle, since we were fifteen people in that house—four Van Dalens, six in our family, two Allied airmen, and three German deserters. All of the inner walls had collapsed into the corridor, showing how right the deserters were and how bad the advice of the Dutch civil defense was. Had we stayed in that corridor, surely most of us would at least have been injured.

The second most urgent thing to be done was to find hiding places for the airmen. Theo knew some addresses of farmers, and they were hurriedly brought there. In the meantime, we started to collect as many things from the ruins as possible. That night, we slept in a farmhouse close by. We were the family Lindekamp, refugees from Nijmegen, and that is what we remained till we were freed by the Allies. The German deserters slept in the ruins of Theo's house. Theo and Father buried the German rifles and other war materials, such as Allied firebomb sticks and ammunition for the rifles, in a bomb crater after wrapping them in cloth filled with axle grease. I helped with the digging and was proud to have been able to do something. In the morning, the German deserters left. They did not know where we were staying, and the next few days were very scary and uncertain since we did not know what the deserters would do.

Most of the rocket bombs had fallen in the orchard next to the house, and it was totally destroyed, trees standing at odd angles, branches torn off. It was clear what had happened. The warning that

Certificate received by Nathan's
father, Isaak Cohen, for aiding Allied
soldiers, ca. late 1940s

The airmen were evacuated to a place in the Veluwe, about thirty kilometers north of us. From there, they were to be picked up by plane. They went in a civilian ambulance and were wrapped with blood-soaked bandages (cow blood), either as head wounds or as lower belly wounds, so they had a reason not to speak in case of a German check.... Some people had to stay bandaged up all the time so that [Isaak] could claim they were too severely wounded to be moved.
NATHAN

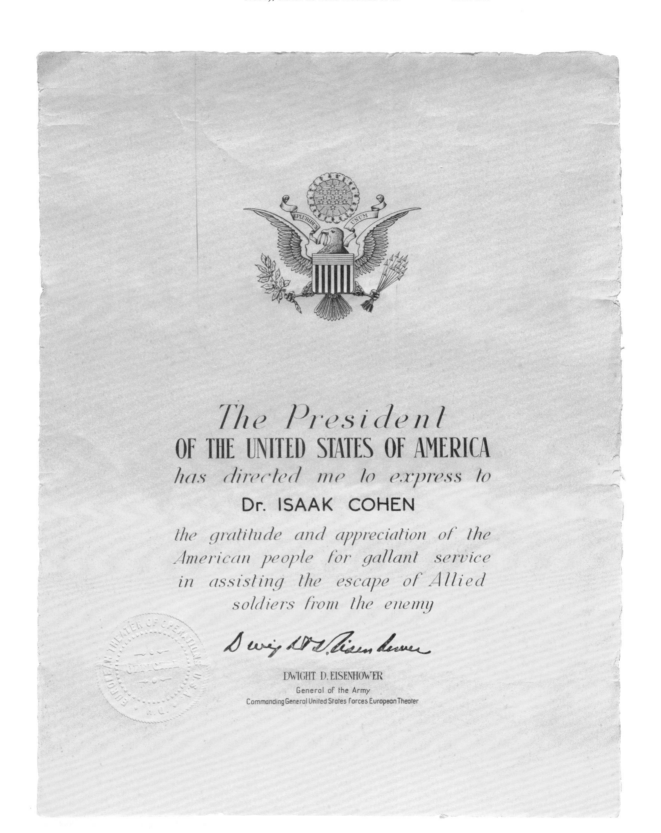

The President
OF THE UNITED STATES OF AMERICA
has directed me to express to

Dr. ISAAK COHEN

the gratitude and appreciation of the
American people for gallant service
in assisting the escape of Allied
soldiers from the enemy

DWIGHT D. EISENHOWER
General of the Army
Commanding General United States forces European Theater

a group of German tanks were in that orchard must have gotten through, and it really was quite an accurate bombing. It was a pity that the tanks were gone before the orchard was bombed. I don't think Theo, Father, or any of the grown-ups realized when sending that sketch of the German tanks that they were inviting the Allies to bomb Theo's house. Maybe, if they had realized this, they would not have sent the sketch.

———

After a few days, we went to another farmhouse close to the dike. This was a big farm; the farmer was hiding English fliers, and he was one of the sources of Theo's food distribution chain. The Germans were evacuating the civilian population from the war zone, sometimes forcibly. Father established a "hospital"; there were nearly no regular patients, but it gave a reason to stay since the grown-ups were convinced that the Allies would advance and free us any day.

The Germans were telling families to go to the confluence of the Waal and the Rhine, where a ferry was still working to take them to a safer place. One night, Father was called to a family who had been thrown out of their house by the Germans and caught in the open during some shelling. A girl of ten years was wounded in the chest by a shell fragment, which opened her flesh like a can of sardines, down to her ribs. Father closed the flap and sent her to a real hospital for treatment.

After a few weeks at the farm, the airmen were evacuated to a place in the Veluwe, about thirty kilometers north of us. From there, they were to be picked up by plane. They went in a civilian ambulance and were wrapped with blood-soaked bandages (cow blood), either as head wounds or as lower belly wounds, so they had a reason not to speak in case of a German check. We stayed in that farm after the entire neighborhood had been evacuated, living on apples from a nearby orchard, meat when a cow was wounded, and the farmer's large reserve of cheese. Some people had to stay bandaged up all the time so that Father could claim they were too severely wounded to be moved. But after about a month of this, the Germans had enough and commanded us to leave. One night at the end of October, the wounded (both real and pretend) were loaded on the wagons, and we were driven in style to the branching of the Waal and Rhine and ferried to the eastern shore. We separated there from the Van Dalens. They went to family in Deventer, and we went to look for somewhere to stay, as close to the front as possible since we hoped to be liberated soon.

We stayed that night at a big farm next to the river. They had accommodation for fifty or more people in their cellar, which in normal times would hold cattle ferried over the river. They had real bread, home baked, and I remember this as a big treat.

The next morning, we traveled with some people who had a horse and wagon—they allowed us to put our stuff on the wagon. We were going northeast in the direction of Doetinchem. Planes were flying overhead all the time, and since it was a clear day, we were told not to walk too close to the wagon and to be ready to jump into a ditch by the roadside in case a plane should dive to fire on our little convoy.

The Mierlo-Staring family sheltered the Cohens for one night in late September 1944 at their farm, located at Het Klooster 9 in Angerlo.

The monks who hid the Cohens for three days, just before the family moved to Halle in October 1944, may have belonged to the order that founded Saint Willibrord's Abbey after the war, though this cannot be confirmed.

When we reached a cloister, we stayed there for the night, receiving a real warm meal, with potatoes and vegetables with salt, and it tasted heavenly. Father told the abbot that we were Jewish and that he would not be offended if the abbot thought that it was too dangerous to keep us there. The abbot said that this was no problem and that in the past many Jewish refugees had stayed there. We remained at the cloister for a few days, Mother and we children, while Father went to a small town where he had heard they needed a doctor.

When he came back, he said that we would move the next day to Halle, a small town next to Doetinchem. The doctor there had been deported by the Germans after he was betrayed for hiding Jews. The doctor's wife said that she did not mind Father being a Jew and that he could take over the practice for the rest of the war. She warned Father that he should not trust any of the farmers in his practice since most were very antisemitic—NSB or sympathetic to the Germans. Father hired a few rooms in a farmhouse, and we left the cloister the next day after thanking the monks. They did not want to be paid, since they said that helping refugees was God's work and one should not be paid for it.

Our two rooms in Halle looked like a palace to me. We were the family Lindekamp and, as good Dutch Christians, were free to move around, a novelty for us children after a year and a half being closed up in one room. We did not go to school. I think, because of the closeness of the battlefront, the schools were closed or maybe our parents decided it was not worth the danger to send us to school in Doetinchem, the nearest town. After about a week, we had settled in, and I started to work as a farmhand. I don't know if I was much help, but I loved feeding hay to the cows from the hayloft. Even cleaning out the pigsty was fun. We had *klompen* (Dutch wooden shoes) for footwear, and I remember having to get used to this since the top of the wooden shoes would chafe my feet.

Food was plentiful, except for eggs, which for some reason were in short supply. Father got paid for his work in farm produce, and soon our living room had a string of smoked hams and sausages hanging across it. Since there was plenty of cow meat, my parents decided that we need not eat swine. Bread was baked by the farmers, and we exchanged smoked ham and sausages for bread and other farm products. There was no soap to be had, so Mother started to make it with fat and soda ash from the apothecary Father kept. This was a hit with the farmers, and Mother's soft green soap was used by all the neighboring farms. We made our own butter in a glass jar with a churn. By pushing the stick up and down, we churned the milk, and either cream or butter could be produced. Buttermilk was a by-product not much appreciated by me.

The western part of Holland is densely populated, and the farm produce there was insufficient for the population, especially since the Germans had first choice. Soon there was a steady stream of Dutch men from western Holland who came on foot or with bicycles with wooden tires. The farmers in the neighborhood established a distribution system whereby each would give or sell some grain, butter, or other foodstuffs to everyone asking for some. My parents gave away all the sausages and hams hanging in our living room. Some farmers sold their food at exorbitant prices or traded the food for jewelry.

The front was static that winter; then, in the early spring, the Allies captured a bridge across the Rhine, in France, and soon established a big bridgehead on the other side. The front became mobile again. Soon, we were hearing the familiar (to us) rumble of faraway gunfire. The Germans were now very disorganized.

The Post family hid David from July 20, 1943, to spring 1944 in the town of Doniaga.

I was taken to Friesland, a little place near Sint Nicolaasga. It was all farm country. I was hidden there with a grocer who lived behind his store. Their name was Post. My story was that I was a nephew from Indonesia; my parents were in Indonesia, and I was stuck in Holland. My parents were supposed to come to Blaricum, and they couldn't because the war broke out, and this is why I stayed with the family in Friesland. The father had five kids. I was the only person hidden. His kids worked with him in the business delivering groceries and all that. I worked on a farm after school milking cows and haying. All the kids had to work. Out of the two years I was in hiding, I spent almost a year with those people.

I went to school and learned the local dialect. After three months, I spoke fluent Frisian, so I could walk the streets because no Jews spoke Frisian. The only problem I had in school was that it was a farm community and when it was haying time, the kids didn't go to school—they worked in the fields. I was way ahead of the other kids because I went to school in the city. It was kind of boring to me, and I got into all kinds of trouble—like bringing cats to school in a bag and releasing them, and in the winter, putting rubber bands on the stove so it would smell so bad they had to let us out.

The Post family was religious, and on Sunday we had to walk to church. I was bored like hell. The kids didn't give a shit either. Every meal they prayed and the whole bit, so I just sat quietly.

The family I hid with was good to me. I was like one of them—I felt very protected. I thought I would wait out the war there and see my parents after. I lived a normal life in Friesland, like all the other kids. I was not any different. When the family went to a fair in Heerenveen, the big city, I went with them.

There was another Jew hidden in town with another family. We were the only two Jews there. Before the war, no one in Friesland had seen a Jew because it was a very isolated area. There were two Nazis—Dutch Nazis. One ran the slaughterhouse; the other was a baker. And the guy from the slaughterhouse came to me and said, "Look, if the Germans ever come to this town, you come to me, and I will hide you, and they won't do a darn thing to you." Everybody in town knew what I was. I told the people hiding me what the man from the slaughterhouse told me. They said to do what he says because it was my best way of surviving if something happened. Then, the other Nazi, the baker, turned somebody in. People from the town took the baker to the woods and beat the hell out of him. It was the last time he tried anything like that because he knew those farmers would kill him.

I had a business selling rabbits with one of the sons from my hiding family. At this time in Holland, there was hunger. We had about seventy rabbits we were butchering, and people came from the cities and bought what they could. We were also growing tobacco and cutting it on the meat machine, which was the only thing the machine was useful for in those days.

Then, the Germans stopped supplying electricity. The people hiding me were Protestant. Very strict Protestants. They sent us to the Catholic village next door because they had these huge beautiful

David

Invisible

David, ca. 1942

I was supposed to be bar mitzvahed at the end of '43, but my father thought, "Well, everyone is still there." He wanted to speed it up because he didn't know what would happen to us. The feeling among the grown-ups was that this was the last time that everyone would be together. A lot of people who were already in hiding could not come.

I left home in March with one suitcase. I was thirteen.
DAVID

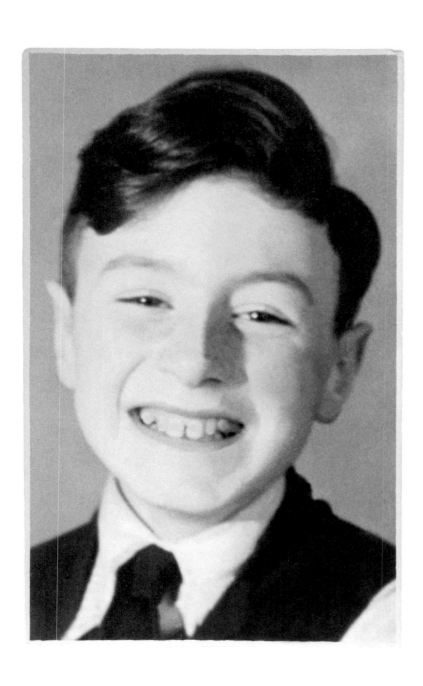

candles in the church there—the kind you pay for and light for whomever. So, they sent us with money and said, "Get the candles; don't light them. Bring them home, so we have light."

Then the youngest son developed tuberculosis, and life changed. The whole family revolved around this child, and there was not much they could do about it.

I was working after school for a farmer, and I had to take a horse to another village with his kid. We had to go through the woods, and we hit a rainstorm. The day after I came back, I developed pneumonia. I realized I was not like the others. I couldn't go to the hospital. A doctor came to me from about four villages away. With a huge needle, he took water out of my back. They didn't think I was going to make it because they didn't have the medication there. I knew what the village did for people who are sick, because we had the son with tuberculosis, and every Sunday the people brought him a piece of cake that they'd made before they went to church. The amazing part was, when I started recuperating, everyone from the village brought me cake too. The whole village was concerned for my well-being. So I recuperated.

———

Then, a rumor came around that the Germans would come to the village, so the family had to move me.

An underground organization picked me up and brought me to the Kuiperses in IJlst. It's a decent-sized village. Like all over Holland, it is filled with connected lakes, rivers, and canals. It was near Sneek, which was the main town. There was a big factory called Nooitgedacht that made wood chisels, wooden tools, and ice skates—things like that. The father was a worker in that factory; they had three or four kids.

I could not go to school, but I could go outside because I spoke the local dialect. I worked on a barge that recovered wood for burning and for wooden shoes. The Kuipers had another Jewish family with them, a man and wife. The wife was pregnant. They were not allowed on the street. They were also from Amsterdam. I got a little more scared in IJlst because of them. They saw the seriousness of the situation and always told me to be careful.

At that time, there were some big razzias. The Germans came to the town looking for bicycles, people, and radios. When they heard the Germans were coming, the people from this village took all their bicycles and threw them in the rivers.

Because I spoke the language fluently, the people where I was hidden told me, "When the Germans come, you go out on the street." So I just walked around calmly with the other kids looking at what the Germans were doing. The Germans came with dogs, and one of the dogs jumped right on top of a whole bunch of bicycles in the water. They started dredging them out. A bunch of us kids were standing around, and the Germans asked us what we knew about the bikes. We said we didn't know anything. A couple of Germans said we should stay there, that we couldn't leave. Well, I saw a way of disappearing because—for me, knowing who the hell I was—it was not the healthiest thing to stay there with the Germans. It was a loose arrangement, and I got away, over to the other side of town where there were no Germans because they were all busy where the bicycles were found.

Pieter and Corrie Kuipers hid David from spring 1944 to January 1945.

Invisible: David

I went into the fields and stayed there until I was sure the Germans were gone. The people where I was hiding were afraid because they didn't know if the Germans noticed that I had disappeared and would come look for me.

So, in early 1945, I moved to a second family in IJlst—Van Kampen was their name. They had a very small house, like labor housing, outside the village about a mile. They also had a four-year-old girl hidden. The husband was a laborer who worked at the quarry. They got me a job at the quarry running a horse that pulled the dump carts. When I was with them, I could only go to work and home. I could not go back to the village. It was very boring. I was with them for two months.

In 1944, the Germans stole all the food they could from Holland and did not pump the water from the low fields. A lot of the farmland was flooded. Some farms were only reachable by rowboat or barge. A lot of ship and railroad traffic went through IJlst. In February 1945, a German troop transport train came through town. The Dutch railroad workers were on strike and left the railroad bridge open. When the German engineers came to close the bridge, the Dutch underground was there in German uniforms. They opened the bridge, so the whole train went into the river, soldiers and all.

And then every man in the village, including myself, took to the fields. I spent ten days alone in the field. I stole food from the farmers, milked some cows, and hid in haylofts at night. When I met an animal in the field, it looked very big in the dark. That was the time I was the most afraid.

After ten days, I went back to my first address in that town. The people took me in. I got a job making wooden shoes. I worked with a guy on a boat that was transporting potatoes and turf.

The Van Kampen family hid David in January and February 1945; afterward, he returned to the Kuipers home and stayed until May 1945.

Dieter Heymann is the son of Erika Heymann, who hid Erwin in her apartment at Argonautenstraat 19, Amsterdam, from early July until September 5, 1943.

Erwin

DIETER HEYMANN

When the Germans began to round up Jews, Erwin Geismar came to live with us, illegally of course, in our apartment on the Argonautenstraat. My mom, Erika Heymann, had run a bed and breakfast there, so it did not seem strange to the neighborhood that he was a renter. Fortunately, our landlord was an avid Dutch nationalist and anti-Nazi who asked no questions, although he suspected what was going on.

ERWIN

July 21, 1943: Why do I begin just today, to write on the day that has brought me the most personal worries of the last three and a half years? Why just today? Most likely, because I am alone with my thoughts and worries, because I am cut off from the things and people with whom I could exchange thoughts at work, because I no longer have my daily occupation, because I can no longer contribute in the way I have been accustomed, because my domestic surroundings are dissolved, because the chance to commit my entire being to help my family and myself has been taken from me, because the daily thrill of danger is missing, this thrill like a narcotic on the nerves, giving one the feeling, to help and to dare, over and over to involve yourself in danger, like a gambler more and more enslaved by his passion.

Surely, these are the reasons that drive me to write down my current thoughts and to explain my activities to others who may perhaps be interested. Perhaps, too, the helplessness in which I find myself, condemned to sitting still, the unaccustomed quiet after a year of sixteen-hour days.

DIETER HEYMANN

In 1943, when Erwin came to live with us on the Argonautenstraat, he had falsified ID papers and pretended to be a Catholic who went to church on Sunday. Erwin was not the only hider in our apartment. Around this time, my mom became a member of the Vrije Groepen (Free Groups) underground resistance organization. We had three hiders: Erwin; a Dutch student, Appie (Albert) Keijzer; and a German in his late teens, Hans (Chanan) Flörsheim. The two younger men pretended to have jobs in town; hence, they went out quite freely. On at least one occasion, an Allied airman who had been shot down but rescued was hidden one night with us on his way back to England.

We had known the Geismar family since July of 1933; they lived in the ground-floor apartment of Van Eeghenlaan 14, the row house where we lived when we first arrived from Germany. Erwin had a business making belts. My mom had fled with my sister, Sonja, and me from Berlin to Amsterdam. My father, Stefan Heymann, had been arrested and imprisoned—not because he was a Jew, not because he was a communist, but because he wrote a scathing article about Hitler.

Eventually, Erwin became my flute teacher. I liked him very much. My sister told me later that this was considered remarkable, as I was very critical of others at the time. Erwin was an excellent flute player who had once been invited to be the soloist for a Mozart flute concerto performed in the famous Concertgebouw (concert hall) of Amsterdam.

HANS (CHANAN) FLÖRSHEIM

When every Jew had to report at the concentration camp of Vught, I had to "disappear." The idea of obeying this decree never entered my mind. I was given an address but warned that it was not certain that I would be able to rent there. A pleasant woman [Erika Heymann] opened the door, and within three minutes everything was settled. Thus, I moved into the attic room, which I was to share with a student [Appie]. The days turned into weeks and the weeks into months. For full board, I paid three guilders per day, and I lived in a friendly milieu. Powerful decrees were promulgated against the Jews who still lived in Amsterdam, and thousands were again on their way to Westerbork.

There were also razzias like the huge one on June 20. On that morning, I was awakened by the shrill loudspeakers of the trucks of the Grüne Polizei. Soon thereafter, the real razzia began. Police and others came into the homes to check IDs and search for forbidden items or persons. My roommate and I paused anxiously while our landlady achieved wonders with her German passport.

My hidden relatives, with whom I had lived during my school days, had been kicked out by their landlady, who had evidently become anxious for some unknown reason. That was on Saturday, the fourth of September. We were just eating dinner when the relatives and their small daughter came upstairs in a dither and begged Mrs. Heymann to give them shelter for that night. Actually, no person except for [four colleagues in the underground] knew where I was living, but my relatives had begged me to give them the address in case I was late in delivering the food stamps, which I regularly provided for them. Thus, they could reach me but only in case of the utmost urgency. And so they had appeared totally unhinged. I had to argue long and convincingly with Mrs. Heymann. She only agreed in the end because her two children, Dieter and Sonja, were not in Amsterdam for the weekend. Thus, my relatives were allowed to stay that night.

I immediately rode my bike across town that evening to find shelter for them, but without success. My attempts during the following day were equally in vain.

DIETER HEYMANN

The Sicherheitsdienst, or SD (Security Service), part of the Nazi SS, came to our apartment on Sunday, September 5, 1943. On the Sunday of the arrest, Sonja and I were in 's-Heerenberg visiting our uncle. Appie was out in town. Erwin and Hans were at home, and there were three more people who had arrived late Saturday night. They were family of Hans and had been kicked out of their hiding place. My mom was furious because that was a serious breach of trust among all "hiders"—you did not give your address to anyone. Nevertheless, Mom allowed them to stay for the weekend.

HANS FLÖRSHEIM

I returned, exhausted, at three p.m. and planned to ride and search again at some later time. I was just about to leave the apartment when the doorbell rang. I called Mrs. Heymann, who was sunbathing on the flat part of the roof, and asked her to open the main front door

Hans Flörsheim hid with Erwin at Erika Heymann's residence.

HISTORY BRIEF, PAGE 236
Raid on June 20, 1943

July 21, 1943: Why do I begin just today, to write on the day that has brought me the most personal worries of the last three and a half years? Most likely, because I am alone with my thoughts and worries, because I am cut off from the things and people with whom I could exchange thoughts at work, because I no longer have my daily occupation, because I can no longer contribute in the way I have been accustomed, because my domestic surroundings are dissolved, because the chance to commit my entire being to help my family and myself has been taken from me.
ERWIN

vielleicht jahrelang gewohnt war.

arbeit Gedanken ausgetauscht habe, weil ich meine gewohnte
tägliche Beschäftigung nicht mehr habe, weil ich nicht
mehr positiv arbeiten, ja beinahe kämpfen kann,
weil meine bäuerliche Umgebung aufgelöst ist,
weil die Notwendigkeit von mir genommen ist,
zu helfen unter Einsatz seiner ganzen Person u
seiner Familie, weil der Reiz der Gefahr, in der ich
mich täglich bewußt befunden habe, dieser Nervenreiz,
der wie ein Narkotikum auf die Nerven wirkt, u
der einem den Schuss des Spielers gibt, zu helfen u zu
ragen, sich immer mehr in die gefährliche Materie ein-
zulassen, wie ein Spieler sich immer mehr an seine Lei-
denschaft versklavt.

Dies alles werden wohl die Gründe sein,
die mich dazu treiben meine Gedanken deutschen Gedanken
aufzuschreiben, u andern, die es vielleicht interessiert von
meiner Tätigkeit zu erzählen. Vielleicht ist es auch die
persönliche Einsamkeit, in der ich mich befinde, der zum
Stillsitzen verdammt sein, die für mich ungewohnte
Ruhe nach einem Arbeitsjahr von täglich ca. 16 Stunden.
Endlich ist es aber auch die Hoffnung u der Trenuel,
daß meine Zeilen vielleicht doch einmal von Men-
schen gelesen werden, die daraus ersehen wie gekämpft
wurde, unter welchen, teils sehr schwierigen Umständen
u daß dann diese treuen Leser den Kampf, den wir
in der vordersten Linie mitgefochten u erlebt haben
aufnehmen mögen, zum Erreichen einer
menschenwürdigeren menschlichen Gemeinschaft

two flights downstairs. Although I had already pressed the electric door opener once, the door had failed to open. Hence, I went downstairs to open the door myself manually. Meanwhile, Mrs. Heymann had pressed the door opener, and this time it had worked. Thus, it came about that four grim-faced men accosted me as I was descending the stairs. I pretended to be unaware and tried to pass them to leave the house. At first glance, I knew exactly who they were. However, they blocked my exit, and thus I returned upstairs where, at the entrance door to the apartment, I overheard the following dialogue between the men and Mrs. Heymann:

"Heymann?"

"Yes, that is me."

"German police! ID documents!"

I had entered the apartment in the meantime and was totally witless. I was engulfed by a terrible fear. So, that is the end of it!

The pulse in my temple throbbed, and my knees trembled. The right back pocket of my pants still contained ten sheets of food stamps, and the left pocket contained a blank identification document. A policeman demanded that I surrender my ID. He put it, as well as the German passport of Mrs. Heymann, in his pocket. I walked through the living room to the bay window and scanned the street in search of possible guards or a car. Nothing!

Then, I heard one of the men command, "Get ready. Get dressed." I walked to the door of the apartment, demonstratively closing my coat as if I was about to walk downstairs. I intended to reach the stairs and to run as fast as I could, but already on the first step, I was rudely pushed back by the guy on guard there. I turned around totally helplessly and unable to think clearly. Almost mechanically, I walked to a small room in the rear of the apartment where a Jewish co-hider, a Mr. Geismar, of about forty years, had already been living for several weeks. I threw the blank identification document behind a small cabinet in the room. Almost as though through a fog, I heard Mr. Geismar asking me, "Will you take your overcoat along?" I answered "Yes," but my mind was really already elsewhere. As if by lightning a new plan was beginning to take form. Through the rear door of the little room, I viewed the balcony and remembered that [a colleague] had tried to save himself when he was already arrested by jumping down from a third floor. I went outside, but when I looked down into the gardens of the interior courtyard, I dropped this idea. However, I had hit on another potential escape route! I thought and acted almost simultaneously. I climbed on the balcony's banister and crossed in one step to the other side of the wooden partition between our balcony and that of the neighboring apartment! Now, the men in Mrs. Heymann's apartment could no longer see me. I repeated this action several times until I was already several apartments away.

Several families were actually sunbathing on the flat roofs all around the square block of approximately one hundred apartments. Meanwhile, I went into an unknown apartment, ran to its exit door in order to leave the house and get into the street. Unfortunately, it was tightly locked because the inhabitants were obviously still absent, possibly on vacation. This was lucky, because what could I have told

Erika Heymann, Erwin's host while
in hiding, ca. 1945

When the Germans began to round up
Jews, Erwin Geismar came to live with
us, illegally of course. Fortunately, our
landlord was an avid Dutch nationalist
and anti-Nazi who asked no questions,
although he suspected what was
going on.
DIETER HEYMANN

them when they had suddenly come home while I was still there? I was about to disappear quickly under a sofa to hide from possible pursuers when a better idea occurred to me. I climbed across one more wooden partition into the next apartment. Luckily, nobody was there, and the front door was unlocked.

I swiftly ran down all stairs, into the street, all the while scanning the scene carefully. As I turned a corner, I noticed an abandoned Mercedes with a German license plate. I ran around for another hour, shaking over my entire body. I certainly had the feeling that I had been saved, but what if the Germans had found my secret papers? It concerned a bread bag with IDs, inkpad, and eighty sheets of food stamps. It would be an unthinkable catastrophe for our organization if these were lost. I dreaded moreover the possible fate of [my colleague from the resistance], whom I had agreed to meet at 4 p.m. in the Argonautenstraat. [She] had indeed innocently gone to my former apartment in the afternoon but nobody had opened the door after she had rung the doorbell. We deduced that, luckily, no guards had been posted in the apartment. Therefore, she returned to the apartment the next day to retrieve the important items from it. She was admitted by Mrs. Heymann's children, who had returned on the evening of that fateful previous day. She could, therefore, hand me the hidden IDs.

Judging from information I gleaned later, my relatives, as well as the older gentleman, Mr. Geismar, were transported to Westerbork, while Mrs. Heymann was first locked up in a jail in Amsterdam and then sent to the concentration camp of Vught.

DIETER HEYMANN

Hans escaped to a neighbor's apartment at a moment when the SD did not watch. My mother was arrested and deported to Vught. (She was released in 1944 but was very sick and died in 1950.) The four others were murdered in Auschwitz. Did my sister and I know what was going on? Yes, we did. I was sixteen and she twenty-one at the time. Our landlord allowed us to remain free of rent as long as Mom was in camp. Sonja and I were incredibly lucky that the SD apparently did not know or did not care that we had two Jewish grandparents and that our Jewish father was in Auschwitz-Monowitz at the time. Had they known or cared, they would probably have come back to arrest us too.

We do know the reason why the SD came to arrest us all. Erwin was reluctant to go to a barbershop to have his hair cut because he suspected that all sorts of gossip about him looking so "Jewish," whatever that means, would arise. He hired a young Dutchman to come to our apartment to cut his hair. I do not know how he found this person. This fellow had a very low IQ as we learned later. He had heard that one could get a monetary reward for every Jew turned in (I believe two and a half guilders).

DAVID

Food was hard to get. My father arranged with his barber to sell food coupons for himself and the other people in the house on the

HISTORY BRIEF, PAGE 235
Rewards for Turning in Jews

black market. This man brought the coupons to my father. Then, when it dried up, he turned all those people in, including my father. The woman, my father, the other people hiding there—they all got turned in.

My father was first put in jail, in Amsterdam, and this barber identified him. My father told this to somebody in Westerbork, and this person came back and told my mother after the war. My father was killed in Auschwitz. We tried to do something after the war. My mother tried to see if she could prosecute the barber, but there was not enough evidence for the Dutch government to prosecute. There was just no way. It got thrown out, hearsay, and they wouldn't do anything.

ERWIN
In the end, I hope that my lines will be read by people who will see how we struggled under terrible circumstances, and that the reader will want to take up this struggle that we have fought and experienced from the front lines for the construction of a worthwhile human society.

The identity of the barber who presumably betrayed Erwin and his housemates is unknown; it is not clear if the barber was the source of the coupon stash Hans amassed for his resistance work, although David states that the barber was selling food ration coupons to those hiding at Erika Heymann's apartment.

HISTORY BRIEF, PAGE 236
Punishment Cases

After

The Allied armies liberated the southern part of the Netherlands in the fall of 1944; the First Canadian Army reached the eastern and northern parts of the country in April 1945. The German forces in the western Netherlands capitulated on May 5. The Dutch counted their losses: 200,000 men, women, and children out of a population of nine million. Of these casualties, over half were Jews murdered in the camps. The Dutch Jews counted their survivors: fewer than 50,000 out of a population of 155,000.

These survivors faced difficult choices. Make a clean break with the past and begin a new life in a new place from scratch? Or return to one's city or town to resume an interrupted life without murdered loved ones? And not only that, but struggle for the restitution of position and property—or to catch up with interrupted schooling—in the presence of neighbors and onetime friends who had been passive bystanders during the persecution. And what about the toddlers and children who had been taken in by Christian families, and who emerged from hiding as orphans?

Some 5,000 survivors left for Mandatory Palestine and countries such as the United States and Canada. The rest remained in the Netherlands, where they had to engage in cumbersome restitution procedures for homes, businesses, and financial assets. Many discovered that personal possessions entrusted to neighbors in 1942 had never existed—at least not according to those neighbors. The Dutch government adopted a policy of treating all Netherlanders equally; it was unwilling to acknowledge the special fate of the Jews. The only way to move forward was to try to look to the future—to forget the horrors of the past and ignore the pain of the present.

1945–
1964

April 1, 1945
Nathan is liberated by the Canadians in Halle.

April 12, 1945
Westerbork is liberated by the Canadians.

April 13, 1945
David is liberated by the Canadians in Sneek.

April 28, 1945
The Allies strike a deal with the German authorities in the Netherlands, allowing humanitarian aid to reach millions of Dutch civilians in the western Netherlands.

April 29, 1945
Great Britain begins aerial food drops in the Netherlands.

April 30, 1945
Adolf Hitler commits suicide in Berlin.

May 1, 1945
The United States airdrops rations in the Netherlands.

May 5, 1945
Led by the Canadian army, the Allied forces finally liberate all of the Netherlands, marking the end of the Nazi occupation.

May 7, 1945
Germany surrenders unconditionally to the Allies. Anton Adriaan Mussert, the leader of the NSB (Dutch Nazi Party), is arrested.

May 8, 1945
Victory in Europe Day is celebrated, marking the end of World War II with the Allies' formal acceptance of Nazi Germany's surrender.

Mid-May 1945
Chaim, Fifi, Mirjam, Judith, and Hadassah are reunited.

Late May 1945
David is reunited with his mother, Grete, at their Amsterdam apartment.

Nathan and his family return to their hometown of Apeldoorn.

June 20, 1945
The De Zoetes sleep in a house of their own for the first time since August 1942.

June 28, 1945
A parade in Amsterdam celebrates the return of Queen Wilhelmina.

August 17, 1945
Indonesia declares independence from the Netherlands. A four-year military struggle between the new state and Dutch military forces ends with Dutch recognition of Indonesian independence on December 27, 1949.*

May 7, 1946
Anton Adriaan Mussert is executed.

October 16, 1946
Arthur Seyss-Inquart, Reichskommissar of Hitler's civilian administration in the Netherlands, is executed.

Autumn 1947
Mirjam and Nathan meet in Gouda, the Netherlands, after joining a Zionist group that prepares youth for immigration to Palestine.

November 29, 1947
The United Nations General Assembly recommends the partition of British-ruled Palestine into two states—one Jewish and one Arab. Jews accept the resolution and Arabs reject it.

December 1947
David goes to Marseilles, France, to work.

January 1948
Mirjam and Nathan immigrate illegally to Palestine.

May 14, 1948
The state of Israel is established as a nation.

May 1948
David immigrates to Israel and joins the army.

December 1948
Chaim, Fifi, Judith, and Hadassah immigrate to Israel.

March 24, 1949
Hanns Albin Rauter, formerly the highest-ranking Nazi police officer in the occupied Netherlands, is executed.

July 25, 1950
Mirjam and David marry.

October 1957
Mirjam and David immigrate to the United States.

January 26, 1959
Hadassah and Zigi marry.

March 23, 1964
Judith and Nathan marry.

* **HISTORY BRIEF, PAGE 239**
Indonesia

MIRJAM

Tante Nel told us about the Allies coming closer and closer. She seemed to get information from the illegal radios and newspapers that the underground supplied. We were told about the Americans, British, and Canadians landing in France (D-Day). The Allies finally came into the southern part of Holland, and we thought it would end. After Arnhem, we thought it would be maybe another month. The people in the southern part of Holland were freed almost ten months before our part of Holland was liberated. We heard stories that the English are coming, the Canadians are coming, the Americans are coming—hoping that one day they would.

HISTORY BRIEF, PAGE 238
The Liberation of the Netherlands

DAVID

We were liberated in April '45 by the Canadians. Just before we were liberated, we saw the Germans leave through the canals in all kinds of boats. They didn't have their elaborate fleet of trucks anymore. We knew they were finished. The Canadians who came to Friesland did not come to the town I was in, but they came to Sneek. The man of the house where I was hidden took us there to see the Canadians with a whole bunch of villagers. He was the only one who spoke English. He could speak with them and translate. I was very impressed.

NATHAN

The end of the war came quite suddenly for us in Halle. One morning, April 1, 1945, we woke up to the noise of sporadic firing and heavy traffic. This was a tank group passing through the village. We were liberated in this undramatic way by the First Canadian Army. They had come from Germany and mistakenly believed they were still there. They behaved quite atrociously to the townspeople, throwing people out of their houses, commandeering houses to sleep in, moving furniture from one house to the next for their convenience, and terrorizing the town. After a half day, signs were put up saying in huge letters: "You have left Germany and are now in Holland, a friendly country. Behave courteously to the civilian population."

MIRJAM

Finally, in May 1945, the Canadians came to Haarlem. On the illegal radios, people started hearing, "They are in Rotterdam!" "They are in The Hague now!" Then, "They are in Leiden!" And, "Now they are in Haarlem and Amsterdam!" That night, for the first time, all four of us could go outside without fear. I was thirteen years old. We went to the center of Haarlem to see the Canadian army drive into the city. Friendly soldiers on trucks and tanks. No one screaming at us. No one was pointing a gun at us. Five years of horror were over.

People were singing and dancing in the street. *We* were walking in the street. Up to that day, although I lived two and a half years in Haarlem, I had never seen Haarlem. We walked, and we saw the stores, and the people, and we saw the army trucks, and people throwing flowers, and people throwing candies to us, and we didn't have to go to bed till very late that night. It was amazing that you could walk in the street without being scared. Just amazing.

I actually think I was happier that day of the liberation—when we were walking around Haarlem, all of us, the entire hiding family—than when I saw my parents. It was just, you know, it was like something got off your back. You didn't have to be scared anymore. And I knew I would see my parents, though I could have been totally wrong. Obviously, if you see the statistics, I had little chance of seeing them, but I didn't know that. I was convinced that I would see them in time.

There was no transportation, so it was very hard to find people, and there was no communication, no telephone, no nothing. It was very hard to get people together again after the war. But the liberation day I will never forget. That was one truly happy moment.

DAVID
The Canadians came, and there was a big celebration. We saw real white bread that we hadn't seen in years. It was like that light Wonder Bread—at that time it was like cake to us. We also got cigarettes from the Canadians.

NATHAN
I remember that we got our first really white bread, which was supplied by the US Army. The same as the bread that was air dropped to the western part of Holland, which was still occupied by the Germans, and where there was real hunger. I remember that, to me, it looked quite nice but was rather tasteless, and that I liked the local bread better.

MIRJAM
American planes threw boxes of food down, including white bread and margarine. After eating tulip bulbs and scraps and being hungry, it was so delicious. We hadn't tasted something that good in a very long time! It was like one big party. Everyone was singing and dancing and waving the Dutch flag. Everyone was just free.

NATHAN
Father told us not to tell anybody that we were Jewish yet, because he was afraid that the front might shift again and leave us with Germans occupying the town once more. He was not so much afraid of the Germans, who, he was sure, had other problems on their minds, but of the Dutch, whom he did not trust, knowing that most were very antisemitic. But after a few days, it became clear that the Germans would not return, and we became Jews again.

One of the Canadian tanks had something wrong with it and remained in the village. I was constantly in and around that tank, which was standing under a big oak tree not far from the farm where we stayed. The tank crew sort of adopted me and showed me around inside the tank, explained its operation, and told tales of their exploits.

My parents invited the crew to our house. They brought chocolate and other sweets and all kinds of exotic (for us) conserves, like pineapple and olives. The soldiers, who were mostly Jewish, told us about

HISTORY BRIEF, PAGE 238
**Operation Manna and
Operation Chowhound**

the concentration camps. Some were clear about the revenge they wanted. One said that he had had twelve relatives in Germany and that for every relative he wanted to kill at least ten Germans; he hoped that the war would go on for some time, since he had only managed to kill about thirty. He said it did not matter if they were civilians or soldiers, as long as they were Germans. This was more or less the attitude of them all. They told about another tank crew who captured a group of about twelve German soldiers, laid them out in a row, and drove the tank over them—"since it was a waste of ammunition to shoot them," they said.

DAVID

In the IJlst Town Hall, they made a list of people who were hidden in the area, and I put my name on that list. The list was given to the Red Cross. There were also lists of people who survived, but I didn't find anyone that I knew. Three weeks later my mother, Grete, saw my name on the list from the Red Cross in Amsterdam.

My mother found an inland boat in Amsterdam that was going to IJlst, where a very busy canal went through the town. She sent a letter with the skipper, the skipper gave the letter to the bridge attendant in IJlst, and he got the letter to me. Everybody knows everybody in those little towns. So, I knew my mother was alive— that was very joyful to me. About my father she wrote, "We don't know at this point."

My mother told me she was back in our old house because the woman who had taken over my father's factory (a German woman who had a Jewish boyfriend) also had taken over our house, so everything was there. She gave it back. My mother wrote that she would like me, as soon as I could, to come back home.

You had to have permission to travel in those days. The people I was with went with me to the town hall to arrange for permission. It took about two weeks, and then I got a travel permit to go to Amsterdam. I went back alone on a train, a boat, and a train again. All I had was a pair of wooden shoes and a suitcase. When I came to the railroad station in Amsterdam, I had to walk home. I really did not know at that time what hunger was—in Amsterdam they did.

The people where I was hidden told me that when I arrived it might be a big shock for my mother. They told me not to ring the bell directly at my mother's. They said to go to the neighbors and ask them to notify my mother that I was there.

I rang the neighbors' doorbell. Downstairs was a dentist who lived there before we went into hiding. The maid answered the door, but she didn't know me. I asked if I could see the neighbors; the wife came out and right away recognized me. She called my mother, and my mother came down. She was very happy. I was very happy to be back in our old place. That was the reunion.

At that time my mother knew my father had been transported to Auschwitz, but she didn't know exactly if there was still a chance of any more survivors. He wasn't on any of the lists. She still had some hopes.

DIETER HEYMANN

After the German capitulation in the Netherlands, it became known that there would be a special parade, mostly military, in Amsterdam, to be reviewed by Queen Wilhelmina. When my mother, Erika, and some of her friends from the concentration camp at Vught learned that the non-military resistance would hardly be represented, they became furious and quickly organized a float to participate in the parade. No one could stop them. When they got to the reviewing balcony, the queen was on the toilet, which infuriated them even more. They were tigresses.

NATHAN

After the Germans surrendered and the war was over, we could go back to Apeldoorn. Since Father was then the only local doctor in Halle, he had to transfer the practice to a physician in Zelhem, a small neighboring village. This took some time. We heard afterward that the local doctor, who had been arrested by the Germans because he had helped Jews, survived the war and safely returned to his family.

We returned to Apeldoorn somewhere at the end of May. Since the house where we had lived, Regentesselaan 18, was now in use, we got the use of an old house in the same street, Regentesselaan 3, which was previously the house of Dr. Hermanides, who was a sympathizer with the Germans and a member of the NSB (Dutch Nazi Party). He had been arrested by the Dutch, and his family evicted from the house.

Until then, we had not heard what happened to the Jews who were sent to Westerbork and on to "work camps" in Eastern Europe. But now stories came back to us about what these camps really were. About the gas chambers, the brutality of the Germans and their Polish and Ukrainian helpers.

After my parents saw and heard what had happened to the Jews, they were convinced that the parents of Gertrude, our foster sister, had been murdered by the Germans—as were most German Jews. They first tried to get some information about the parents (as well as about our family, of course), but when after a few months there were no results, they started the adoption process for Gertrude and told her that from now on she should call them Mother and Father, just as my siblings and I did.

A short while later, we had a visit from someone from the Red Cross, who told my parents that Gertrude's parents were alive and in Sweden. This was a big surprise, and although we all thought of Gertrude as part of our family, we were all happy for her.

Gertrude's parents had been exchanged with Sweden in 1943 or 1944. In exchange for what, I don't know. For prisoners of war? Or Swedish steel? But they were among the lucky few who were exchanged.

The story of that family is really miraculous. The parents survived. Gertrude survived together with us. Gertrude had a brother, Alfred, and a sister, Lilly, who were also sent to Holland by their parents in 1938 and stayed in a Jewish refugee house in Deventer. Sometime during 1942, Alfred and Lilly were sent to Amsterdam to

Nathan had ten aunts and uncles and eight cousins who were murdered in the concentration camps.

be sent on to Westerbork camp. From the train, they went on foot to the Schouwburg, where all Jews were processed before being sent on to Westerbork. Alfred, at one street corner, went to the right instead of going straight on with all the other children and knocked on the door of a house, saying that he was a Jew looking for a hiding place. The chances of him knocking on the door of someone willing to risk his life hiding a Jew were infinitesimally small. But he was lucky and survived the war hiding somewhere in Limburg, in the southern-most part of Holland. Lilly did not survive; she was murdered with all the other refugee children. Of a German family of five, four survived the war and were reunited.

MIRJAM

Now life would be good and normal again. Well, that is what we thought, but not really. There were many more sad days, weeks, and months ahead of us. And for many people, life never really returned to normal.

HADASSAH

Tante Riek (the underground friend of our family) picked Judith up in Rijnsburg and brought her to Wassenaar—to me.

MIRJAM

My mother's brother Ben came to pick me up to bring me to my sisters, who were in Wassenaar. Because of his connections in the underground, he found my sisters and me. Since he was a doctor, he got to have a car, because there were lots of sick people, and he had to get around. He got gasoline from the Canadian army.

I wasn't sorry to leave the home where I had been living. I was always waiting for that moment.

I first saw my sisters at the Van Gelders, the family with whom I hid for the first half year. They were friends of our family. My sisters were already there when I came in, and we looked very strange to each other. I don't think we kissed; we just looked at each other and smiled. I was so happy to see them.

Hadassah was totally bald. She had lice, and they couldn't get rid of them, so they shaved off her hair. My sisters had less hunger than me. Judith had lived with a butcher. They didn't look that bad physically. I was pretty skinny. I had not matured physically at all yet because there was no food.

HADASSAH

Mirjam and Judith did not recognize me (neither did Mammie) because I was well fed, having had the benefit of the good food that my hiding family got from the Germans. And, instead of my light brown hair, I was now bald. So they said, "Who are you? You are not our sister!" I, in tears, said, "But I am! Look at my ring and yours. They are the same!" We all looked and compared, and they were exactly the same—a narrow golden band with a light blue aquamarine stone. Well, that and some more watching and talking convinced them.

Fifi and Chaim had given three identical rings to Mirjam, Judith, and Hadassah before they separated to go into hiding.

After

JUDITH

Uncle Ben had arranged it so that the three of us sisters arrived at the reverend's house, where my parents were hidden, at the same time. The reverend, who had been picked up by the police for illegal actions at the end of the war, was back from prison at that time.

MIRJAM

We all cried when we saw each other. Only my parents couldn't stop crying. I remember how bad I felt about them crying. You hate to see your parents emotional. It's terrible to see them crying and hugging and crying. You get very uncomfortable. I do. You know, you don't see your kids for almost three years, and they're so different. We were now teenagers instead of children. And we probably didn't look too good.

JUDITH

Mammie was a brunette when we left but now had completely white hair, which was a little shock for us to see. She also had lost a lot of weight. Uncle Ben (the funny one of her brothers) tried to cheer us up. He said to the reverend, "I see you still have all the benches in your church; I am amazed you did not use them for heating." Or, to make us laugh some more, he started to read backward all the biblical verses that were hanging on the walls. It was an awkward situation.

MIRJAM

My father had lost most of his teeth because he couldn't go to the dentist, and my mother was addicted to sleeping pills, as she was forced to stay in bed for two years so as not to be heard by the church parishioners below the attic where she and my father were hiding. My mother was a vivacious person. She liked to talk, and my father didn't talk, so she had nobody to talk to. He could read, and he was fine. But she just couldn't. She just couldn't. She was addicted to sleeping pills, and it took her more than ten years to get over it.

HADASSAH

We stayed for a while with a woman friend of Mammie's sister Annie. How that woman did it was amazing. Also staying there were Mammie's sister and her husband. It was quite a small apartment, but somehow everybody managed not to get in each other's way. All that was very sad for Tante Annie and Oom Jacques, because they had lost their four sons and saw our "complete" family every day right before their eyes.

Harry, Bob, Sally, and Bernhard Maarssen, Fifi's nephews (all four murdered, Auschwitz, August–September 1942, 22, 21, 19, and 18 years old, respectively).

FIFI

June 20, 1945: The first time that the five of us slept in a house of our own again (albeit temporarily).

When you see the havoc created in both our families and then, looking beyond that, see all the suffering in so many other families, you can hardly comprehend that our family emerged from that hell in one piece.

June 20, 1945: The first time that the five of us slept in a house of our own again (albeit temporarily). When you see the havoc created in both our families and then, looking beyond that, see all the suffering in so many other families, you can hardly comprehend that our family emerged from that hell in one piece.

20 Juni 1945. Hebben we weer van het eerst met ons vijven in een eigen huis (al is het dat huis misschien tijdelijk) geslapen.

Als je de ravage in ons beider families ziet en dan verder kijkende alle ellende in zoveel gezinnen kun je toen haast niet bevatten dat wij niet ongezien zo heel uit de hel tevoorschijn zijn gekomen.

7. augustus 1959.
Hier liggen dus ruim 14 jaar tussen. Had ik toen ik pas goed de grootte van de ravage ging onderkennen, niet meer de moed om verder te schrijven?
Wat was het wat mij die 20ste Juni 1945 die paar regels liet schrijven om even zo plotseling op te houden?
Ik houd er van om mijn gedachten op te schrijven maar hier miste ik toch blijkbaar de moed om verder te gaan.
moeder weg, Hartha weg. Annie en Jacques zonder kinderen. Jetje en 't hele gezin weg. Sam op een hongertransport aan de weg blijven liggen. Hans in Dagou gestorven. Behalve tante Keetje alle zusters en broers van moeke weg. Moeke zelf te vroeg in Amsterdam overleden.
John Bennie en vrouw weg. Sam en hele gezin weg. Man van Rietje gefusilleerd. Rietje onthoofd achtergebleven later zelfmoord.
Geen een van de zusters van Chaim's ouders me

August 1, 1959: So, fourteen years have gone by. Did I lack the courage to continue writing once I truly began to acknowledge the enormity of the havoc?

What was it that made me write those few lines on that twentieth day of June 1945 and then just as abruptly made me stop?
FIFI

2.

...ver. Onze vrienden gedecimeerd.
...at is wat je direct waarneemt. En de geeste-
...ijke ellende die de oorlog achterliet? Hoe is 't daarmee
Van 20 Juni 45 tot 1 December 48 woonde we
in ons laatste huis in Holland
December '48 gingen we met de "Mendoza" een
nieuw K.N.S.M. schip naar ~~Holla~~ Israël
waar we 27-12-48 de 2e dag Chanukah
...een verduisterd schip (hoewel de oorlog
was afgelopen) aankwamen.
...emand en kolo haalden om af.
...irjam die eind Januari '48 met haar
...ouda groep illegaal naar Israël was ge-
...aan waren natuurlijk ook. Alle bij waren
...e blij weer bij elkaar te zijn Mirjam
...oonde in kijat Bialik in Workad + Aha-
...a, waar ze evenals in Gouda een hele
...oedejeugd had. Men hield veel van haar
...men waardeerde haar ijver en plichts-
...vel. In de Chewrah was ze een goed
...d.
...es ik nu achter af bedenk waar we de
...wed van daan haalden. Of ik ben ge-
...aald voor deze stap, ik weet het niet
...e hadden alleen maar een schriftelijk
...ericht van Bernard, waarin stond dad
...voor een apotheker zeker plaats kou hij
...aar dad stond volkomen op losse gron-
...en koals later zou blijken.
...was, een goede gesalarieerde baan
in Holland. Een prettige werkring voor
Chaim

Sam Polak, Fifi's brother; Sam was in the resistance and was arrested and deported to an unknown location (he is thought to have died in Eastern Europe in a death march).

Riekje Polak-van Zuilekom, Fifi's cousin (committed suicide, February 22, 1947, 30 years old); Steef van Zuilekom, Riekje's husband (murdered, Sachsenhausen, February 7, 1945, 39 years old).

FIFI

August 1, 1959: So, fourteen years have gone by. Did I lack the courage to continue writing once I truly began to acknowledge the enormity of the havoc?

What was it that made me write those few lines on that twentieth day of June 1945 and then just as abruptly made me stop?

I like writing down my thoughts, but apparently, in this case, I lacked the courage to continue.

Mother gone, Martha gone. Annie and Jacques without children, Jetje and the whole family gone, Sam left behind, lying in the road during a hunger march, Hans died in Dachau. Except for Aunt Lea, all Moeke's sisters and brothers gone. Moeke herself died in Amsterdam all too soon. Uncle Bennie and wife gone, Sam and the entire family gone. Riekje's husband shot, Riekje left behind shattered—suicide followed.

Not one of the sisters of Chaim's parents remains, our friends decimated. That is what you notice right away. And the emotional anguish that the war left behind. What about that?

MIRJAM

We really didn't know how bad things were until after the war. Then came the really sad times. Many people were waiting for their family, their husbands, their wives, their children to come back, and they didn't come back. We were one of the few families that stayed intact. The four sons of my mother's oldest sister, Annie (the one we always went to for Passover), were betrayed by a friend who was supposed to help them escape. They died in the camps. So did my mother's other sister (Jet), her husband, and two children. Her oldest child, Mirjam, was my best friend—I think a lot about her, about her sister, and about my four other cousins. What would have happened to them if they had lived, and how come I'm still alive and they're not? It affects me. Two other brothers of my mother were killed in the camps. The same with my father's mother (my grandmother Naatje) and sister, Martha. I also lost many great aunts and uncles and second cousins. And the list kept on growing. It took months and months for the whole story to get out.

Every time they heard about someone who didn't come back, my parents were crying, and they were always whispering. We weren't told right away. We were still protected. They didn't want to make us too upset, but we knew. Everything was sad. And you felt guilty because you didn't get killed.

My parents took in people who had nowhere to go. It was a strange kind of time.

JUDITH

In hindsight, I am sorry that I did not ask my parents more questions about the things that happened to our family, and especially to them. Maybe we did not ask because one was not supposed to ask too many painful questions. And they never talked about it on their own initiative. Pappie was a very quiet person who only offered his opinion when asked for it, and after the war Mammie was so depressed and down

Fifi's closest relatives who were murdered by the Germans

Left column, from top:

Nephews Bernard, Sally, Bob, and Harry Maarssen, ca. 1940

Brother Sam Polak, pictured with his wife, Fiejte, ca. mid-1930s

Nieces Hetty and Mirjam de Lange, ca. 1938

Right column, from top:

Brother Hans Polak, 1940

Sister Jet Polak-de Lange, ca. 1913

she made herself forget by taking sleeping pills. We did not ask our aunt Annie, Mammie's sister. She was too hurt and withdrawn by the loss of her four sons; so was her husband, of whom we were always a bit afraid. And the only one who survived (besides us), Uncle Ben, was not quite the person to ask personal questions of unless one was on intimate terms with him.

These are the names of close family who were murdered by the Germans. On Pappie's side: Naatje, his mother; and Martha, his sister. On Mammie's side: her older brother, Sam; her youngest brother, Hans (Chaja's father); Harry, Bob, Sally, and Bernhard—the four sons of her eldest sister and her husband, Annie and Jacques— who were betrayed by a (so-called) good friend who had promised to get them to the Swiss border (for money) and then (again for money) gave them over to the Germans; her middle sister, Jet, with her husband, Karel, and two daughters, Mirjam and Hetty. They were ordered to come to the train station, and as good law-abiding citizens, they did as they were told to do and never were heard from again.

MIRJAM

The parents of Dolf, Ans, and Hans (the other children hiding with me) were all killed in a concentration camp. The children found this out only months later. The little boy, Hans, went to an aunt. I was the only lucky person.

ANS AND DOLF VROMEN

After the war, Mirjam went back to her parents. Our parents, and the parents of Hans, did not come back. Hans went to an uncle and aunt, and we stayed with Tante Nel, who became "Mam."

HANS (ZWI) GOLDBERG

At the beginning of the war, there was a connection with my parents (I don't know if they knew where I was). Then they were betrayed by some Dutch woman, sent to Auschwitz, and were murdered there.

MIRJAM

Hans Goldberg was very young when he went into hiding, and he thought of Sonja as his mother. And she wanted to keep him after his parents were killed by the Germans. But an uncle and aunt got him. And that's when the Holocaust started for him. The war wasn't over when the war was over!

SONJA VAN VLIET

We are very fortunate that we got through the war. Afterward, everyone was so happy that it was over, we all believed life would get better. But if you look at the world now, you wonder whether man ever learns from misery.

FIFI

As a Jew, to come back to everyday life, staying alive, being back in the world—is it surprising if you lost your rhythm a little?

MIRJAM

Hitler and his collaborators, the Nazis all over the world—in Holland, in France, Poland, Ukraine, and many other countries—killed six million Jews. Babies, old people, young people, everyone! Not because they were bad but because they were Jewish. Before the war, there were 140,000 ("full") Jews in the Netherlands. By the end of the war, only one-quarter of them were left!

DAVID

Slowly it became clear that my father didn't survive. He wasn't on any lists. He was arrested a few weeks after I left him.

In 1948, my mother received an inheritance certificate that said my father died in Auschwitz on November 19, 1943. It said we— Margarete Karoline Geismar-Heinsheimer and Dietrich David Geismar—were his heirs. A strange thing was that it also said my mother and I were not "enemy subjects" and my father's property was not "enemy property."

Erwin Geismar, David's father (murdered, Auschwitz, November 19, 1943, 41 years old).

NATHAN

I met my old friends, but they and I were changed, and I could not reconnect with them. Henk, who was formerly my best friend, had a girlfriend, the daughter of the director of the De Bijenkorf, a big store.

Theo van Dalen went back to Gendt after the war. When the former mayor, Becude, came back, nothing was done to him by the Dutch authorities. Theo got mad, went to him, and gave him a thrashing. The mayor sued Theo for assault. He was suspended from the police and had to go to court. Father was there as a witness, but evidence of the mayor's misdeeds was not admissible, being unrelated to the "crime" Theo had committed. That Theo had saved at least one Jewish family and helped save about ten Allied airmen was thought to be irrelevant—which it probably was, even though the ex-mayor was part of the system that killed most of our family. When the judge started to berate Theo about his behavior, Theo asked him what he had done during the war. This, of course, was not a good thing to ask, since the judge probably had not done anything, the same as most Dutchmen. The judge fined Theo one guilder. This was really saying that he was not guilty, but since Theo was a policeman, and he now had a file, this meant that he could not be promoted in the future. Theo resigned from the police in disgust, and after a few months immigrated to Australia. Father helped him financially as much as Theo would let him, which was not much. In the 1950s, a tree was planted for Theo in the Avenue of the Righteous Gentiles at Yad Vashem in Jerusalem.

After the war, we found that the Germans had murdered most of our family: Uncle Moos, Aunt Fietje, and cousins Gerda and Salomon Cohen; Aunt Mietje, Uncle Jonas, and cousins Bram and Henny Wijnberg; Aunt Betje and Uncle Julius de Haas (they went into hiding and were betrayed by a Dutch person for money; their four children went separately and survived); Aunt Elly and Uncle Hans Heijmann; on my mother's side, Aunt Clara and Uncle David, and cousins Adolph, Nathan, Mimi, and Jack Rosenbaum.

HISTORY BRIEF, PAGE 239
Why Were So Many Dutch Jews Murdered?

Nathan with his parents and sisters,
left to right: Henny, Isaak, Nathan,
Rivka, and Annemieke, 1945

*After the war, we found that the
Germans had murdered most
of our family.*
NATHAN

Some of Nathan's family members who were murdered, 1934

Back row, from left: Aunt Fietje and Uncle Moos Cohen (murdered with their children, Salomon and Gerda); Uncle Hans Heijmann (murdered); Aunt Mietje and Uncle Jonas Wijnberg (murdered with their children, Bram and Henny); Aunt Anna and Uncle Isaac Levij (survived); and parents Rivak and Isaak Cohen (survived)

Front row, from left: Aunt Betje de Haas (murdered with her husband, Julius); grandparents Salomon and Hendrika Cohen (died before the Holocaust); and Aunt Elly Heijmann (murdered)

Max Heinsheimer, David's maternal grandfather (died returning from Bergen-Belsen, January 7, 1945, 72 years old). Luzie, Eugen, and Felix Peter Eschenheimer, David's aunt, uncle, and cousin (all murdered, Auschwitz, March 9, 1943, the parents were both 39 years old, and their son was 6).

DAVID

My grandfather must have spent close to a year in Westerbork, and then he went to Bergen-Belsen. He died of dysentery on the train back to Holland from Bergen-Belsen. He went through the whole thing. My aunt, uncle, and cousin (the Eschenheimers) were all murdered in Auschwitz.

MIRJAM

I thought we would all be back together again and everything would be like it was before the war. My parents "overlived" their ordeal and my sisters "overlived" theirs. I was one of the lucky ones who could go home. Even though we had no home.

JUDITH

The three of us sisters never talked about our war experiences. It was over, and it was time to start a new life, so why bother each other with it?

MIRJAM

You were not supposed to talk about it. You were supposed to forget about it as quickly as possible and live a normal life because there was no sense in rehashing the past. There was no way you could possibly think about it and build a normal life, so you had to just forget.

JUDITH

After the war, Pappie said that he regretted not having put his family first and his job second.

HADASSAH

After the war, I was afraid to go outside. When Tante Petronella saw that I had lice, in the spring of 1945, she shaved my head. I remained bald till the end of the war and for a short time after. I was twelve years old, just a child (not old enough to collaborate with the Germans), but after the war, some women had their heads shaved as a sign of and punishment for fraternizing and collaborating with the Germans. I did not dare show myself.

MIRJAM

And now what? Everything had been stolen from us. My father had hidden some small items and photographs, and we got those back. There were still major food shortages. We stayed here and there with friends (family members either had died, been murdered, or were in the same situation we were).

Slowly, the situation got better. We got permission from the Dutch government to move into a house that was owned by an NSB Nazi who had either fled with the Germans or was put in prison. It was on Kralingse Kerklaan. We got the house with furniture and everything in it under the stipulation that we could use it as long as we wanted but had to return it to the city of Rotterdam when we moved out. We lived there for two years. I thought the owners would come back and kill us. I was scared to death. I would never go to the attic or the basement. They hated us, and we were living in their house.

After

Between 1946 and 1968, David's mother, Grete, received a series of letters from the Red Cross in response to her search for her sister, Luzie; Luzie's husband, Eugen; and their son, Felix Peter. One letter states, "reason for detention: 'Jew.'"

April 10, 1946: In connection with your letter of December 19, 1945, I have to inform you that, according to the records, [Luzie, Eugen, and Felix Eschenheimer] were deported in the direction of Sobibor (Poland) or Auschwitz on 8.31.43. It does not establish that this was their last residence. After all, in many cases, the deportees were transported again to unknown destinations. Experience tells us that the chance of deportees returning should generally be excluded. THE NETHERLANDS RED CROSS

INFORMATIEBUREAU VAN

HET NEDERLANDSCHE ROODE KRUIS

OPSPORING JOODSCHE PERSONEN
TELEFOON 43066 - HEERENGRACHT 479 - AMSTERDAM C.

Nr.   TYPE: vR. 1154

Nr.

BIJLAGEN:

BETREFT:

'S-GRAVENHAGE

BIJ BEANTWOORDING DAGTEEKENING EN NUMMER
VAN DIT SCHRIJVEN AAN TE HALEN

AMSTERDAM, 10 April   1946

Mevrouw Gr. Geismar Heinsheimer
Pieter de Hoochstraat 76 II
A m s t e r d a m.:.Z.

Mevrouw,

In verband met Uw schrijven van 19 December 1945 moet ik U mededelen, dat blijkens de registers van het aan hoofde genoemde Bureau onderstaande personen met bestemming, althans in de richting van Sobibor (Polen) of Auschwitz op 31.8.43 werden gedeporteerd.

Lizie Eschenheimer, geb. 14.903
Eugen Eschenheimer   geb. 4.12.03
Felix Eschenheimer   geb. 5.4.36

Hieruit komt niet bij voorbaat vast te staan, dat gezochten aldaar hun laatste verblijfplaats hebben gevonden. Immers, in vele gevallen werden de gedeporteerden naar voorshands onbekende bestemming verder gevoerd. De ervaring leert ons echterm dat de kans op terugkeer van gedeporteerden, op een uitzondering na, vergeleken bij het geheel, uitgesloten dient te worden geacht.

Hierbij zend ik U een lijstje met namen van personen, die van bovengenoemde transporten terugkeerden. Wellicht kunt U zich met hen in verbinding stellen, ten einde nog nadere inlichtingen te verkrijgen,

Vertrouwende U hiermede van dienst te zijn geweest, verblijf ik

hoogachtend,
HET NEDERLANDSCHE ROODE KRUIS
de chef der afdeling

S. Broekman

K 281

Remembered

Chaim de Zoete's family

Naatje de Zoete	mother	age 70	07.16.1943	Sobibor
Martha de Zoete-Zwarenstein	sister	age 38	07.16.1943	Sobibor
Rosalie de Zoete	aunt	age 69	10.29.1942	Auschwitz
Johanna de Zoete-van Goor	aunt	age 67	04.16.1943	Sobibor
David van Goor	uncle	age 63	04.16.1943	Sobibor
Regina van Goor	cousin	age 37	09.30.1942	Auschwitz
Juliette de Zoete	aunt	age 63	11.19.1942	Auschwitz
Flora de Zoete-van Klaveren	aunt	age 56	11.05.1942	Auschwitz
Benjamin van Klaveren	uncle	age 52	11.05.1942	Auschwitz
Betty van Klaveren	cousin	age 17	06.04.1943	Sobibor
Fransie de Zoete-Anolt	aunt	age 71	05.21.1943	Sobibor
Nel de Zoete-van der Lijn	aunt	age 69	07.09.1943	Sobibor
Abraham van der Lijn	uncle	age 67	07.09.1943	Sobibor
Gonda van der Lijn	cousin	age 38	07.16.1943	Sobibor
Helen de Zoete-Carsch	aunt	age 70	12.03.1942	Auschwitz

Fifi Polak's family

Harry Maarssen	nephew	age 22	09.04.1942	Auschwitz
Bob Maarssen	nephew	age 21	08.25.1942	Auschwitz
Sally Maarssen	nephew	age 19	09.09.1942	Auschwitz
Bernhard Maarssen	nephew	age 18	09.19.1942	Auschwitz
Jet Polak-de Lange	sister	age 49	06.11.1943	Sobibor
Karel de Lange	brother-in-law	age 42	07.23.1943	Sobibor
Mirjam de Lange	niece	age 13	06.14.1943	Sobibor
Hetty de Lange	niece	age 08	06.11.1943	Sobibor
Sam Polak	brother	age 45	03.15.1945	Poland
Hans Polak	brother	age 28	02.20.1945	Dachau
Boelea van der Heim-Polak	aunt	age 70	04.09.1943	Sobibor
Samson Levy with wife & five children	cousin	age 70	04.09.1943	Sobibor
Steef van Zuilekom	cousin's husband	age 39	02.07.1945	Sachsenhausen
Riekje Polak-van Zuilekom	cousin	age 30	02.22.1947	Suicide

Nathan Cohen's family

Mietje Cohen-Wijnberg	aunt	age 52	02.12.1943	Auschwitz
Jonas Wijnberg	uncle	age 58	08.10.1942	Auschwitz
Bram Wijnberg	cousin	age 19	09.30.1942	Auschwitz
Henny Wijnberg	cousin	age 17	02.12.1943	Auschwitz
Elly Cohen-Heijmann	aunt	age 42	03.13.1943	Sobibor
Hans Heijmann	uncle	age 54	03.13.1943	Sobibor
Betje Cohen-de Haas	aunt	age 49	12.07.1942	Auschwitz
Julius de Haas	uncle	age 59	12.07.1942	Auschwitz
Moos Cohen	uncle	age 54	08.31.1942	Auschwitz
Fietje Meijer-Cohen	aunt	age 48	08.31.1942	Auschwitz
Salomon Cohen	cousin	age 23	06.11.1943	Sobibor
Gerda Cohen	cousin	age 17	08.31.1942	Auschwitz
David Rosenbaum	uncle	age 44	06.11.1943	Sobibor
Clara Cohen-Rosenbaum	aunt	age 40	06.11.1943	Sobibor
Adolph Rosenbaum	cousin	age 18	03.31.1944	Auschwitz
Nathan Rosenbaum	cousin	age 16	07.09.1943	Sobibor
Mimi Rosenbaum	cousin	age 13	06.11.1943	Sobibor
Jack Rosenbaum	cousin	age 07	06.11.1943	Sobibor

David Geismar's family

Erwin Geismar	father	age 41	11.19.1943	Auschwitz
Max Heinsheimer	grandfather	age 72	01.07.1945	Bergen-Belsen
Luzie Heinsheimer-Eschenheimer	aunt	age 39	03.09.1943	Auschwitz
Eugen Eschenheimer	uncle	age 39	03.09.1943	Auschwitz
Felix Peter Eschenheimer	cousin	age 06	03.09.1943	Auschwitz

Zigi Mandel's family

Zygmunt Rappaport	father	age unknown	1942	Bukhara
Basia (Barbara) Rappaport	mother	age unknown	1942	Bukhara
Lilka Mandel	sister	age 20	1940	Warsaw

The De Zoete sisters with friends, from left: Mirjam, Ruth, Fientje, Judith, Sim, Hadassah, and Nita, 1946

The three of us sisters never talked about our war experiences. It was over, and it was time to start a new life, so why bother each other with it?
JUDITH

HADASSAH

We got the house of that Nazi sympathizer, and there was a cellar with lots of stuff, wine, and lots of books and journals. I read all the Jules Verne books and all the books for teenage girls. I loved it!

MIRJAM

My parents also took in a guy who lost his parents and a girl who lost her parents. She stayed with us for a year or two. Everyone tried to help people coming back from the camps and kids coming back from hiding who didn't have parents.

JUDITH

Pappie very soon got his old job back and started earning money again. The man who had replaced him was a pharmacist from India and was chosen for the job because he only needed it temporarily. So, if Pappie made it through the war, he could get his old job back. His replacement went back to India after the war.

HADASSAH

After the war, Mammie spent a lot of time being drowsy from sleeping pills or just lying in bed.

MIRJAM

I was impatient with my mother. I was embarrassed by her because she was often only half there. She would sometimes fall because she was on sleeping pills. My father hid them. He forbade all the pharmacies in Rotterdam from selling her pills. Later on, in Jerusalem, the same thing. And she always somehow managed to get them. I felt sorry for my father. I loved my parents very much, but I found it depressing being home.

My parents were so different, yet they had a lot in common. They loved classical music, fine arts, contemporary furniture, traveling. They loved their kids and sent us to private schools. They were not wealthy, but that would not prevent them from giving us the best education there was. I think that their marriage was better before the war than after. Probably because my mother was so addicted to sleeping pills. It made life difficult for both of them. Also, the loss of her family—brothers, a sister. The sadness and concern for Mammie's oldest sister, who lost all four of her children, made for a life full of sorrow.

JUDITH

We went back to Montessori school and did not have to pay at the beginning because they took money according to one's income. We actually lost three years—1943, '44, and '45—but were set back only one year for a few reasons: first, we got private lessons during part of our hiding period; second, the Dutch non-Jewish children had also fallen behind because schools were closing due to shortage of fuel for heating the classrooms; third, a lot of absenteeism by students and teachers due to illnesses, especially during the hunger period; fourth, men (teachers and fathers) taken away to German work camps. So, we really fit in, the three of us, quite comfortably in grades only one year behind. And besides, in the Montessori system, grades are not all that important, and it is easy (with the help of teachers) to catch up if you want to.

MIRJAM

We were sent to Zionist organizations, and we became very involved as teenagers. For me, it was an escape to get away from home. My parents sent us to a Zionist organization because at that point they were more convinced than ever that Israel would be the answer for the Jewish people. One country for the Jewish people, standing behind us: that made sense to me after the war. *Shluchim* from Israel came to talk to us and convinced us that they really needed us in Israel right then. They needed people to work on farms, and they didn't need people who thought for themselves. They convinced me, or more or less brainwashed me. I was the only one (of my sisters) who quit school. Saying "I want to help Israel" was a good excuse for me; it was hard to sit down and learn after not going to school for so many years.

Shluchim are emissaries sent around the world to connect Jews to their heritage.

I quit school in tenth grade, two years after the end of the war, and went to a place in Holland that prepared us for life in Israel. We worked half days and studied half days. We had to learn a whole new language. We studied Hebrew, the history of Israel, and the history of the Old Testament.

Once I was in *hachshara*, I was happy to go home for a weekend, but I wanted to get away from my parents. They were still living the war and mourning all the brothers and sisters they had lost.

Hachshara is a Zionist movement that prepares youth for immigration to Israel.

NATHAN

In the autumn of 1945, I went back to school but did not study at all. I had no interest in what went on in the class, and my report cards were marked accordingly. I think I got bad grades in all subjects except English, which I knew better than the other children since I had learned it while hiding during the war. I know that my parents were quite exasperated by my behavior. They told me that if I did not want to study, then maybe I should start learning a useful profession, like watchmaking or some such, but I was not interested in anything. I went to Zionist summer camps, and there I heard about going to *hachshara*, or preparation for life in Israel. I really do not remember much of what went on around me, but somehow I decided that was what I wanted to do. One of the main reasons was that I would not have to study; in Palestine agricultural workers were what was needed. I remembered how I enjoyed working on the farm in Halle during the last few months of the war, and that may have influenced me to ask my parents if I could go to Gouda, where they prepared you for life in Palestine. My parents agreed to let me go.

That autumn, I went to Gouda. It was a big change from anything I had experienced before then. We were about sixteen to twenty boys and girls, mostly orphans. There was a Madrich (a leader-teacher), a housemother, and a cook. Half the day was study time: modern Jewish history, mostly about the building up of the Jewish community in Palestine; Hebrew lessons (learning the Hebrew alphabet, grammar,

Nathan and Mirjam belonged to the same youth group in Gouda; David was part of another group, also in Gouda.

some words); and some geography of Palestine. The second part of the day was work in the vegetable garden behind the house where we lived. We grew vegetables that were sold on the *veiling* (vegetable auction). This was hard work, at least for me: weeding, pulling carrots, and covering asparagus so that the shoots would not turn green—all bend-work. The farm was run by a Dutch farmer and his helper. The vegetables were put on a boat that was poled through waterways to the auction house very early in the morning. In the evening, we did some communal things, like learning Hebrew songs, playing games, or sometimes, not very often, going to a free concert in a church in Gouda. This was the first time that I heard classical music. I loved it.

We were a mixed group, all about the same age but from very different backgrounds. A few of us had big emotional problems as a result of the war. Some had been in the camps during the war, and the rest had gone into hiding. Most had lost one or both parents. All of us had lost family members. As far as I remember, the war was never mentioned in our conversations.

MIRJAM

Nathan and I met on a vegetable farm in Gouda, Holland, in 1947. We were preparing ourselves to become useful citizens for the state of Israel. I met David in Holland the same year; I was sixteen. We were dancing the horah in the street because the United Nations had voted to make Israel a state. I twisted my ankle badly and couldn't walk. David and a friend brought me to my uncle Ben, a doctor, who didn't live far from where we were. They carried me up to my uncle's apartment, and that's how we met.

NATHAN

In the autumn of 1947, the United Nations voted on the partition of Palestine into Jewish and Arab states. The outcome of the vote was that Palestine would be partitioned. We all went to a big meeting in Amsterdam, where we danced the horah in the middle of the street. I think there were several thousand people there, and it was very exciting.

DAVID

After the war, it was hard to adjust to normal life because I was kind of on my own. My mother didn't understand kids, and we never got along that well. Her way of life and my way of life were different.

I got involved in a Zionist organization. I went to *hachshara* when I was sixteen. I think one of the reasons I went was that I didn't know what to do in Holland. First I went to Gouda. We did farming half a day, and we went to school half a day. And then I had a crazy idea: I thought I should find out how religious life is. So I went to a religious *hachshara*. After a year, I found out it's big bullshit. I told the leader, and he was very upset. He said, "You got to be thankful." I said, "For what the hell do I have to be thankful? My life is nothing. Everything I got, I got myself. There's nothing to be thankful about." He made sure at the dinner table he was always sitting between the potatoes and me so when he handed me the potatoes I had to say, "Thank you."

HISTORY BRIEF, PAGE 239
The Partition of Palestine and the State of Israel

After

Second row from top, from right:
Mirjam and Nathan, with their
Zionist youth group, 1949

On the back of Nathan's copy
of this photo:
*Those who sow in tears will reap
with songs of joy.*
PSALM 126

On the back of Mirjam's copy
of this photo:
*A time to weep and a time
to laugh.*
ECCLESIASTES 3:4

A guy from Holland who was supposed to help arrange for aliyah (immigration to Palestine) didn't show up. So, I drove a truck in Marseilles for half a year. I brought immigrants from Germany, from the *Exodus*. I brought them to Marseilles to ship 'em to Israel.

NATHAN

Shortly after the UN vote on the partition of Palestine, we were told our group would go on aliyah. We went to Marseilles. Our passports were stamped with false tourist visas to Palestine, which was still a British mandate. The freighter departed from Marseilles, then went to Alexandria, on to Piraeus, and then to Haifa.

Though the sea was very calm, some of us became seasick and stayed that way for the entire voyage, which took about two weeks. Early in the morning, we all were on deck to watch our arrival in Haifa. We arrived well after first light and watched Mount Carmel rise out of the sea.

We arrived at the *merkaz* (port or center) without incident and were put up in a small hotel, where we stayed for a day or two. I was overwhelmed by the abundance and variety of food and clothing that was being sold, which I was not used to, since things were still scarce in Holland.

When we arrived, there were separate houses in which different groups were housed. We were housed with a group of Polish Jewish boys and girls, also new immigrants, who had survived the camps and had arrived in Haifa a few days before us. We, of course, did not have a common language, and I think that was the whole idea of mixing the two totally different groups—so we would have to learn Hebrew to communicate.

The British decided to leave Palestine in mid-May. That day, the state of Israel was declared by Ben Gurion. We listened to the radio speech from the National Assembly in Tel Aviv. The radio reception was very bad, and we could barely understand what was said. But we understood that our new state was called Israel. (Till then, we did not know what the name would be.) It was a very tense and emotional time. Fighting immediately broke out on all sides.

MIRJAM

We immigrated to Israel in January 1948. First, our whole group was sent to a children's home because we were too young to join the army. We celebrated together with our *chaverim* (friends) when Israel became a Jewish state in May 1948.

After one year in Mossad Ahava (a youth village), Nathan and I and the rest of the "Hollandim" were drafted into the Israeli army. After three months of drilling, running, shooting, and bad food, we were released and had the honor of starting a new *moshav shitufi* (cooperative village) in the northeastern part of Israel.

I felt good about being Jewish, good about doing something useful, building up a country. It was nice to be young with other people my age. During the war, I hadn't been home for three years, so for me it was easy, not being home.

Mirjam was later skeptical of her experience with the *shluchim*, and it is possible she is using the word "honor" here ironically, as Israeli communal living disillusioned her.

After

DAVID

In May 1948, I went to Israel. They took me straight into the army. This is a very difficult subject. I have the philosophy that I don't want to do to somebody else what I don't want done to myself. The Palestinians have rights. I would be pretty pissed off if somebody came, took my house away, threw me out, and said, "You have no home." I know how that feels. We were thrown out of our houses in Holland.

JUDITH

We left for Israel in December 1948. We were one of the very few Jewish families in Holland still intact (I mean parents and children). We had tickets on a cargo boat from Rotterdam through the Atlantic Ocean, via the Strait of Gibraltar and the Mediterranean. This boat had accommodations for a few passengers as well as cargo.

Mirjam was already in Israel. She arrived there at the beginning of 1948 when Israel was not yet a state. She, together with a Zionist youth group who had been trained to be pioneers in the future state, went the illegal way.

My sister Hadassah and I were seasick most of the trip. My mother, whom my father had provided with anti-seasick pills, had the time of her life, being the only passenger at the dinner table with the captain. My father didn't want us children to take the pills, because they were, at that time, still in a trial stage. We arrived in Haifa on December 27.

FIFI

Chaim gave up his job, we took Judith and Hadassah out of their school and, fortunately, didn't leave by plane. This way, we had the transition of a fine journey by ship, which, for two reasons, took extra long: first of all, we had to stop in many different ports because there was a lot of freight; and, secondly, our boat was held up on Cyprus because of the Christmas holidays.

All five of us were glad to be together again. Mirjam was living in Kiryat Bialik in Mossad Ahava. People really loved her and appreciated her diligence and sense of duty.

In retrospect, as I now reflect upon the courage required to take this step and where it came from, I just don't know. All we had was a written message from Beresh that said there would definitely be a place for a pharmacist, but as we would later find out, there was absolutely no basis for this.

In Holland, *there was* a job with a good salary, a pleasant working environment for Chaim. Appreciation from both sides. Chaim was "in," as they say—when the doctors needed advice in the pharmaceutical area, they knew they could turn to Chaim.

We had a lovely home, dear family, and many dear friends. But we were also very idealistic and had an urgent sense we had to do something, to give a living response to the outrage of 1932 to 1945. Our response was to go to Israel.

JUDITH

While we stayed with Mammie's brother Beresh, his wife, and three daughters, my father crisscrossed the country looking for work. My

Beresh Polak and Lolo Polak, two of Fifi's brothers, emigrated from the Netherlands to Palestine in 1930.

David, ca. 1948

In May 1948, I went to Israel. They took me straight into the army. This is a very difficult subject. I have the philosophy that I don't want to do to somebody else what I don't want done to myself. The Palestinians have rights. I would be pretty pissed off if somebody came, took my house away, threw me out, and said, "You have no home." I know how that feels. We were thrown out of our houses in Holland.
DAVID

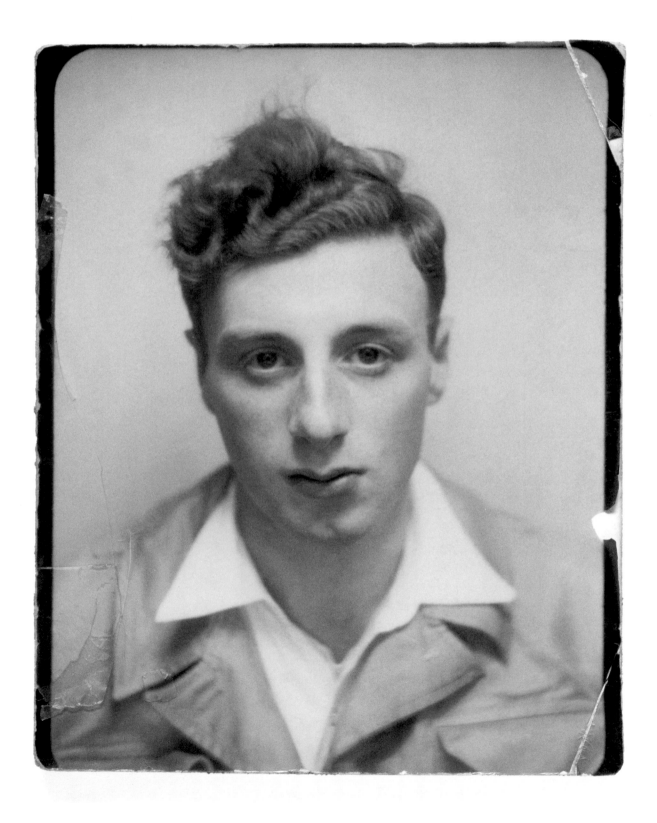

mother found work in a children's house (mostly immigrant children who survived the war), and my sister Hadassah and I spent our days picking oranges for a real salary! We felt great. What's more Israeli than picking oranges?

My father finally found work in a pharmaceutical company called Teva—at that time a small and not-very-profitable company. The place was near Jerusalem, and that is where he made arrangements for a place to live.

While our parents were getting organized, Hadassah and I were sent to Ben Shemen, an institute (village) for children—mostly survivors of World War II or children whose parents had trouble taking care of them. We were the only two Dutch girls there. The others were mostly from Eastern European countries. They lived six to eight in a room or even in tents, but my sister and I were lucky to get a wooden shipping container just for the two of us, which very soon became a sought-after spot in the village. We always had visitors. We wrote our name on the door in misspelled Hebrew, which made the whole thing even more attractive.

Our days were spent in school in the afternoons and at work—mostly agricultural—in the mornings. Hadassah with the chickens, and I with the cows. In the evenings there were all kinds of activities under the supervision of a coach.

After about a year or more, we left Ben Shemen and came home to our parents in Ein Kerem (a village near Jerusalem). Mirjam was with her group in a *moshav shitufi*; Hadassah and I lived at home. But after a short while, I left for nursing school, and Hadassah went into the army.

I did not like the idea of going into the army, and that must have been one of the reasons I chose to go to nursing school and become a registered nurse.

MIRJAM
The first few years in Israel were difficult for my parents. My mother was fifty-two, my father forty-five. It's hard to emigrate, for sure, at an older age. To learn a whole new language, alphabet and all. Meeting and getting along with people who themselves were all immigrants from over thirty other countries made for a lot of anxiety. Ten years after the war, my mother signed herself into a hospital back in Holland for a cure from dependency on sleeping pills. Finally, life got a little better for both of them, I think. They had a circle of friends, mostly Dutch friends, who lived in Israel, and family and friends visiting them from Holland. I like to think that their last few years together in Israel were happy years.

DAVID
After serving in the Israeli army, I was a truck driver with a Dutch group on a kibbutz. Then I joined the group where Mirjam was, in Moledet, in the Galilee. I'd already met her briefly in Holland.

MIRJAM
David and I had lost contact and then re-met when he joined our group— we were in a *moshav shitufi* in Israel, almost like a kibbutz. Then we

moved to start a new community and that's where we started going together. I was eighteen.

NATHAN

Around 1949, we went as a reinforcement group to a collective farm in Arbel, situated not far from Tiberias. Arbel was a well-organized group of World War II veterans who had decided to form a community. It had its own agriculture, a few tractors, a truck, a herd of cows, sheep, and a chicken coop. There were wooden huts, and we moved into one of them. In a short while, we were more or less integrated into the village and it was no longer "us" and "them." We felt part of the community.

A boy, David Geismar, who had joined our Dutch group, and a girl from our group, Mirjam de Zoete, were married at about this time. They were the first to be married in our group.

At about this time, I got a motorcycle as a present from my parents. This left me much more mobile, and in the afternoon I could easily go to the beach at Lake Tiberias or Haifa.

FIFI

When Mirjam married David on July 25, 1950, both were still kids, but smart kids. They lived in Arbel, worked hard, and were known for their determination and helpfulness. It wasn't a pleasant farm community, but coming to their house was always a pleasure. Their son was born on April 26, 1951. Mirjam worked till the end of her pregnancy. Her friend had to force her to stop working in the henhouse. If she hadn't, the baby would have been born between the little chickens.

NATHAN

I started working in the carpentry shop, which was in another village close by. We worked at building our permanent housing. Each family had a house, and the bachelors each got a house too. The bachelors in the community were assigned to families who cooked for them, and, if my memory serves me correctly, also did the clothes washing. Since my house was next to the house of Mirjam and David Geismar, I became "their bachelor."

In 1954, the Geismars decided that they wanted to be independent and left Arbel.

I started to work in a navy camp as a draftsman, and in the evening went to night school at the Technion (Israel Institute of Technology). I still had my Dutch citizenship, and since I still struggled with my Hebrew, I finished my studies in Holland.

JUDITH

Hadassah went into the army, where she met her husband, Zigi.

MIRJAM

Hadassah married a Jewish guy from Poland. So he was in the war too. He was actually a transport child brought to India—British India. All of his family died, and they put him on a train to India.

Nathan, ca. 1950

Around 1949, we went as a reinforcement group to a collective farm in Arbel, situated not far from Tiberias. Each family had a house, and the bachelors each got a house too. The bachelors in the community were assigned to families who cooked for them, and, if my memory serves me correctly, also did the clothes washing. Since my house was next to the house of Mirjam and David Geismar, I became "their bachelor."
NATHAN

ZIGI MANDEL

December 27, 1958

Shalom Mirjam and David,

Hadassah speaks often about you, and therefore I know about you much more than you about me. I'm thirty-one, in Israel from 1943. I was born in Kraków, Poland. During the war years, till '42, I was together with my family (parents and one sister) in Russia—mostly Siberia. Then a year ('42–'43) in British India and then Israel. In Israel, first about two years in Magdiel Agricultural School, then a year in the British army. After that, I worked as an electrician in Tel Aviv till the end of '47. From then and up to now I'm in the army—first till January '52 as a soldier, and from then on as a civilian.

As Hadassah has perhaps already written, we plan to marry on January 26th in Lydda Airport, and from there to fly to Eilat for a short honeymoon. In the meantime, we succeeded to find a flat in Ramat Gan. It is a small flat—only one room and conveniences.

We bought a Vespa, and I am learning to drive it. I hope to go to the test next week and pray to succeed at first try. They say here that it is quite impossible to succeed the first time. Well, we shall see.

Shalom,

Zigi

NATHAN

In 1963, after finishing my studies, I returned to Israel. I started work as a mechanical engineer in the Haifa refineries.

Mirjam came to Israel for a visit from the United States, where she now lived. The three De Zoete sisters visited me at my parents' house in Haifa. Judith and I continued to meet, and after a short while we decided to marry.

MIRJAM

Nathan saved himself so he could marry Judith after fourteen years!

JUDITH

Nathan lived and worked in Haifa as an engineer in the oil refineries. We got married and lived for about two years in Haifa. There, I worked again as an operating room nurse in a local hospital. Nathan wanted a change of jobs—I liked the Negev—and so he applied for and got a job at the Dead Sea Works. We bought a house in Arad, which, at that time, was thought of as a model town for the future.

NATHAN

For several years, Judith was the only operating room nurse in the whole south of Israel.

MIRJAM

Nathan is my oldest and best friend. I have known him since I was sixteen years old. I'll be forever grateful that Nathan and Judith got married. For Judith, because she could not have found a nicer man. And for me, because I did not have to lose my best friend ("my bachelor").

Left: Mirjam and David,
married July 25, 1950

Right: Hadassah and Zigi,
married January 26, 1959

Bottom: Judith and Nathan,
married March 23, 1964

FIFI

We have lived here in this house, in Ein Kerem, contentedly, for more than ten years, and we now have electricity, gas, running water, a refrigerator, radio, and gramophone. It is a house in the real sense of the word because it is wonderful to live in it. We can entertain our children here, and soon, when Annie, Jacques, and maybe Fietje come, we have enough room to entertain them as well. Only when the home is good can you find meaning outside.

CHAIM

January 14, 1950

Dear Children,

When the war was over and we were free once again, days of great happiness arrived. I don't think I need to remind you, as that period must be sharply etched in your memory. But it wasn't just our freedom that was returned to us; it was as if life itself had been put back into our hands. For our very life had been stripped from us. From us, which is to say from European Jewry. People had actually bid us farewell as if we were really dying. And it wasn't because we deserved it that death, passing by us so closely, had spared us.

And we went through the streets with this new life, singing on the inside, seeing everything in a different light. To be overcome by emotion is but a feeble way of describing the feeling that repeatedly took hold of us. For instance, when I saw one of you beneath the copper beech tree entering the garden of the Montessori Lyceum. Or much later, as I stood on the other side of the canal overlooking the vast lawn, I saw you get off your bicycles right under the blossoming chestnut tree only to disappear through the old gate of the Lyceum.

Gladness and gratitude overwhelmed me. Gratitude to all of those who had supported us during the war years. But part of it, too, was an emotion of thankfulness that, for now, I will call divine. But this feeling was almost immediately stifled, remembering just one of the millions of cases where the children had not returned. Surely countless ones among them must have been a thousand times more deserving than we.

This is the opening text of a seventy-page letter that Chaim wrote to Mirjam, Judith, and Hadassah to provide guidelines and stability for "moments that require answers to questions about life" in the aftermath of the mass murders and crimes committed during the Holocaust.

Chaim's seventy-page letter to Mirjam, Judith, and Hadassah, January 14, 1950

Ein - Kerem 14 Januari 1950

Lieve kinderen,

Toen de oorlog voorbij was en wij onze vrijheid terug kregen,
braken dagen van groot geluk aan. Ik geloof niet dat het nodig is dit in
herinnering te roepen,zoó sterk zal deze tijd in jullie geheugen gegrift
staan. Maar het was niet alleen onze vrijheid die wij terug kregen,ook het
leven werd als het ware opnieuw in onze hand gelegd. Want wij hadden ons
leven verbeurd. Wij,d.w.z. het Europeesche Jodendom. Men had zelfs afscheid
van ons genomen als van stervenden. En het is niet onze verdienste geweest
dát de dood,die dicht langs ons heen is gegaan,ons niet heeft gevonden.

En met dit nieuwe leven gingen we,in eindig zingend, langs de straten
alles ziende in een ander licht. Ontroering is maar een zwak woord voor het
gevoel dat ons herhaaldelijk overviel.Zoo b.v.toen ik een van jullie onder
de bruine beuk in tuin van het Montessori-Lyceum aan de Beschenweg in zag
gan,of later,staande aan de overkant van de Watersingel en kijkend over
het brede gazon,juist onder de bloeiende kastanje door,jullie van de fiets
zag afstappen om in het oude poortje van het inmiddels verplaatste,Lyceum
te verdwijnen.

Geluk en dankbaarheid overviel me. Dankbaarheid tegenover allen die ons
in de oorlogsjaren tot steun waren geweest. Maar ook een,laat ik voorlopig
zeggen bovenaarda gerichte,dankbaarheidsgevoel was daarmede gemengd.

Doch dit laatste gevoel werd bijna op hetzelfde moment getemperd.Want het
was voldoende slechts een van de gevallen uit de vele miliomen te herinner
waarbij de kinderen niet waren teruggekeerd,om te zeggen:maar dan heeft
een ,,hogere macht" ook dát gewild.

Zeker,ik heb anderen horen zeggen:,, niet te lang bij wat achter ons ligt
stil staan; streep erdoor; God heeft ons gespaard met een doel;we moeten
verder."

" God heeft ons gespaard met een doel" Maar dan heeft Hij ook de anderen
onder laten gaan met een doel. De ,,anderen". Waren daarbij niet talloozen
duizend maal beter dan wijzelf. En als we nog af willen zien van de volwas-
senen,wie zou willen beweren dat de reine kinderzielen de dood hadden verdie

,, Ik zal altijd zoet zijn,ik ben nog zoo jong" moet herhaaldelijk tot
de beulen gezegd zijn. Is met dit ene zinnetje deze God die het kind tóch
liet sterven niet veroordeeld?

Moge over dit antwoord nog onzekerheid bestaan,het was voor ons ieder
in elk geval mogelijk in het domein van het dagelijkse leven een antwoord
op het gebeurde te geven. En het zou een Joods antwoord moeten zijn,zo o mogelijk een honderd procentig Joods antwoord. En waar zou dit anders gegeve
kunnen worden dan in Israel?Maar ook daar blijft de vraag voor velen bestaan
wat is volledig Joods? De Israëlische staat zonder meer geeft het antwoord
niet. Het is een klein staatje zooals er meerdere op de wereld zijn.

Een bijzonder religieus fundament of in ieder geval een bijzonder geesteli
fundamenk structuur,die ook in het dagelijkse leven,in de gemeenschapsvormer
tot uiting zou moeten komen,zou nodig zijn.

Een opnieuw zich verdiepen in de hoofdlijnen van het Jodendom zoowel op
geestelijk gebied als op het terrein van het dagelijkse leven is voor de
de beantwoording dezer vragen noodzakelijk.

En,omdat het Joodse antwoord op geestelijk-religieus gebied er één is uit
meerdere mogelijke antwoorden(al zal de orthodoxie beweren dat het het enig
mogelijke antwoord is zal,aan een onderzoek naar de hoofdlijnen van het Jodendom,een bestudering moeten voorafgaan van de algemene bodem waarin deze
antwoorden wortelen.

Zigi

Zigi Mandel became part of the De Zoete family when he married Hadassah in 1959. As a European Jew, Zigi shared the experience of surviving the Holocaust with his in-laws. But instead of hiding, Zigi spent most of World War II in flight—a journey that took him from his native Poland to Russia, through Afghanistan and Pakistan to India, and onward to Palestine. Zigi's escape provides a compelling counterpoint to that of the De Zoetes, Cohens, and Geismars, and underscores the vastness of the war, the resilience of the persecuted, and the immeasurable losses suffered by the survivors.

Zigi; his British army ID number
is handwritten on the photograph,
April 1943

ZIGI

My story is quite different from those of Mirjam, Judith, Hadassah, David, and Nathan. I never met a German soldier face-to-face. I was born in Kraków, in a house at 22 Rynek Główny, one of the oldest town squares in Poland, built in the fourteenth century. I remember my father's hands, or rather his palms. They seem to me now very large, perhaps since I was so small. I can feel even now his hand covering my face. I can almost smell the aroma of the cigarettes he smoked, and I love it. I think my father loved my mother very much. My sister, Lilka, was about eight years old when I was born. I loved her very much.

Growing up, I knew that we were Jews, but we weren't religious at all—we were assimilated. I thought of myself as a patriotic Pole. In school, I had a friend, Leszek. We both were at the top of the class. When he intended to celebrate his name day, as was customary in Poland, he did not invite me. He told me, in his naiveté, that although he wanted to invite me, his parents said, "No, we don't have Jews in our home."

———

The "winds of war" were felt in Kraków for weeks before the war actually broke out. Everybody was equipped with gas masks, and people were digging trenches and filling sacks with sand in every park and on every empty plot. I'm not sure that I understood what was going to happen, but I knew that something bad would happen.

The war began for us when the first bombs fell on Kraków at about six o'clock in the morning, on Friday, September 1, 1939. I remember going out onto the street with a lot of other children and grown-ups and looking at the falling bombs and the resulting fires. We didn't live in the center of Kraków, so we saw it from far away, and we were more curious than afraid.

The next day, my parents decided—as did thousands of other people in Kraków—to leave the city. My parents and I left Kraków on Sunday, September 3, 1939, on foot with backpacks on our shoulders. It was the beginning of a very, very long trek that ended, for all my family, in death.

The first part of our trek took us to the eastern Poland town of Kowel, over 350 kilometers from Kraków, and then to Lwów (now both towns are in the Ukraine). We were not alone: hundreds of people—Poles and Jews of all ages—trekked with us. We tried to go by side roads to avoid being bombed and strafed by German planes, but we didn't escape them. We were on our way for thirteen or fourteen days and were strafed a few times and bombed at least once, in the town of Lublin. That was the first time I saw wounded and dead people around me.

We didn't have a car, and at the beginning we envied those who did and overtook us, but as we progressed, we saw more and more cars abandoned for lack of gas.

We slept wherever we could, sometimes in a peasant's cottage or barn, and sometimes by the roadside. After a few days, we realized that the villagers were unfriendly, and we tried to avoid the cottages—there were rumors that some people were robbed while sleeping there.

We bought food and sometimes even water at outrageous prices. For a few days, we traveled in comparative comfort after my father bought a cart and a horse. I cannot imagine how much he had to pay for it, but those were the best days for me. I don't know what happened to the cart and horse, but when we were bombed in Lublin—not far from our destination, the town of Kowel—we were again on foot.

On the 16th or 17th of September, we arrived in Kowel. There we went to a very large Bata footwear store belonging to a relative of my father. We weren't alone; other relatives had arrived earlier. We all slept in the shop on mattresses spread on the floor.

A day or two later, in the evening, a cousin of my father, an officer in the Polish army, came riding on a horse and without dismounting told us that the Russians were on the outskirts of the town, then galloped back to his unit. We knew already that on the 17th of September, the Red Army had crossed the eastern border of Poland. We didn't know then that it was according to a German-Soviet agreement, signed in August 1939, to divide Poland.

We were in Kowel only a few weeks and then in mid-October 1939 found ourselves in Lwów, where we remained until June 1940. We lived in a rented, furnished apartment that once belonged to a Polish aristocrat who fled from the Russians to the German-occupied part of Poland. One day a Russian officer came, looked around, and told us to vacate a room in the apartment. From then on he was our neighbor.

In June 1940, there were rumors that there would be another repatriation into Russia, and my parents decided that we would leave our apartment for a few days. As Lilka was already an adult, we separated temporarily—she slept at a friend's place and we three somewhere else. After a few days, on June 22nd, my parents decided that it was safe again to return to our apartment and so we did. Lilka remained for one more night with her friend. That was the night they came for us.

We were told that, being "an unsteady element," since we lived in western Poland before the war, we were going now to be resettled. We were given an hour or two to pack—we could take with us everything we wanted except furniture. As an afterthought, judging by the final outcome, this "resettlement" probably saved my life and surely spared my parents and me unspeakable suffering.

We were taken to the railroad station and there waited for a train consisting of cattle cars, in which we were to spend the next few weeks, although we didn't know it then, of course. Again we were not alone—hundreds of people, whole families with old people and small children, crowded at the station, and more arrived every hour. In the middle of each car, there was a heating oven, and in one corner there was a primitive toilet. On both sides of the car, there was something like shelves and bales of straw to sleep on. Into each car, intended for sixteen horses, about thirty people were crowded.

We spent the first day and night without moving from the station. The next day Lilka somehow found us and tried to come with us. My parents refused. They did not know what the future held. Lilka wasn't a child anymore. She worked in Lwów in a big hotel and had a boyfriend. How we regretted that decision.

HISTORY BRIEF, PAGE 229
Soviet Deportations of Former
Polish Citizens

Our voyage from Lwów to Tesma, our final destination, took almost four weeks, although the distance, about 2,500 kilometers, could be covered in a few days. Sometimes we were waiting for hours at a station, and other times it just seemed that we were stranded in the middle of nowhere, as if everybody forgot about us.

During the voyage, nobody threatened us physically. We had enough to eat—not lavishly, but not much worse than we were used to by then, and not much worse than the average Russian ate at the time.

Farther on, when the train stopped, we were allowed to get off for a short time, car by car. After a week or so, all of us were allowed to get off—I suppose the guards didn't believe that somebody would try to escape deep inside Russia.

Finally, in the middle of July, we arrived in Sosva in the eastern Ural Mountains. From there we were driven some fifty kilometers by horse-drawn carts into the Taiga, to the very small village of Tesma, where we spent over a year.

Tesma consisted of three not-very-long parallel streets crossing the "main" street. Along the streets were small cottages. Each family was allotted a cottage—sometimes to a not-very-large family a single person was added. For some time we had a single woman in our house.

The first few days were spent acclimating. We tried to bring the house to a state that made living in it possible; we figured out where the shop and the dispensary were and so on. The most pressing activities were ensuring that we had something to eat, making beds, repairing the roof, and repairing the big oven, which was almost completely ruined. We made the beds using planks. With time we improved them and placed their legs into cans with kerosene. This was to guard against a swarm of bedbugs, which were a real plague—we were told they came from the moss that filled the cracks between the logs of which the walls of the house were made. Later we found that it didn't help much—the bedbugs fell down from the ceiling.

We were given some food and told that in the future we would have to buy it with the money we earned. Most of the men were directed to work felling trees and bringing them to the river Tesma using a two-wheeled cart to which a horse was harnessed—summer and winter. Tesma was a tributary of a bigger river, Sosva, and the logs traveled down the two rivers to the town of Sosva. In Sosva, there were lumber mills where the logs were processed.

Every working person was allotted a kilogram of bread per day; nonworking persons were allotted a half kilogram—so at first, we had two kilograms of bread a day. The dark, wet bread was almost impossible to eat as is; when toasted, it was passable. Everything else we had to buy either in the communal shop or from the Russian families. In the shop, there were typically only one or two products available for a week or two. Sometimes it was sardines, and we ate them for weeks, at other times potatoes. Sometimes it was vodka or even eau de cologne, which we bought and then bartered for eggs, meat, or milk with the local Russians.

We quickly learned that if we didn't find a way to find some healthy food, sickness would prevail. Here the Taiga helped. The local people advised us to go into the woods and gather a kind of red berry—they told us that it's very healthy food, free and abundant. We spent hours doing that in the spring and summer. We ate it every day and stored a big crate for the winter, as advised. That helped us to remain alive and healthy.

My father was one of the lucky ones—somehow he managed to get a job as a helper to the Russian "expert" on repairing the big ovens, which were ruined in almost every house, so he had assured employment for a long time. The *pieczka* (oven) was made of bricks and served us well in the cold winter. The shelf served as a bed— I slept there often, and it was much more pleasant than sleeping in a cold bed. My father worked mostly inside, could come home for lunch (such as it was), and earned steady daily pay. Men who worked in the woods were paid according to the part of a "norm" they succeeded to fulfill on a given day. To fulfill 100 percent of the norm was almost impossible for somebody not used to this kind of work— and most were not.

In September, we were sent to school. There were two classrooms, one for first and third grades, and one for second and fourth grades, and one teacher. We all learned simultaneously, so the teacher had to attend to all four grades at once. For some time we had an unsympathetic teacher named Nina. Later on, another teacher, Anna, replaced her—she was much nicer. That is where I learned most of my Russian.

There I found my first love (one-sided!), a Polish girl my age named Zosia, daughter of a professor. I was very much in love, and I quietly asked the teacher to change places so that I could sit near her. For her birthday, I presented her with all the exercises in our math book—solved.

A short time after we arrived, all women who didn't have children below some given age were required to work in the woods. Although that brought us some more earnings and an additional half kilogram of bread daily, it was very hard on our mothers. So after some time, we, the older boys (twelve and up), organized and asked the *nachal'nik* (commander) to discontinue school and let us go to work in place of our mothers, and he agreed. From then on we helped in the woods, doing the lighter jobs. That preserved our full ration of bread and gave us even more earnings, since by some rule children were not required to fulfill a norm but instead were paid a daily wage.

Winter in Tesma was long and savage. There were days when the thermometer outside the *nachal'nik*'s office showed minus thirty degrees Celsius. Work in the woods was stopped only when the temperature fell below minus thirty-six.

In August or September 1941, we received good news—we were to be freed! What irony. The Germans brought about our release by attacking Russia (Operation Barbarossa). Now Poland and Russia were allies.

Sometime later, we were issued passports stating that we were now free to move in all of the USSR, except—and here came a long list of exceptions, such as towns greater than a defined size, locations nearer than a defined distance from international borders, security zones, and so on. What remained were probably only the southern republics like Uzbekistan and Kazakhstan. Representatives of the Polish

HISTORY BRIEF, PAGE 230
The Polish-Soviet Agreement of 1941

Zigi

government advised us to try to go south. Together with thousands of others, both Poles and Jews, we did. Later, we realized that it was a wrong move. But who could know it beforehand? And what would have happened if we had remained in Siberia?

The journey south resembled the journey to Tesma. As before, we traveled in cattle cars; we were stranded for hours and days in the middle of nowhere. The whole journey took almost a month. There was a heating oven in the car, and there was *kipiatok* (boiling water) at every station. We needed them more than ever since this journey was in autumn and much colder. And like before, we didn't know what awaited us at the other end.

But there were some very significant differences. Although the distance was similar, it took us much longer—possibly because Russia was now fighting for its life, and there were a lot of military trains with higher priority than ours. We went voluntarily. We had to pay for it. The cars were much more comfortable, and there were fewer people in each car. There were no guards. Nobody gave us food—we had to find it and pay for it ourselves. We were not afraid—we hoped that a better future awaited us.

We were completely disillusioned by what we found in Bukhara. In October 1941, we "landed" in the old part of the city. In the southern republics, there were already some millions of refugees from the Ukraine, which was overrun by the Nazis. And now there was a new stream of hundreds of thousands of "free" Poles and Polish Jews.

We found in Bukhara a city of poverty, hunger, dirt, lice, and sickness. There was no chance whatsoever of finding any kind of work. Our money had run out paying for the journey from Siberia. In Bukhara, we felt for the first time what real hunger is. The only place we could find to live in was a hovel, maybe three by three meters, without a window. My parents and I lived there for some months, together with a woman. We slept on the clay floor without even the simplest furniture. My father was very weak and had to lie in bed all day long.

I'm almost ashamed to admit it, but there I experienced a most shameful episode: one night I noticed that the woman who lived with us had a piece of bread near her—and thinking that she was deeply asleep, I simply stole it. But then she woke, or perhaps she wasn't sleeping at all, guarding her "hoard," and caught me at it. That was one of the very few times that I remember my parents being angry with me.

I spent most of my time foraging for food. We tried to find some Uzbek who would buy some of our clothing. I tried to find a "line" before some shop to buy anything they sold on a given day. That was a typical "sport" in Russia—while going along a street you saw a line forming, so you immediately took a place there, and only then did you ask, "What is this line for?"

On some days, my mother somehow succeeded to prepare a few sorry-looking, very small sandwiches, and I would go on the street with a big plate and try to sell them at exorbitant prices. Usually, I succeeded and could buy some bread, also at exorbitant prices.

We felt filthy, and so we were, and full of lice. As hard as we tried, we couldn't get rid of them. Only the "richest" (and there were such) families among us could afford to live in more normal conditions. We knew one such family. My parents showed me where they lived and told me that if at any time we separated and I was left alone, I should go to them and they would care for me.

And then with the lice, there came typhus. I was the first one to get it and was admitted to a hospital very far away from our hovel, in the new part of Bukhara. That was the last time I saw my mother. I was hospitalized for five or six weeks, and during all that time nobody came to visit me. Afterward, I realized that my mother fell sick and went to another hospital, and my father caught typhus a week or two later.

While in the hospital, I heard terrible stories from other children about *detskiye doma* (Russian orphanages). I was very slight and weak, but I did somehow defeat typhus. Since nobody came to visit me, I was afraid that I'd be sent to an orphanage.

The hospital authorities let me go home with another patient, a grown-up Uzbek, who promised that if we didn't find my parents, he'd bring me to the police station. On our way, I somehow persuaded him to let me finish the journey alone.

When I came "home," I found my father alone, very sick with heavy bedsores. He told me that my mother had been taken to a hospital a few days after me. The next day, I went to look for her. I went to the hospital and told one of the gatekeepers that I was looking for my mother and gave him her name. They had a list of patients, but he couldn't find her name there. He went inside to find out and after a few minutes came out, saying in broken Russian: "Mother dead." I don't remember what I told my father, but I'm sure I didn't tell him that Mother died.

My father's condition deteriorated, and I brought him by truck to the hospital. A few days later, I learned that he had died there. I was alone and on my own.

I took a small bundle of things, including a woolen shawl, which I later bartered for a few pickles, and went to the "rich" family as told to do by my parents. I stood on the threshold, and they did not invite me inside.

In June 1942, I arrived at a Polish orphanage in Samarkand, about 200 kilometers from Bukhara. The orphanage was in a building near the railway station in the old city. We spent most of the day in the very large hall in which we slept. There were about a hundred children of all ages and a few grown-ups who took care of us. Most of the children were Christians, but there were also a few Jews. We thought that one of the grown-ups, Michael, was a Jew, but he did not identify himself as such.

I don't remember what we did all day. Every few days, three or four older boys (of which I was one) were sent to the Polish consulate in the new city, quite a long way away—or so it seemed to me then— to pick up a few sacks of bread for the orphanage. We fought to be chosen for this task, since on our way back we had an opportunity to scrape all the crumbs from the outside of the bread—when we arrived back at the orphanage, every loaf was cleanly "scrubbed."

At the end of June or beginning of July, we were told that some of us, perhaps twenty or thirty, would be going the next day to Ashgabat in Turkestan and from there to India. A list was compiled and read out, and all of us thought and spoke of nothing else. I wasn't on the list! We didn't know much about India, but it was a place exotic enough to fire our imagination. We didn't know what would happen in India, but any change was more than welcome.

The next day, a truck or two came, and the list of the lucky children was read again. And then there was a commotion—one of the girls on the list was sick in the night and whoever was in charge decided that she couldn't go. So there was an empty place, and they had to decide at the last moment who would go instead of the sick girl. Everybody hoped to be the lucky one. And to my surprise, I was the one! Michael, the one who we thought was Jewish, told me to board quickly and then added me to the list. I think that I was the only Jewish child on board. (Much later, in India, we realized that, among the 500 or so children, there were only eighteen Jews in all—six who came with the first transport from Russia and twelve in our second transport.)

Our first destination was Ashgabat, not far from the Persian (now Iranian) border, where there was a big and very well-organized Polish orphanage. We were there for some weeks in much better conditions. We slept on new mattresses with clean blankets. The food was, for us, almost luxurious.

On the first night, on the mattress next to mine, I found a new friend, Eddy. We spoke deep into the night, sharing our stories. Eddy told me, in good Polish but with a strong foreign accent, after I vowed not to tell anybody, that he wasn't Polish. He was born in Vienna and educated in an Italian boarding school. Sometime before the war, he was sent to an uncle in Poland—his parents thought that he'd be safer there. He was afraid that somebody would find out that he was not Polish and he'd find himself back where he came from.

On the 14th of July 1942, about 200 of us, accompanied by a few women, boarded ten or so big Polish army trucks and the whole convoy, accompanied by Polish soldiers, moved toward the Persian border. At the border, we transferred to smaller lorries, driven by Indian drivers. The leader of the convoy was Dr. Konarski, a captain in the Polish army who had come all the way from India. We were guarded by armed men. For us, the older boys, it was the beginning of an adventure.

Then began the real journey to mysterious India, which was over 2,200 kilometers long, through Persia and Afghanistan—the playing ground of Kara ben Nemsi, the hero of my Karl May books. What could be more exciting?

We drove to the Persian city of Mashhad, where we spent a week or two in a kind of quarantine, getting some fat on our bones and getting rid of possible illnesses. Then we drove south to the eastern border of Persia and across the southwestern part of Afghanistan to Quetta, in what is now Pakistan, and then to the Polish School in Balachadi, near Jamnagar. We didn't know then that we, the Jewish children, would stay there for only a few months.

Balachadi is a small village not far from the city of Jamnagar. Near the village, Maharaja Jam Saheb (ruler) Digvijaysinhji Ranjitsinhji of Nawanagar had one of his palaces. Not far from there he built a camp for over 600 Polish children evacuated from Russia, most of them orphans, of which I was one.

The camp was managed by Father Franciszek Pluta, a priest. There was a staff of about thirty teachers, all of them women. We lived in wooden one-story buildings, each well equipped for some tens of children. We slept in clean beds with white bedspreads covered by mosquito nets, each of us with his or her own small locker beside the bed. We were never hungry—on the contrary, sometimes we overate. There was plenty of everything, including many exotic foods that we did not know.

Eddy, whom I mentioned earlier, tried everything he could to leave the camp. Around December 1942 or January 1943, he succeeded. Once in a while, a dentist from Bombay came to the camp. Through her, he left for Bombay and was hosted by a German Jewish family, Lotte and Walter Daus.

At the end of February '43, the remaining eleven Jewish children left the camp for Bombay. In Bombay, there was a representative of the Jewish Agency, Mr. Cynowicz, who arranged for our certificates of entry to Palestine. We had to wait some time for appropriate transport, which, in that time of war, was difficult to arrange. Therefore we were temporarily "adopted" by European Jewish families in Bombay. Eddy asked the Dauses to take me in, and so they did.

At the beginning of April 1943, we boarded a cargo ship bound for Suez through the Arabian Sea, the Gulf of Aden, and the Red Sea. From Suez, we traveled by train to Haifa, where we arrived on the 24th of April 1943, in the middle of World War II.

In all the newspapers, there were articles about us, mostly to help our relatives—if there were any—to find us. I didn't realize it then, but here, at last, a short time after my fifteenth birthday, I had found my home and started my new life.

The boarding school in Magdiel was my first home in the land of Israel. It was also my first taste of the melting pot into which entered people from every imaginable background, land, and environment. There were about one hundred children from all over Europe: Romania, Poland, Greece, Holland, Turkey, and more. We learned mathematics and physics, Hebrew, modern Jewish history and literature, secular teachings of the Old Testament, and Israel's history and geography. Part of each day we worked in different agricultural jobs. At first, I was assigned to the vegetable garden, and then I somehow succeeded in being transferred to the most sought-after job—the donkey cart driver.

In early 1945, shortly after my seventeenth birthday, I enlisted in the British army with forged papers issued by the Jewish Agency, stating that I was eighteen. I was eager to take my revenge on the Nazis. I did not see combat before the war in Europe ended.

I can no longer visualize my mother or father, Basia and Zygmunt. I was with my mother until I was fourteen years old, and yet I cannot "see" her face! I loved her very much. Aunt Mania, my mother's sister, and her daughter, Inge, didn't survive the Holocaust. Mania's husband, Uncle Natek, gave me the only picture I have of my family: it is of Aunt Mania with my older sister, Lilka, who didn't survive either.

The picture was taken in Krynica in 1934, when Lilka was fourteen, and I was six years old. When we were forcibly taken to Siberia and Lilka remained in Lwów, we lost all contact with her. A few years ago— more than fifty years after the war—I learned from the Yad Vashem site that Lilka died at the age of twenty in Warsaw. This information was submitted by a Mrs. Janina Ferber, who identified herself as Lilka's "school and best friend." I contacted her, and she told me that she lived during the war in Kraków, but she was in contact with Lilka, who traveled all over Poland with false papers till some girlfriend delivered her to the Germans. Without knowing the circumstances, having only this information, it is difficult for me to blame her. Maybe they tortured her or threatened to kill her parents and she couldn't stand it? How would I behave in such circumstances?

Later Years

Chaim de Zoete
Fifi Polak-de Zoete

It was rare for an entire nuclear family to survive the Holocaust, as Chaim, Fifi, Mirjam, Judith, and Hadassah did. From their three daughters, Chaim and Fifi had nine grandchildren and twenty-one great-grandchildren. Among the six million Jews who did not survive were Chaim's mother and sister, two of Fifi's brothers and a sister, and twenty-four other close family members. Mustering the courage to construct a new life, Chaim and Fifi left the Netherlands for Israel. When they arrived at the end of 1948, Fifi, still addicted to sleeping pills, spent much of her time dazed and in bed while Chaim, worrying that she would overdose, traversed the country looking for a job. He found a position with a small pharmaceutical company called Teva, now one of the world's largest manufacturers of generic drugs. Despite her addiction, Fifi also found a job, working with children who survived the Holocaust.

In 1950, Chaim and Fifi moved into a government-provided house in Ein Kerem, a historic Jerusalem village, with agricultural terraces, stone houses, churches, monasteries, and an aqueduct and spring. (In the Christian narrative, Ein Kerem is the fourth-holiest site, where the pregnant mothers of Jesus and John the Baptist met by the spring in the center of the village.) Chaim and Fifi's house had previously belonged to Palestinians who fled Ein Kerem during the 1948 Arab-Israeli War. For the first four years, Chaim and Fifi shared the house with a young couple and their child. There was no water, sewage, electricity, or gas for the first seven years; the outhouse was down a long stairway beneath the stone patio.

The year the De Zoetes moved to Ein Kerem, Chaim completed his seventy-page letter to his daughters, hoping it would serve as a guide in the aftermath of the mass murders and crimes committed during the Holocaust. Chaim attempted to explain the individual's place in the world, drawing from a long list of writers, philosophers, and scientists, including Bertrand Russell, Rilke, Spinoza, and Darwin as well as from Judaism, Christianity, and Buddhism. Chaim was convinced that a spiritual entity grounded the universe. He did not believe that any one religion was better than another and felt that those who do "are not in the innermost sense of the word, religious."

Chaim fervently believed in Israel as a homeland for the Jews and in the need to fight for its existence. In a letter to relatives in the Netherlands, written just after the 1967 Arab-Israeli War, Chaim proudly details Israel's "miracle of victory," but ends his letter with tempered triumph because "in war there is killing and maiming, and man deviates from his explicit dedicated mission as 'human being.'" Chaim's writings reveal his ethical conflicts. Feeling that "the current spiritual and moral level (in Israel) is unworthy of the sacrifices of the Galuth (exile of the Jews) and of the sacrifices of the battle for liberation," Chaim yearned for a society that would, among other things, strive for truth and justice, respect all living things, and encourage fulfilling work and a rich cultural experience for all. This society would fight against intolerance, class struggle, worship of money, and fanaticism and coercion in religion and politics. Chaim filled notebooks with his ideas on life, religion, God, being Jewish, parapsychology, philosophy, dreams, music, history, and tolerance. A good friend reflected that Chaim "was a man of few words, but big thoughts."

Ten years after arriving in Israel, Fifi checked herself into a hospital in the Netherlands to conquer her addiction. When she returned, she was able to fully engage, making friends and feeding all the cats in Ein Kerem. Fifi had a big heart, but could also be critical and difficult—albeit in an endearing way, as described by one of her friends: "In some sort of captivating fashion Fifi knew how to twist you around her little finger. Sometimes she would make you dead tired, and of course she would interfere a lot, but that didn't really matter, because Fifi was Fifi, and Fifi was a dear—she gave you much more than you could ever give her."

Fifi and Chaim's love for each other ran deep. They shared interests in reading, writing, classical music, and art. They traveled together to the Netherlands and the United States to see family and friends. They had plans to fulfill Chaim's dream of a trip to Japan in 1970, but Chaim died unexpectedly in 1969, at the age of sixty-six, while the couple was in the Netherlands. Fifi's heart was broken. She filled a notebook with beautifully tragic poems about Chaim's death, life, and their relationship. Toward the end of this notebook, Fifi found her strength:

Am I still asleep?
Well, it's about time
To wake up
It's about time
To shake myself up
Because it's cowardly
All that sleeping
Can't I realize that?
I don't like cowards
Thus it's about time
To set myself right.

Fifi died in 1986.

David Geismar
Mirjam de Zoete-Geismar

In late 1948, Mirjam, David, and about thirty other young men and women started their new lives in Israel with a few tents, two donkeys, some guns, and one truck as part of a *moshav shitufi* (cooperative village) in the town of Moledet in Galilee. In 1950, Mirjam and David, who had resettled (along with Nathan) on a collective farm in Arbel, were married under the grapevines and fig trees on the terrace of Chaim and Fifi's house in Ein Kerem, Jerusalem. In Arbel,

David drove a truck and Mirjam worked with the cows and chickens. She gave birth to a son and then a daughter.

In 1954, the young family left the collective to live independently in Beit Yitzhak. David opened an appliance store and repair shop in the nearby town of Netanya, but had to close the business in 1956 when he was called back into the army for the Suez War.

Tired of wars, David and Mirjam immigrated to Jersey City, New Jersey, in 1957. There, David drove for a trucking company by day and worked at a five-and-dime store by night. Not one to express regrets, David once said that he made a big mistake after the Holocaust when he followed the *shluchim* (emissaries) who convinced him to focus on his Jewish heritage rather than on resuming his education.

After three months, David and Mirjam moved to Norwalk, Connecticut, where David worked a day job as the maintenance plant manager in a factory and repaired washing machines at night. Mirjam took in ironing. Two years later, they moved to Weston, Connecticut, where they started Dave's Electric Appliance Service. David sold and repaired large appliances; Mirjam was the business manager. They had two more daughters.

In Weston, David joined the volunteer Emergency Medical Services (EMS) and responded to thousands of calls over the next four decades. Serving as EMS chairman for twenty-four years, he tirelessly fought to bring the best possible services to the town. In 1992, David was named Weston's Citizen of the Year. David's successor as chairman of EMS wrote, "His greatness derived from his love of people, his self-sacrifice and his commitment to doing right."

After David and Mirjam's youngest child was in school, Mirjam also became an emergency medical technician, volunteering for twenty-two years. In addition, she worked as a nurse's aide in the public schools. Between raising four children, working, and volunteering, Mirjam found time to learn photography, developing and printing her photographs in a darkroom that David built for her. She also hooked rugs, learned to weave on a large floor loom, and attended classical music concerts and plays. Mirjam was at once tough, telling her children not to fuss about "tiny little nothings" (which was almost everything when compared to the Holocaust), and vulnerable. For example, she gave her children a secret code to use over the phone to signal they were okay in case someone—say, a kidnapper—should ever hold a gun to their heads and demand they call their parents. Mirjam also kept a decoy purse in the closet, to be readily handed to a would-be burglar; her real purse was hidden in a spot that required acrobatics to retrieve every time she left the house.

David worked tirelessly, played hard, and helped whenever help was needed. On weekends, after spending time welding, forging, and woodworking, he would rise from his basement shop through a cloud of smoke, wearing his welding helmet and Dutch wooden shoes. He rode a motorcycle and owned several boats, teaching himself to sail. A sailing companion who became his son-in-law said, "I don't know anyone as fearless and as full of life as David."

In 1995, David and Mirjam sold their appliance business to an immigrant from Iran whom David had trained and mentored. His name was Sam, but everyone called him Dave. Mirjam helped Sam's wife adapt to life in the United States. The families shared meals from their respective cultures. In retirement, after a life of terror, hard work, raising a family, and humanitarian efforts, Mirjam and David finally found time for themselves, camping, bicycling, reading, going to flea markets, and picnicking on the beach.

They also visited schools and spoke about their experiences during the Holocaust. Mirjam told one group of students, "It makes me sad to tell you about my life during the war, but it also makes me feel good because it's so very important that every generation hears what happened to me and millions of Jewish people—when evil people tried to run the world. Now you can tell your own children, and they can tell theirs. And we can try to do something when we see it happening again somewhere else in the world."

When David and Mirjam were in Israel visiting family in 2003, David died unexpectedly, and Mirjam returned to the United States alone. With characteristic unflappability, Mirjam pressed on despite her loss; a decade later, she began to lose her memories to dementia. She died in 2019.

Nathan Cohen
Judith de Zoete-Cohen

After the war, Judith resumed her Montessori education before immigrating to Israel with Chaim, Fifi, and Hadassah. Initially, Nathan couldn't focus on his studies but enjoyed physical work and riding his motorcycle; he eventually returned to his schooling as well, through a correspondence program offered by the British Council, after spending eight years doing agricultural and carpentry work on collective farms in Israel.

Nathan wanted to do all he could to support Israel, enthusiastically serving in four wars and one month per year of military reserve duty. Always a man of principle, Nathan noted that he had been in the reserves for thirty years and "never fired a bullet in anger." Judith went to nursing school so she wouldn't have to join the army.

After graduating, Judith worked seven days a week in a hospital in the Negev desert—she was the only operating room nurse in southern Israel. Judith lived in the hospital compound so she could be accessible around the clock, sharing a house with the head of pediatrics. During the Suez War of 1956, wounded soldiers occupied every space in the compound, but working conditions were more manageable for Judith with help from the mobilized army medical units. After seven years, when the hospital closed in 1960, Judith decided to leave Israel to participate in an exchange program in the United States, working as a surgical nurse in Massachusetts, New Jersey, and New York, and spending time with Mirjam and her family in Connecticut. After two years in the United States, Judith returned to Israel, living with

Hadassah and Zigi in Petah Tikva and working in the operating room at a local hospital.

Nathan also left Israel in 1960 after studying mechanical engineering for two years at Technion–Israel Institute of Technology. Taking classes in Hebrew was difficult, so he resolved to complete his studies in the Netherlands. After graduating in 1963, Nathan returned to Israel to work as a mechanical engineer at the Haifa Oil Refinery.

Shortly after Nathan's return, Mirjam traveled to Israel to see her family. While there, she called on her close friend Nathan, bringing Judith and Hadassah along for the visit. Judith and Nathan connected, and they married the following year. Initially, the couple lived in a small flat in Haifa before moving to the southern desert town of Arad. Judith worked as a surgical nurse, and Nathan took a job as a mechanical engineer for the Dead Sea Works.

In 1967, during the Six-Day War between Israel and the Arab states of Egypt, Syria, and Jordan, Judith worked long hours to receive the wounded from the Sinai Peninsula. She was pregnant with the couple's first child, a daughter born four months later. Two more daughters followed. When the girls were young, Judith didn't work, except for an intense spell assisting in surgeries for the wounded when Egyptian and Syrian forces launched a surprise attack on Israel in 1973. Once the children were school age, she took a job in a neonatal intensive care unit three nights a week, returning home in the morning to see the girls off to school.

In 2003, Judith and Nathan moved to the small town of Shimshit, near Nazareth, where two of their grown daughters lived with their families. In Shimshit, Nathan spent time in his workshop inventing, building furniture, and constructing toys for his grandchildren and the local kindergarten. He listened to classical music on his headphones and made homemade ice cream. He was interested in technology, keeping himself current on personal computing and sharing his knowledge with others. He also volunteered in the community, driving those in need to the hospital. Nathan was magnanimous—noble, honest, generous, kind, and charitable. He spoiled his daughters and gave outrageously big tips. Throughout his life, he took photographs (which he developed in his bathroom) of his growing family, who loved him dearly. Nathan died in 2012.

Judith's daughters describe her as a liberal, modern feminist who is mistrustful of people due to her experiences during the Nazi occupation of the Netherlands. She is terrified by the current rise of nationalist leaders and demagogues, and fears bureaucracy and modern surveillance to the point of tears. Judith is most fearful of white supremacist hate groups, thugs, and men who victimize women. Nathan was similarly wary, pointing out that there were far more Nazi collaborators in the Netherlands than helpers. Today, Judith prefers reading books in her armchair at home to being out in the world. Her daughters observe that Judith "will close her eyes and smile if you put on country music and give her a cigarette and piece of chocolate. And, if you play some old rock-and-roll, she will get up and show you how to dance the twist."

Zigi Mandel
Hadassah de Zoete-Mandel

Zigi and Hadassah were both fifteen years old when they arrived in Israel—Zigi in 1943, Hadassah in 1948. Both were situated in boarding schools where they continued their education and did agricultural work with other teenagers from across Europe. Some of the adolescents were orphans, many traumatized during the war.

Zigi was seventeen when he enlisted in the British army with false papers, sparking a forty-year military career as an intelligence security specialist in the Israel Defense Forces (IDF) Signal Corps, later retiring with the rank of lieutenant colonel. Hadassah was conscripted when she turned eighteen, fulfilling the required two years of mandatory military service before working from 1955 to 1964 for the IDF, where the two met. They married and had two sons.

Hadassah and Zigi had an ardent love that lasted a lifetime. "There is no love story like theirs, even in Hollywood's most exciting stories," recounted their sons. The solidity of their relationship encompassed the entire family. After being separated from her parents and sisters for three years during the Holocaust, Hadassah valued family above all else. She lived fully in the moment, realizing there was no way to know what the future would bring. With this philosophy, the Mandels lived simply, in a small house with few belongings, and used a scooter for transportation. Hadassah was thrifty, cutting open a tube of toothpaste to get every last bit, but generous in nature. Zigi also preferred to indulge his family with kindness and care rather than material possessions. He believed these principles would nurture strong, optimistic sons who would be able to survive even if they found themselves alone in a terrifying world. Hadassah and Zigi were also gracious toward friends and extended family—especially Fifi—inviting her to live next door and providing companionship in the last decade of her life. Hadassah was Judith's best friend.

While raising her sons, Hadassah worked and volunteered in various forms: as a cosmetician, in a bookstore, and for the Israeli Labor Party from 1987 to 1997. She was a free spirit with interests in music and fashion, and she maintained a healthy lifestyle, keeping a vegetarian and vegan diet long before it was common to do so. Hadassah taught her sons that they *only* needed to be good people—the rest would be a bonus. They contributed to Hadassah's care when she became ill. After Hadassah's death in 2009, Zigi wrote, "I love her enormously, endlessly. We truly found happiness in each other and it's wonderful that we were together for so long."

Hadassah's relaxed nature was balanced by Zigi's intensity. He was intelligent and curious. When the World Wide Web was introduced, he was amazed by the wealth of information that opened up to him. He utilized the internet for in-depth research into a variety of subjects, including learning all he could about Hadassah's medical situation in an effort to keep her from suffering and death.

Zigi described his ethics, formed by his experiences during the war and his life in Israel, as a struggle to reconcile his two fundamental beliefs:

1. As a human being, I believe that the highest moral value is that of honesty and integrity.

2. As a Jew and an Israeli citizen, I believe that the one and only raison d'être for the existence of the State of Israel is its "being there" ready to receive any Jew in need.

The trouble is that these two beliefs often contradict one another. Therefore, I've no other option but to establish priorities. My belief as a Jew comes first. I see it as a simple case of survival. To some that may seem harsh and possibly even unfair.

Let me try to explain. Sometimes we Jews have a few "good" years or a few "good" decades. But, in the end there always comes a time of oppression or even persecution. There is a supreme need to prepare a place of safety for any Jew who may need it. Nobody will do it for us. That, for me, is the quintessence of Zionism.

Why didn't I confine myself to honesty and integrity? Why didn't I add some universal values such as an end to all wars, universal love, world peace, equality, etc.?

I am fully aware that my second belief is a very dangerous statement, since it can lead to a complete moral decline for its promulgator. But I see no other way. I truly believe that honesty and integrity are the most important human values. But when I try to think on a "lower," more pragmatic level, and contrast it with the existence of the State of Israel (always, as a "city of refuge"), I can't find another way out. Although the universal human values will rule, on the Jewish level there may come a catastrophe. And this level is, to me, indescribably more important and more precious.

Zigi died in 2015.

Erwin Geismar

Erwin was murdered in Auschwitz on November 19, 1943. He was forty-one years old. He was survived by his wife, Grete, and his thirteen-year-old son, David. The memoir he wrote while in hiding, discovered more than sixty years after his death, offers his descendants an extraordinary glimpse of his humanity. After the German occupation of the Netherlands, Erwin was driven to assist the many Jews who could not work due to antisemitism, guiding them to help themselves and one another. In observing the suffering of his community, he wrote, "My measure of compassion is full." After David became a parent himself, he reflected on Erwin's death: "My father would have enjoyed knowing my kids. It gets me every time I think about it."

Family Members

Listed on the following pages are members of the three primary family groups who narrate this book, including the two generations of narrators and the parents of the older generation. Birth dates follow each name. Familiar forms rather than proper names are used. Names in gray are not mentioned in the narratives.

Individuals marked with a Jewish Star were killed by the Germans. See page 191 for a comprehensive list of close family members who were murdered—sixty-one relatives from three generations.

Zondag. 7 November 1948.
Rotterdam.

Afscheid van:
Chaim en fifi de Zoete-Polak.
Judith Ruth
Mirjam   en
Hadassah.
Bij hun vertrek naar ?

A page from Fifi's diary,
June 20, 1945–1963

Sunday. November 7, 1948. Rotterdam.
Farewell from: Chaim and Fifi
de Zoete-Polak, Judith Ruth, Mirjam
and Hadassah. On their departure
to the land of Israel.

De Zoete Family

Chaim de Zoete
1903

Fifi Polak-de Zoete
1896

Mirjam de Zoete
1931

Judith de Zoete
1932

Hadassah de Zoete
1933

Chaim's Parents
Moses de Zoete: 1867
✱ Naatje de Zoete: 1872

Chaim's Sisters & Their Spouses
Grentje de Zoete-Hartog Klop: 1901
Gus Hartog Klop: unknown

✱ Martha de Zoete-Zwarenstein: 1904
Maurits Zwarenstein: 1901

Fifi's Parents
Moses Polak: 1871
Goldine van der Hove-Polak: 1873

Fifi's Siblings & Their Spouses
Annie Polak-Maarssen: 1892
Jacques Maarssen: 1892

✱ Jet Polak-de Lange: 1893
✱ Karel de Lange: 1901

✱ Sam Polak: 1900
Fietje van Gigh-Polak: 1894

Beresh Polak: 1901
Pauki Lipschütz-Polak: 1904

Lolo Polak: 1902
Regina Polak: 1901

Ben Polak: 1913
Petra Eldering: 1909
Mireille Smit: 1931

✱ Hans Polak: 1916
Annetje Kupferschmidt-Polak: 1914

Fifi's Nephews & Nieces
✱ Harry Maarssen: 1919
✱ Bob Maarssen: 1921
✱ Sally Maarssen: 1922
✱ Bernhard Maarssen: 1924

✱ Mirjam de Lange: 1930
✱ Hetty de Lange: 1935

Chava Polak: 1929
Rivka Polak: 1931
Rachel Polak: 1939

Edna Polak: 1936

Peter Polak: 1940
Freek Polak: 1942

Chaja Polak: 1941

Cohen
Family

Nathan's Parents
Isaak Cohen: 1899
Rivka Rosenbaum-Cohen: 1902

Nathan Cohen
1931

Nathan's Sisters
Henny Cohen: 1927
Annemieke Cohen: 1934

Nathan's Maternal Grandparents
Nathan Rosenbaum: 1860
Bietja Godschalk-Rosenbaum: 1865

Nathan's Maternal Aunts & Uncles
✱ Clara Cohen-Rosenbaum: 1902
✱ David Rosenbaum: 1898

Mieke Rosenbaum-de la Penha: 1900
Bram de la Penha: unknown

Nathan's Maternal Cousins
✱ Adolph Rosenbaum: 1925
✱ Nathan Rosenbaum: 1926
✱ Mimi Rosenbaum: 1930
✱ Jack Rosenbaum: 1936

Nathan's Paternal Grandparents
Salomon Cohen: unknown
Hendrika Rosenbaum-Cohen: 1866

Nathan's Paternal Aunts & Uncles
✱ Moos Cohen: 1888
✱ Fietje Meijer-Cohen: 1894

✱ Mietje Cohen-Wijnberg: 1890
✱ Jonas Wijnberg: 1884

✱ Betje Cohen-de Haas: 1893
✱ Julius de Haas: 1883

Anna Cohen-Levij: 1897
Isaac Levij: 1895

✱ Elly Cohen-Heijmann: 1901
✱ Hans Heijmann: 1889

Nathan's Paternal Cousins
✱ Salomon Cohen: 1920
✱ Gerda Cohen: 1925

✱ Bram Wijnberg: 1922
✱ Henny Wijnberg: 1925

Jaap de Haas: 1920
Sallo de Haas: 1922
Ina de Haas: 1925
Henk de Haas: 1930

Iwan Levij: 1925

Geismar
Family

★ Erwin Geismar
1901

David Geismar
1930

David's Mother
Grete Heinsheimer-Geismar: 1905

David's Paternal Grandparents
Dietrich Geismar: unknown
Rosa Geismar: unknown

David's Paternal Aunt & Uncle
Jul Geismar-Bloch: unknown
Leo Bloch: unknown

David's Maternal Grandparents
★ Max Heinsheimer: 1872
Auguste Lehmann-Heinsheimer: 1876

David's Maternal Aunt & Uncle
★ Luzie Heinsheimer-Eschenheimer: 1903
★ Eugen Eschenheimer: 1903

David's Maternal Cousin
★ Felix Peter Eschenheimer: 1936

Except where otherwise indicated, all documents are held in a consolidated family archive.

Main Narrators

Chaim de Zoete

Unpublished manuscript. "The Warning Dream." 1939.
Translated from Dutch by Mirjam Geismar.

Unpublished manuscript. "The Raid on the Breeplein
Church." 1947. Translated from Dutch by Marjolijn de Jager.

Letter to Mirjam, Judith, and Hadassah de Zoete.
January 14, 1950. Translated from Dutch by Marjolijn de Jager.

COMMEMORATION REQUESTS SUBMITTED TO YAD VASHEM,
THE RIGHTEOUS AMONG THE NATIONS DEPARTMENT,
JERUSALEM, ISRAEL

"Data Concerning the Family Saved." 1963.

Report on Hendrika (Riek) Dekkers. September 30, 1963.

Report on Gerrit and Gerda Brillenburg Wurth.
November 14, 1963.

Report on Jacobus (Hendrik) and Annigje (Anna) de Mars.
November 20, 1963.

Report on Jacob Groeneveld. November 28, 1963.

Report on Jan and Nan van Gelder. November 28, 1963.

Report on Petronella (Nel) van Vliet. December 2, 1963.

Report on Alida Wouters-van der Lely. December 4, 1963.

Report on C. and P. H. December 9, 1963.

Report on Hendrik and Jans van der Leer. December 30, 1963.

Report on Franciscus and Petronella Lafontaine.
January 5, 1964.

Report on Johanna Leepel-Labotz. January 5, 1964.

Report on Tjeerde and Antje Miedema. November 25, 1964.

Fifi Polak-de Zoete

Diary. March 21, 1937–September 29, 1941.
Translated from Dutch by Judith de Zoete-Cohen.

Diary entry. April 23, 1943.
Translated from Dutch by Marjolijn de Jager.

Diary. June 20, 1945–1963.
Translated from Dutch by Judith de Zoete-Cohen and
Marjolijn de Jager.

Mirjam de Zoete-Geismar

Note and drawing for Chaim and Fifi de Zoete. 1943.
Translated from Dutch by Mirjam de Zoete-Geismar.

Diary. January–February 1945.
Translated from Dutch by Mirjam de Zoete-Geismar and
Judith de Zoete-Cohen.

Unpublished hiding account. 1979.

Audiovisual testimony. Recorded for the Fortunoff Video
Archive for Holocaust Testimonies at Yale University.
New Haven, Connecticut. 1980.

Unpublished hiding and liberation account. N.d., ca. 1990s.

Audiovisual testimony. Recorded for the USC Shoah Foundation, Visual History Archive. Los Angeles, California. 1997.

Interview with Diane L. Wolf. University of California, Davis. June 2, 2000.

Correspondence with Judith de Zoete-Cohen. 2003.

Interview with Andrew Thomas. 2006.

Interview with Sharon Cohen-Strauss. 2007.

Email correspondence and conversations with Daphne Geismar. September 23, 2008; October 16, 2008; April 26, 2010; May 10, 2010; and August 2, 2013.

Letter to Chaja Sondak. 2011.

Judith de Zoete-Cohen
Unpublished hiding account. 2004.

Unpublished hiding account. 2005.

Interview with Sharon Cohen-Strauss. 2007.

Email correspondence with Daphne Geismar. May 8, 2015; June 18, 2015; and November 18, 2015.

Hadassah de Zoete-Mandel
Speech delivered at Breeplein Church, Rotterdam. November 11, 2006.

Unpublished hiding account. 2007.

Interview with Sharon Cohen-Strauss. 2007.

Nathan Cohen
Unpublished memoir. 2004.

Unpublished postwar account. 2007.

Erwin Geismar
Unpublished memoir. July 21–September 1943.
Translated from German by Robert Bjornson.

David Geismar
Audiovisual testimony. Recorded for the Fortunoff Video Archive for Holocaust Testimonies at Yale University. New Haven, Connecticut. 1980.

Unpublished hiding account. N.d., ca. 1990s.

Interview with Diane L. Wolf. University of California, Davis. June 2, 2000.

Castellano, Terry. "Holocaust Survivor Recounts Tales of Terror." *Weston Forum*, January 24, 2002.

Zigi Mandel
Letter to Mirjam and David Geismar. December 27, 1958.

Unpublished memoir. 2007.

Supporting Narrators

Grete Heinsheimer-Geismar
(David's mother; Erwin's wife)
Declarations of Oath. August 2, 1956, and September 2, 1969.
Translated from German by Robert Bjornson.

The Netherlands Red Cross. Letter to Grete Geismar.
April 10, 1946.
Translated from Dutch by Judith de Zoete-Cohen.

The Netherlands Red Cross. Letter to Grete Geismar.
June 6, 1968.
Translated from Dutch by Judith de Zoete-Cohen.

Chaja Polak
(Fifi's niece; Mirjam, Hadassah, and Judith's cousin)
Hiding account. December 23, 2017.

Isaak Cohen
(Nathan's father)
COMMEMORATION REQUESTS SUBMITTED TO YAD VASHEM, THE RIGHTEOUS AMONG THE NATIONS DEPARTMENT, JERUSALEM, ISRAEL

Report on Jo and Anne Bakker. December 6, 1964.
Translated from Hebrew by Noam Strauss.

Report on Theo and Betsy van Dalen. January 28, 1965.
Translated from Hebrew by Noam Strauss.

Hans (Zwi) Goldberg
(hidden with Mirjam)
Interview with Sharon Cohen-Strauss. 2013.

Ans and Dolf Vromen
(hidden with Mirjam)
Hiding account. 2005.

Sonja van Vliet
(helped her mother, Nel van Vliet, hide Mirjam)
Letter to Mirjam de Zoete-Geismar. July 20, 1997.

Dieter Heymann
(his mother, Erika Heymann, hid Erwin)
Email correspondence and conversations with Daphne Geismar. February 2, 2015, and June 8, 2016.

Hans (Chanan) Flörsheim
(hidden with Erwin)
"He Who Dares Wins: Across the Pyrenees to Freedom—1923–1944." N.d.
Translated by Dieter Heymann. http://www.hassia-judaica
.de/Lebenswege/English/Floersheim_Hans_Chanan
_English/ChananFloersheim_He_Who_Dares_Wins.pdf.
Previously published in German as *Über die Pyrenäen in die Freiheit: Von Rotenburg an der Fulda über Leipzig nach Amsterdam und durch Frankreich und Spanien nach Israel 1923–1944.* Edited by Heinrich Nuhn and Erhard R. Wiehn. Konstanz, Germany: Hartung-Gorre Verlag, 2007.

History Briefs

Robert Jan van Pelt & Jennifer Magee

The Breeplein Church

Located in Rotterdam, the monumental Breeplein Church was built in 1931 to serve both as an urban marker for the city and as a home for the local parish of the Reformed Churches in the Netherlands. The denomination, established in 1892, split from the dominant Dutch Reformed Church. The Reformed Churches in the Netherlands were against the social and theological liberalization supported by the Dutch Reformed Church, and instead held to a strict interpretation of Calvinist doctrine. A theologically, politically, and socially disciplined denomination, it had an outsize influence on the Netherlands in the late nineteenth and early twentieth centuries through the political Antirevolutionary Party created by the group's leader, Abraham Kuyper. In the 1930s, the denomination forbade the faithful to join the Nationaal-Socialistische Beweging, or NSB (Dutch Nazi Party). During the German occupation, the church leadership provided little moral leadership, but many members of the Reformed Churches engaged in resistance activities. The two most famous resistance newspapers, *Trouw* (*Fidelity*) and *Vrij Nederland* (*Free Netherlands*), emerged from this community.

The Dutch East Indies

Between 1815, when the Netherlands was recognized by the representatives of the Great Powers assembled in Vienna, and 1914, when the political order established a century earlier collapsed, the Netherlands was classified as a European state of the second rank. As such, it pursued a policy of non-attachment versus the five major European powers: Russia, Britain, France, Germany, and Austria-Hungary. Yet in the Dutch imagination, the Netherlands was superior to the other second-rank states, such as Italy and Spain, and in some ways even to Germany and Austria-Hungary, because of its vast colonies in the East. The history of the Dutch East Indies went back to 1595, when a Dutch fleet sailed east to take control of the lucrative spice trade hitherto controlled by the Portuguese. In the two centuries that followed, the Vereenigde Oost-Indische Compagnie, or VOC (United East India Company)—the first public company listed at a stock exchange—established trading posts in the Malay Archipelago, bringing great wealth to its shareholders. In 1796, the Dutch government nationalized the VOC, transforming its holdings on Java, Sumatra, Borneo, Sulawesi, and the other islands into a proper colony. In the nineteenth century, the economy of the main island, Java, was made to serve the needs of the Dutch economy, imposing a great burden on the local population. The Dutch suppressed the resulting resistance to colonial rule. By the twentieth century, a policy of economic exploitation had morphed into a more enlightened one that envisioned a full emancipation of the Dutch East Indies as an equal partner of the Netherlands within a single state. This project, which was practically contradicted by the rigid social order that separated the small Dutch colonial population (200,000) from the native populations (60 million), collapsed as the result of the Japanese occupation of the East Indies in 1942.

Zwarte Piet

Since the nineteenth century, Netherlanders of every denomination, and also non-believers, have celebrated Sinterklaas on December 5, the eve of the Roman Catholic feast day of Saint Nicholas. Unlike the church-sanctioned observance, the secular Dutch version celebrates the journey of a white-bearded bishop, Sinterklaas, from Spain to the Netherlands to deliver goodies to well-behaved children. Sinterklaas is assisted by a dark-skinned boy named Zwarte Piet, or Black Pete. In recent years, the story of Sinterklaas and its accompanying festivities have come under fire for the figure of Zwarte Piet, who is seen by many as a racist caricature of a black slave.

The Committee for Jewish Refugees

In 1933, due to the growing numbers of Jewish refugees arriving in the Netherlands from Germany, the well-known entrepreneur Abraham Asscher and the academic David Cohen founded the Comité voor Joodse Vluchtelingen, or CJV (Committee for Jewish Refugees). It provided relief services for Jewish asylum seekers from Germany, helping them to secure visas and tickets for passage to countries of refuge and providing financial assistance to those who remained in the Netherlands and were unable to support themselves. After the German occupation of the Netherlands, the committee was forced to disband in 1941; its activities were taken over by the Joodse Raad (Jewish Council) of Amsterdam, co-chaired by Asscher and Cohen.

Relations between Dutch Jews and German Jews

The great majority of Dutch Jews were poor, while the majority of German Jews who arrived in the Netherlands in the 1930s had middle- or upper-middle-class backgrounds. Many of them had to survive in the Netherlands on the charity of the Dutch Jewish community. To cope with the humiliation, they would often remind their Dutch brethren that, back in Germany, they had been important. Sadly this defense mechanism won little sympathy from their Dutch cousins, who interpreted it as a denigration of Dutch Jews, of the Dutch Jewish community, and of the Netherlands.

Antisemitism in the Prewar Netherlands

While antisemitism did not shape the attitudes of non-Jewish Netherlanders to their Jewish neighbors, it became a political issue when, in the late 1930s, the Nationaal-Socialistische Beweging, or NSB (Dutch Nazi Party), began to adopt a partially antisemitic platform in order to fall in line with developments in Germany. The NSB, established in 1931, was originally modeled on Italian fascism, which did not blame the Jews for every political, social, or economic ill. But the changing geopolitical situation in the mid-1930s, with Germany ascendant under a National Socialist dictatorship led by Adolf Hitler, caused the NSB to realign itself from Rome to Berlin. In the early 1920s, the Nationalsozialistische Deutsche Arbeiterpartei (National Socialist German Workers' Party), or Nazi Party, had adopted a radical form of antisemitism as a core element of its worldview, calling

for the expulsion of Jews from German society. After the Nazis' ascent to power in 1933, the German government had initiated such a policy of expulsion without articulating where the German Jews might go. In 1938, in an attempt to become a serious player in the eyes of Berlin, Dutch NSB chief Anton Adriaan Mussert developed a plan to resettle European Jews overseas in a Joods Nationaal Tehuis (Jewish National Home) that consisted of British Guiana, Suriname, and French Guiana. At the same time, the NSB closed its ranks to Jewish Netherlanders.

The Invasion and Partition of Poland

On August 23, 1939, German foreign minister Joachim von Ribbentrop and Soviet foreign minister Vyacheslav Molotov signed a non-aggression pact that included a secret protocol preparing for the partition of Poland. On September 1, Germany invaded Poland. Fulfilling their promise to defend Poland's borders, the United Kingdom and France declared war on Germany two days later. On September 17, the Soviet Union invaded Poland from the east. During the campaign, the German *Luftwaffe* (air force) bombed Polish cities, acts of terror against civilians that were proudly presented in German propaganda newsreels. Footage of German Stuka dive-bombers attacking Warsaw was also included in the weekly *Polygoon Journaal* shown in Dutch cinemas. On October 1, Warsaw capitulated, and the last Polish army unit surrendered five days later. Germany and the Soviet Union divided the country more or less evenly in terms of surface. The Soviet Union annexed the whole of its share, declaring its inhabitants Soviet citizens—a declaration many Poles rejected. Germany incorporated only half of the Polish territory it obtained into the Greater German Reich, offering citizenship only to those of German descent, and preparing for the expulsion of the ethnic Polish and Jewish population to the other half of its share of Poland. Designated "General Government," that area was to serve as a colony providing cheap labor for the Reich.

Soviet Deportations of Former Polish Citizens

After the annexation of eastern Poland into the Soviet Union, Moscow initiated a policy to quickly integrate the local economy and its inhabitants into the Communist system. Businesses and farms were nationalized, and the labor force was reorganized to fit the planned economy. Many poor people accepted seemingly attractive job offers in the old Soviet Union. Bitterly disappointed on their arrival, they returned without permission to their former homes—a crime under Soviet law. Hundreds of thousands of Polish refugees, many Jewish, had crossed from the German-controlled General Government territory into the Soviet area, but they refused to accept Soviet citizenship, which would preclude any future return to their homes and require a permanent separation from family members who had remained behind. In the late spring of 1940, Moscow decided to deport the Poles who had violated Soviet laws and those who were considered unreliable—which included all the refugees who had not become Soviet citizens—to the Arctic region of

European Russia, Siberia, or the Soviet republics of central Asia. There they were put to work in often terrible conditions, without proper shelter, clothing, or food. Typhoid, tuberculosis, dysentery, malaria, and accidents on the job decimated the exiles. Paradoxically, for those Jews among the exiles who survived this ordeal, the deportation of 1940 proved a blessing in disguise: they were out of reach when, in the summer of 1941, Germany broke its non-aggression pact of August 1939 as German forces overran the Soviet part of Poland. Special murder battalions soon followed and began to massacre Jewish men, women, and children.

The Polish-Soviet Agreement of 1941
The German invasion of the Soviet Union prompted the Soviet government and the Polish government in exile, now both at war with Germany, to establish diplomatic relations. That, in turn, led to the amnesty and release of Polish exiles in the Arctic, who were now officially placed under Polish diplomatic protection. The agreement also stipulated that Polish prisoners of war in Soviet captivity—those who had survived the murder of 20,000 of them by Soviet security forces in 1940—were to join the newly established Polish armed forces in the East. This army was to fight the Germans in alliance with the Red Army. The collaboration between what came to be known as Anders's Army, named after its commander, General Władysław Albert Anders, and the Soviet forces proved difficult. Facing the continuing assault by the Germans, the Red Army had few resources to share, and Moscow's insistence that only those Poles of Polish ethnic descent (and not those of Ukrainian, Belarusan, or Jewish descent) could enlist in Anders's Army led to an early breakdown in the collaboration. In March 1942, the Soviet, Polish, and British governments decided on what was both a practical and face-saving solution: the almost 79,000 soldiers of Anders's Army would be redeployed to strengthen the British forces in the Middle East. Its journey to its new base in Mandatory Palestine passed through Mashdad in Iran, which became a major collection and transfer point. Some 37,000 Polish civilians who had been amnestied followed Anders's Army: they included family members of the soldiers but also many unaccompanied children, including a thousand Jewish orphans. When the men of Anders's Army arrived in Palestine, the small number of Jewish soldiers who had been allowed to enlist, mostly medical personnel, left the force with the tacit approval of their commanders. Their experience proved useful in the Haganah and Irgun militias (Jewish paramilitary organizations in Mandate Palestine). The Jewish orphans were only given permission to enter Palestine in early 1943.

The Invasion of the Netherlands
Despite the scrupulous policy of the Dutch government to maintain the Netherlands' neutrality, the Germans launched a surprise attack on the country on May 10, 1940, as part of its *Blitzkrieg* (lightning war) against the Netherlands, Belgium, Luxembourg, and France. A large airborne operation to conquer The Hague, residence of the Dutch queen and the seat of government, and the Rotterdam harbor heightened the panic of the Dutch population, as 2,000 German paratroopers and 12,000 airborne soldiers were flown in by aircraft and gliders that landed on highways. On May 13, the Germans broke through the defensive lines at the Grebbeberg, and Queen Wilhelmina left the country on a British destroyer. Now crowds that included non-Jews who had spoken up against Nazism and Jews who feared an immediate pogrom, and who had heard a rumor that special ships had been chartered to evacuate Jews to England, assembled in various ports—most importantly the harbor of IJmuiden, which was in easy reach of Amsterdam. Only 3,000 secured passage on departing ships before May 14, when the Royal Netherlands Army, in an attempt to frustrate any future use of the port by the German navy, scuttled an ocean liner in the IJmuiden harbor as a blockship.

The Bombing of Rotterdam and the Capitulation of the Dutch Army
Planning their May 1940 attack on the Netherlands, the Germans expected that the Dutch would surrender within a day or two. Key to the success of this schedule was the quick occupation of The Hague by means of the airborne operation, which had been personally planned by Hitler. Successful Dutch resistance led to the failure of this attack; paratroopers and airborne soldiers dropped and landed near The Hague were captured, and those dropped in Rotterdam were contained in a bridgehead. Enraged, Hitler ordered on May 13 that the Dutch defenses be broken using maximum force. A day later, German bombers dropped 106 tons of bombs on the historic center of Rotterdam, destroying it completely; between 650 and 900 people were killed, and 80,000 became homeless. An ultimatum followed: if the Dutch did not capitulate, Utrecht would suffer the same fate. With most of the Dutch Army Aviation Brigade shot down and no air defenses around Utrecht, the commander in chief of the Dutch armed forces, General Henri Winkelman, decided on capitulation.

Reichskommissar Arthur Seyss-Inquart
Born in the Czech part of the Austro-Hungarian Empire, Arthur Seyss-Inquart grew up in Vienna. He served as a soldier in World War I and became an active member of the outlawed Nazi Party in the Republic of Austria, established in 1918, which sought unification of Austria with the German Reich. Seyss-Inquart became chancellor of Austria on March 11, 1938, and during the two days that he was in office he played the key role in the *Anschluss* uniting the two countries on March 13. His appointment as Reichskommissar (Reich commissioner) in the Netherlands, which took effect on May 29, 1940, was his reward. During the five years of Nazi rule in the Netherlands, Seyss-Inquart consistently violated the Law of War, codified in the 1907 Hague Agreement. He allowed for the systematic plunder of the Dutch economy, oversaw the shooting of hostages, and facilitated the forced labor of 250,000 Dutch workers in Germany. He also enforced the isolation and expropriation

of the Jews and the deportation of 105,000 of them to Sobibor, Auschwitz, and the other camps. Arrested in May 1945, he was tried in Nuremberg, convicted of crimes against humanity, and executed in October 1946.

The Dunkirk Evacuation

Germany's quick and violent onslaught on the Netherlands, Belgium, Luxembourg, and France forced British, French, and some Belgian troops in northern France to retreat to the coastal town of Dunkirk. Between May 26 and June 4, 1940, a motley fleet of warships, fishing vessels, and sailing boats delivered 338,000 soldiers across the English Channel to safety in what Winston Churchill, the British prime minister, so memorably called "a miracle of deliverance, achieved by valor, by perseverance, by perfect discipline, by faultless service, by resource, by skill, by unconquerable fidelity."

The French-German Armistice

On June 14, 1940, the Germans arrived in Paris, which had been declared an "Open City" by the French government, meaning that it would not be defended. Eight days later, France surrendered and signed an armistice agreement in Compiègne at the same location where, in 1918, the armistice that ended the hostilities of World War I was signed. The ceasefire terms allowed the Germans to occupy the northern half of France. The French government relocated to the spa town of Vichy, located in an unoccupied part of the country, and decided on a formal policy of collaboration with Germany. While technically in charge of the whole of France, its actual authority was limited to the unoccupied region.

Radio Oranje and Radio Hilversum

After the fall of France, London became the last refuge of democracy in Europe, offering a home to the governments in exile of Poland, Norway, the Netherlands, Luxembourg, Belgium, Czechoslovakia, and the Free French Movement— and from 1941 onward, Greece and Yugoslavia. The BBC provided facilities to these governments to reach their captive citizens on the continent. Beginning July 28, 1940, the BBC aired a nightly fifteen-minute Dutch-language program called *Radio Oranje*. Despite German warnings not to do so, the majority of the Dutch population tuned in to *Radio Oranje* for their news, and listened to the German-controlled Dutch program *Nederlandse Omroep*, broadcast via Radio Hilversum, a public radio station located in the eponymous Dutch town, for entertainment only. In retaliation for the Dutch refusal to take Radio Hilversum seriously, the Germans sequestered all radio receivers in May 1943.

The Dutch Nazi Party

From the moment of the German invasion on May 10, 1940, the great majority of Dutchmen considered the generally pro-German members of the Nationaal-Socialistische Beweging, or NSB (Dutch Nazi Party), to be traitors. This is one of the reasons that the German proconsul in the Netherlands, Arthur Seyss-Inquart, did not give Anton Adriaan Mussert or other NSB leaders a role in his administration: too close

a relationship with the NSB would impede his quest to win the hearts and minds of the Dutch population. However, he took note of mayors who did not fully cooperate with the occupation regime and replaced them with members of the NSB, and also considered the NSB a ready pool of candidates for militarized Nazi organizations.

The SS

With the German occupation came not only German soldiers belonging to the *Wehrmacht* (armed forces) but also German officials wearing various uniforms that carried the insignia of the SS. The SS, short for Schutzstaffel, began as Hitler's personal bodyguard. In 1929, Heinrich Himmler became the head of the SS, and he transformed the paramilitary organization into the ideological avant-garde of the Nazi party that, through its internal intelligence operation, the Sicherheitsdienst, or SD (Security Service), also controlled the party. After 1933, Himmler had a steep ascent in the German state, acquiring control first over the Geheime Staatspolizei, or Gestapo (Secret State Police), then over the newly established Ordnungspolizei, or Orpo (Order Police), which unified the state, municipal, and rural police forces. Himmler consolidated his power within Germany when, in 1939, he merged the SD, Gestapo, and some other police departments into the Reichssicherheitshauptamt, or RSHA (Reich Main Security Office). Each time that Himmler expanded his authority over these police and intelligence organizations, he offered its officers the equivalent SS rank, while offering SS members positions within those organizations. The result was a dynamic symbiosis between the enforcement apparatus of the German state and the SS, which was energized by the convenient fact that another wing of the SS, the SS-Totenkopfverbände, or SS-TV (SS-Death's Head Units), had exclusive control over the concentration camps that allowed for the extrajudicial imprisonment of anyone. Most men wearing a uniform with SS insignia who had a function within the German occupation administration were officials of the RSHA, more specifically of its SD branch.

The Security Service Headquarters in Amsterdam

In 1940, the Sicherheitsdienst, or SD (Security Service), the Germans' principal intelligence organization in the Netherlands, sequestered a girls' high school in the Euterpestraat, a street in the Amsterdam neighborhood where Jewish refugees from Germany settled in the 1930s. The building, which faced a little square, acquired a sinister reputation because people arrested on suspicion of resistance activities were brought there for interrogation, along with Jews who had been discovered in hiding. In 1941, the Central Office for Jewish Emigration, which was a department of the SD, took possession of another high school on the opposite side of the little square. The two buildings became the nexus of German terror. After liberation, the Dutch renamed both the girls' high school and the Euterpestraat after Gerrit van der Veen, a Dutch artist who established the underground organization De Vrije

Kunstenaar (The Free Artist), published a newsletter calling for resistance, and produced—with the help of printer Frans Duwaer—some 80,000 false identity papers. He also led daring raids on the Amsterdam population registry to destroy records vital to the Final Solution (the German plan to annihilate the Jewish population), on the government printing office to obtain blank identity papers, and on a jail to liberate captured comrades. Found in hiding, Van der Veen was executed by a German firing squad.

The Green Police and Hanns Albin Rauter

German rule in 1940s Europe was supported by police battalions of the Ordnungspolizei, or Orpo (Order Police), which were dispatched to the occupied territories. In each occupied territory, the Orpo, often referred to as the Grüne Polizei (Green Police) because of their green uniforms, were under the control of Himmler's personal representative in that territory, the Höhere SS- und Polizeiführer, or HSSPF (Higher SS and Police Leader), a person who typically had the power of life and death over the civilian population and who proved key in carrying out the genocidal policies against the Jews and the Roma. The HSSPF in the Netherlands was Hanns Albin Rauter.

Underground Newspapers

With the German occupation of the Netherlands, the Dutch press was no longer free to report and discuss local and international news objectively. The Nazis' media censorship gave rise to a variety of so-called *ondergrondse* (underground) publications. An estimated 1,200 clandestine periodicals, ranging from handwritten bulletins to professionally produced newspapers, appeared during the occupation, some only for a very short time. Publishing these papers came with grave risks: the Germans arrested, convicted, and executed many involved in the underground press.

The Great Surrender

When the Dutch government left for London, they left the country in the hands of the commander in chief of the armed forces, General Henri Winkelman, who was to govern the Netherlands with the help of the secretaries-general who ran the government ministries. After the capitulation, the Germans removed General Winkelman, leaving the secretaries-general—efficient bureaucrats who always had loyally served their political masters—without a boss and without guidance. At the end of May, they accepted Reichskommissar Arthur Seyss-Inquart as their new boss, trusting that he would govern in accordance with the 1907 Hague Convention. This convention, which codified the laws of war, stipulated, among other things: "The authority of the legitimate power having in fact passed into the hands of the occupant, the latter shall take all the measures in his power to restore, and ensure, as far as possible, public order and safety, while respecting, unless absolutely prevented, the laws in force in the country," and "Family honor and rights, the lives of persons, and private property, as well as religious convictions and practice, must be

respected." In August 1940, Seyss-Inquart issued a decree giving him the power to dismiss civil servants at will. The secretaries-general did not protest, despite the fact that it violated an important right enjoyed by civil servants. In September, the Germans asked for a list of all public servants who were wholly or partly Jewish. The secretaries-general ought to have refused this, as the Dutch Constitution explicitly did not allow limiting a person's rights on the basis of religion. Instead they instructed all on the payroll of the state, the Dutch provinces, and municipalities to declare whether or not they had Jewish grandparents and, if so, how many. Almost all in the pay of the three levels of government complied. An attempt to support the few who refused making the declaration failed when the Dutch Supreme Court ruled that no legal basis existed for refusal. Subsequently, all those who were defined as Full Jews—those with three or four Jewish grandparents—were dismissed from their posts. The secretaries-general went along, grudgingly, in the interest of "public order and safety." From that moment onward, Seyss-Inquart knew that he had been given a free hand to dispose of the Jews.

The Census

In early 1941, a Jews-only census sorted the Jewish population in the Netherlands, including both Dutch citizens and foreigners, into "Full Jews" (140,522), "Half Jews" (14,549), and "Quarter Jews" (5,719). Interestingly, the number defined by the Germans as Full Jews—that is, those with three or four Jewish grandparents, or Half Jews who were married to a Jew, or Half Jews who belonged to a synagogue—was equal to the number of Halachic Jews—those who are counted as Jewish according to the Halacha, or Jewish tradition. (A Halachic Jew is a child of a Jewish mother, or a grandchild of a Jewish maternal grandmother who is not a member of a non-Jewish religious community.) Of these, the so-called Full Jews and Half Jews—or 155,000 people—would face direct persecution, with varying intensity: while 350 Half Jews, or 2 percent of the target group, were murdered by the Germans as part of the Final Solution, 105,000 Full Jews, or 75 percent, lost their lives as a result of the persecution. In the year 2000, the Dutch government decided that the survivors classified in 1941 as Full Jews and Half Jews were eligible for material and moral compensation.

The First German Raid on Jews

On February 10, 1941, forty members of the uniformed militia of the Weerbaarheidsafdeling, or WA (paramilitary arm of the Dutch Nazi Party), staged a march through Amsterdam's Jewish quarter and randomly attacked its inhabitants. The locals defended the neighborhood, and one of the WA men, Hendrik Koot, was mortally wounded. In retaliation, 600 German police officers sealed off the Jewish quarter and rounded up 427 young Jewish men to be sent to an internment camp in Schoorl, then deported, via Buchenwald, to the Mauthausen concentration camp, where all of them were murdered within weeks after their arrival.

Mauthausen Concentration Camp

In 1938, the SS established a concentration camp near the Austrian town of Mauthausen, adjacent to a granite quarry. The camp's conditions were deplorable: many prisoners were worked to death; sick inmates were left to die from exposure; many were beaten or shot; and German doctors used prisoners in medical experiments, one of which involved removing a person's essential organs to see how long he could survive. Conditions were so appalling that a number of captives jumped to their deaths from the quarry's cliffs. All 1,300 Jews from the Netherlands who were taken to Mauthausen between February 1941 and the beginning of regular deportations in July 1942 perished at the camp within a short time after their arrival. In 1942, the threat of Mauthausen, which Dutch Jews knew to be a death sentence, made many of them comply with orders for deportation to Westerbork, which proved to be an anteroom to Auschwitz and Sobibor. The Gestapo official in charge of deportations, Adolf Eichmann, once observed that in the Netherlands, "the transports ran so smoothly, it was a joy to watch them."

The February Strike

Appalled by the Germans' cruel treatment of the Jews following the first raid, Dutch civilians participated in a strike organized by the Communist Party that effectively shut down much of the infrastructure of Amsterdam—docks, factories, streetcars, and almost all public services—in February 1941. The strike buoyed the spirits of many Jews, but the resistance was short lived: the Germans informed the Joodse Raad (Jewish Council) that more Jews would be arrested unless the strike came to a swift end. The Jewish Council now pleaded with the strikers to return to work. At the same time, the Germans decided on a big show of force, killing dozens in shootings and arresting hundreds in mass raids. After two days, the strike was quelled; the city returned to work.

Dutch Accommodation

Despite the legendary proportions that the February Strike assumed in postwar Dutch national memory, the great majority of non-Jewish Netherlanders were not concerned with the fate of their Jewish neighbors during the first three years of the German occupation. Part of their indifference can be explained by the pillar structure of Dutch society, which tended to limit one's social relations to people within one's own pillar. In addition, the German occupation initially produced a general economic upswing. Due to the austerity policy of the Depression-era Dutch government, unemployment remained high throughout the 1930s, and the forced integration of the Dutch economy into the German one, which was overheated during wartime, meant a return to full employment. By early 1941, it appeared that the policy and attitude of accommodation served the self-interest of the Dutch. However, the separation from the wealth of the Dutch East Indies (occupied by Japan beginning in 1942) and the cessation of American investment led the economy to slow by the middle of 1941. In 1942, a rapid economic decline began due to the forced labor of an ever-growing number of

Dutch men in Germany and the requisition, with "payment" in worthless IOUs, of an ever-larger part of Dutch industrial production to support the German war effort. By early 1943, the Dutch GDP was half that of 1938. The Germans were by now very unpopular, and sympathy for their primary victims, the Jews, increased. But it was too late to matter to the majority of Dutch Jews, as they had already been deported and murdered.

The Jewish Council

In February 1941, the Germans established the Joodse Raad (Jewish Council) for Amsterdam, appointing Abraham Asscher and David Cohen, who had previously jointly run the Comité voor Joodse Vluchtelingen, or CJV (Committee for Jewish Refugees), to lead it. Both men believed they could expand the charitable work done in the CJV through the Jewish Council. The Germans immediately began using the council as a means to control first the Jews of Amsterdam and soon thereafter all Jews in the Netherlands. A major tool was the *Joodsche Weekblad* (*Jewish Weekly*). Published by the council to communicate German orders to the Jews, it was the only Jewish publication allowed during the occupation. As Jews were expropriated, the Jewish Council tried to preserve basic living conditions. It never took a principled stand against the German measures, believing that accommodation would allow them a residual measure of control. When the deportations began, the Germans granted the council 40,000 exemptions from deportation, to be issued by the council to people of its choice. The council accepted the deal and began to issue the exemptions to its own employees (and their families), to Jews who were employed in industries that were useful for the German war effort, and to those considered crucial for the reconstruction of the Dutch Jewish community after the war. The poor did not qualify. From time to time, categories of exemptions were canceled, and the council again faced the question of who was too important or useful to be deported. Finally, in September 1943, the council itself was abolished, and the remaining 5,000 exemptions were annulled. Asscher and Cohen ended up in the Theresienstadt ghetto, which they survived. When confronted after the war with the catastrophic decision to go along with the policy of exemptions and the failure of the council to urge Jews to flee or go into hiding, Cohen justified the policy, stating that he and his colleagues had expected deportations to be relatively slow, that they thought the war would end soon, and that he honestly believed going along with the Germans would enable the council to save as many lives as possible.

The Central Office for Jewish Emigration

After the *Anschluss* (union) of Austria with the German Reich, Gestapo official Adolf Eichmann established in Vienna the Central Office for Jewish Emigration to streamline the expulsion of Austrian Jews. In 1939, he also established a similar operation in German-occupied Prague. In both cases, the Central Office was under the direct control of the Gestapo, which from 1939 onward was a branch of the Reichssicherheitshauptamt or RSHA (Reich Main Security Office), controlled by Reinhard Heydrich. From 1939 until his death in 1942, Heydrich was the architect of the Final Solution within Germany and in the German-occupied territories in the East. When Reichskommissar Arthur Seyss-Inquart gained control of the Netherlands, he chose to articulate his own policy to identify the Jews and push them out of the economy and civil society, and he did not coordinate with Heydrich. To assert his power and ensure a share of the loot, Heydrich established in 1941 a Central Office for Jewish Emigration in Amsterdam, which answered to him and not to Seyss-Inquart. Realizing that information was crucial, the Central Office established a comprehensive registry of all Jews, using the labor of employees of the Joodse Raad (Jewish Council) and data in the municipal registries. After the Wannsee Conference in January 1942, the Central Office, which was directly managed from Berlin by Adolf Eichmann, pushed Seyss-Inquart and his men to the sidelines; for all practical purposes, it was in charge of the final liquidation of the Dutch Jewish community by means of its registry, which informed arrests and deportations to the death camps.

Germany Invades the Soviet Union

On June 22, 1941, the German army invaded the Soviet Union. The attack, codenamed Operation Barbarossa, initially overwhelmed the Red Army, and by the late fall of 1941, the Germans were in view of Moscow and Leningrad. Just as collapse seemed certain, fresh reserves brought from Siberia and the onset of winter were enough to stop the German advance. The Soviet Union was saved—at least for the time being—but Soviet citizens in the German-occupied territories had to endure a very harsh occupation, while specially trained murder brigades and police battalions began to slaughter the Jewish population.

Jewish Symphony Orchestra

In the summer of 1941, Jewish musicians were pushed out of Dutch music academies and orchestras. The newly established Joods Symfonieorkest (Jewish Symphony Orchestra) provided seventy-five Jewish instrumentalists the opportunity to continue playing professionally in the Hollandse Schouwburg (Dutch Theater), a popular venue in the Jewish quarter of Amsterdam, which was renamed the Joodse Schouwburg (Jewish Theater). The orchestra was briefly allowed to play music of its choosing, but on German orders the repertoire was quickly limited to the works of Jewish composers, such as Mahler and Mendelssohn—music that non-Jewish orchestras were no longer allowed to perform. Few of the musicians who performed the Jewish symphony's inaugural program were alive by 1945.

Japan Attacks the United States

On the morning of December 7, 1941, hundreds of Japanese fighter planes swooped down over Hawaii's Pearl Harbor and bombed the US Pacific Fleet. The surprise attack killed more than 2,400 service members and civilians while destroying and severely damaging the American battleships and aircraft stationed at the naval base. In response, the United States declared war on Japan. Although Germany was also caught off guard by Japan's attack, Hitler was quick to declare war on the United States—an act he had promised Japan but had not yet formally agreed to under treaty. The United States reciprocated by issuing a declaration of war against Germany and Italy, the Germans' other major ally, thus fully drawing America into World War II. While the United States had been neutral, Hitler had treated the Jews of Western and Central Europe as hostages to ensure the neutrality of Washington. With the Americans on the side of Britain and the Soviet Union, those Jews had lost their utility, and were to be included in the genocide that had already begun in the German-occupied Soviet Union.

Japanese Occupation of the Dutch East Indies

In late 1941 and early 1942, Japan made significant advances throughout the Pacific: the Japanese attacked the Americans at Pearl Harbor, took control of Singapore from the United Kingdom, and defeated the Dutch navy in the Java Sea. The Japanese war machine needed natural resources to continue, making the resource-rich Dutch East Indies an ideal target to exploit—especially given that the Netherlands was occupied by Germany and unable to defend its territory. On March 1, 1942, the Japanese invaded the archipelago and remained in control until their surrender in August 1945. More than 100,000 Dutch civilians were sent to Japanese internment camps, and 40,000 Dutch military personnel became prisoners of war. Initially, Indonesians were buoyed by the occupation, believing the Japanese were liberating them from their colonizers. Instead, the occupation delivered death and suffering to the native population: 4 million Indonesians were forced into labor—180,000 of whom died due to terrible conditions—and an estimated 2.4 million inhabitants of Java, the Dutch East Indies' most populated island, starved to death.

The "Ghetto"

While closed ghettos existed from the 1940s onward in German-occupied Poland and, from 1941 onward, in the occupied parts of the Soviet Union, such places were not established in Western Europe. However, beginning in January 1942, Jews from various towns and rural regions in the Netherlands were forced to leave their homes and move to Amsterdam. There they were billeted with Jewish families, often in crowded conditions. Two neighborhoods in Amsterdam had a high concentration of Jews: the traditional Jewish quarter in the eastern part of the old city, and a newly constructed area in South Amsterdam. The former had a large proportion of poor inhabitants and was often referred to as the "ghetto."

The Jewish Star

On April 29, 1942, all Jews in the Netherlands were forced to wear a yellow Star of David on the left breast of the outermost layer of clothing. The star had already been imposed on Jews in Poland in the fall of 1939, and in the German Reich in the fall of 1941. Penalties for not following the order included a 1,000-guilder fine and imprisonment, with the possibility of a harsher punishment: execution. For a few days, a small number of non-Jewish Dutch citizens wore yellow stars to protest the order.

Westerbork

In 1939, prior to the German invasion of the Netherlands, the Dutch government built the Centraal Vluchtelingenkamp Westerbork (Central Refugee Camp Westerbork) to house Jewish refugees who had entered the Netherlands illegally. In October 1941, Reichskommissar Arthur Seyss-Inquart decided that Westerbork, which at that time had 1,100 inmates, would become an internment camp for all Jews in the Netherlands who did not have Dutch citizenship—some 20,000. However, it took until the early spring of 1942 before the first German Jews living elsewhere in the Netherlands were summoned to move to the camp. The Germans took full control over Westerbork on July 1, 1942, designating it as a police transit camp. This required the construction of many new barracks, a barbed-wire fence with guard towers, and a railway spur connecting the camp to the national railway system. The first train to Auschwitz left on July 15. In the next twenty-six months, passenger trains dispatched from Amsterdam, other towns, and a couple of internment camps brought 105,000 Jews and a few hundred Roma and Sinti to Westerbork. Ninety-three transports of freight wagons shuttled over 105,000 Jews from Westerbork to unknown destinations "in the East," which proved to be Auschwitz (58,380), the Sobibor extermination camp (34,313), the Theresienstadt ghetto (4,894), and Bergen-Belsen (3,751), with smaller numbers being sent to other camps. Of this group of deportees, only 5,500 survived the war. Compared to the eastern camps, Westerbork offered relatively tolerable conditions—especially to the original group of German Jewish refugees, who occupied positions of privilege and relative comfort in the camp, and who were generally shielded from deportation. The rest of the inmates faced the possibility of being loaded, without warning, onto the weekly train to the east. For almost all of them, that frightening possibility became a miserable reality between July 15, 1942, and September 13, 1944, when the last train left the camp.

The Dutch Theater

Officially known as the Joodse Schouwburg (Jewish Theater) since 1941, when it became the only legal theater where Jews could perform or attend concerts, the former Hollandse Schouwburg (Dutch Theater) was sequestered in the summer of 1942 to become a holding pen and deportation center for the Jewish population of Amsterdam. People who complied with orders to report at the theater, as well as those who were rounded up in raids, were detained there while their fate was determined. A small number of Jews were able to leave the theater if their exemptions proved to be valid, but most were sent from there to Westerbork. Because of the overcrowding in the theater, young children

were kept in a nursery across the street. Hundreds of them were smuggled out of the nursery via an adjacent teachers' college and brought to hiding places. In 1958, the Dutch Theater was designated a monument to the Holocaust in the Netherlands; together with the teachers' college, it would ultimately become the location of the National Holocaust Museum.

Looting and the Abraham Puls & Sons Moving Company

The Central Office for Jewish Emigration coordinated not only the arrest and deportation of Jews but also the plunder of the personal possessions left in their homes. It employed one of Amsterdam's largest moving companies, Abraham Puls & Sons. Puls had received the contract because of his membership in the Dutch Nazi Party. The sight of vans lettered A. PULS loading up furniture outside of empty Jewish homes was so common that *pulsen* became a Dutch verb synonymous with looting. The bulk of the stolen goods was shipped to Germany, although many possessions, including homes, were given to Germans living in the Netherlands.

Flight Options

When the deportations began, Jewish families had to weigh their options: obey the summons and hope for the best, try to obtain an exemption, or go into hiding. Very few considered a fourth option: flight to a neutral country such as Sweden, Switzerland, or Spain, or to Great Britain. A journey to any of these countries was very difficult at best and impossible for families with children. The North Sea stood between the Dutch coast and England, and Germany blocked the road to Sweden. While Dutch refugees seeking safety might find sympathy and support from Belgians and the French, the practical reality was that borders between the Netherlands, Belgium, France, Switzerland, and Spain were sealed, and everywhere police checked papers of those who were traveling by train or bus—private cars had ceased to operate as a result of the lack of gasoline—or who were staying in hotels or other lodgings. Nevertheless, some 4,000 Dutch Jews embarked on these clandestine journeys. Neither trained in covert missions, nor necessarily physically fit, nor equipped with gear for a long mountain hike through the Jura or the Pyrenees in inclement weather, around 1,500 were caught before reaching the Swiss or Spanish border, or were sent back into occupied France by Swiss border guards. However, a small number of clandestine networks evolved to provide help. The largest one, the Dutch-Paris network, involved 300 helpers and *passeurs* who smuggled people over the borders. One-third of the 2,500 Dutch Jews who successfully reached Switzerland or Spain were aided by the Dutch-Paris network.

Rewards for Turning in Jews

For each hidden Jew turned over to the Germans, informants would receive a reward of between 5 and 7.5 guilders. The Germans increased the reward significantly near the end of the war, and informants were paid as much as 40 guilders for each Jew they betrayed, which represented two weeks' wages for an unskilled laborer. Dutch Nazi collaborators were eager to claim the bounty, and the reward also inspired the founding of the Henneicke Column, a group of men who made their living hunting Jews in the Netherlands. Most of the thousands of hidden Jews they exposed were subsequently murdered in the Germans' death camps. Nazi moles also frequently exposed Dutch people who were hiding Jews.

Punishment Cases

Jews in hiding who were discovered were sent to Westerbork as *strafgevallen* (punishment cases), and typically they were placed on the next train to Auschwitz or Sobibor: for them there were no exemptions. Of course, when the trains arrived at the final destination, it did not make any difference if one arrived as a regular deportee who had obeyed the German summons, or as a punishment case: the SS physician who conducted the selection in Auschwitz didn't know and didn't care, and decided on the basis of one's perceived utility: who would live and could work for a bit longer, and who should be murdered immediately. In Sobibor, there was no formal selection, and almost all were murdered on arrival.

Apeldoornse Bos

Founded in 1909, Apeldoornse Bos was a Jewish psychiatric hospital with an official capacity of 500 patients. Situated next to a large forest in Apeldoorn, the hospital also cared for troubled and/or neglected youth. In 1941 and 1942, the population—both inmates and personnel—tripled, not only because Jewish patients were expelled from other institutions and needed a place to stay but also because Apeldoornse Bos was considered a safe place for elderly Jews. And as Jews were excluded from the Dutch economy, the hospital became, with the Joodse Raad (Jewish Council), one of the few places where Jews could be employed. During the night of January 21–22, 1943, the SS and German police raided the hospital, forcing all 1,200 patients and 50 caregivers into trucks that delivered them to the Apeldoorn railway station, where a deportation train awaited them. It brought them straight to Auschwitz, where all were murdered on arrival. The remaining caregivers were sent to Westerbork to be deported a few weeks later.

German Forces Surrender at Stalingrad

The battle for control of Stalingrad, a major industrial and transportation hub strategically located on the Volga River, began in August 1942. The largest military confrontation in World War II, engaging over 2.2 million soldiers, it also was one of the bloodiest, with around 2 million casualties, and it proved decisive. In November, the Red Army surrounded the German Sixth Army, which had been given explicit orders not to retreat. Trapped in the ruined city, the Germans continued to fight until their surrender, violating Hitler's orders, on February 2, 1943. If, in the words of Winston Churchill, the German defeat in November 1942 at El Alamein marked "the end of the beginning," the German defeat in Stalingrad was generally perceived to be "the beginning of the end."

Vught Concentration Camp

In August 1942, the commander of the SS and German police in the Netherlands, Hanns Albin Rauter, established a concentration camp near the city of 's-Hertogenbosch in southern Holland. The official name was Konzentrationslager Herzogenbusch, but it was popularly known as the Vught camp because it was located in the Vught municipality. The camp consisted of two parts: the larger one, classified as a *Judenauffangslager* (reception camp for Jews), was to serve the Final Solution by accommodating and employing Jewish diamond workers and laborers in the armament industries who had exemptions from deportation to the east; the smaller part was to be a regular concentration camp for non-Jewish Dutchmen. The camp was designed to hold 7,000 inmates. It opened in January 1943, was evacuated in September 1944, and liberated by the Canadians in October 1944. Some 31,000 people, including 12,000 Jews, were imprisoned in Vught during that time. At the beginning of May 1943, after the arrival of Jews from the provinces, it counted 8,600 Jewish inmates. Most of them stayed no more than a few months before their deportation. Around 1,500 remained during their employment with the Philips electronics company, which was headquartered in nearby Eindhoven. Compared to other concentration camps, mortality in Vught was relatively low: 329 prisoners were executed, and another 420 died as the result of starvation, disease, or mistreatment. These 749 fatalities do not include the almost 12,000 Jews who were murdered in Sobibor and Auschwitz after their forced sojourn in Vught.

April 23, 1943: All Jews Must Leave

An order given on April 13, 1943, required that all remaining Jews in the Netherlands had to be sent to the Vught concentration camp by April 23, with the exception of Jews living in Amsterdam. Clearing Jews from Dutch provinces was one of the Germans' final steps toward their goal of making the country *judenrein* (cleansed of Jews).

Raid on June 20, 1943

The June 20 raid in Amsterdam, one of the Germans' final razzias, caught the remaining Jewish residents in the city's south and east completely by surprise. Some 5,550 Jews were captured, and 5,524 of them arrived in Westerbork a day later, to be sent on to Sobibor in the weeks that followed. After June 20, only 14,000 Jews lived openly or semi-openly in the Netherlands. These included those whose racial status was still under investigation (3,000), those married to a non-Jewish partner (8,000), and the board and employees of the Joodse Raad, or Jewish Council (2,000).

Failed Bombing of the Fokker Airplane Factory

With approval from the Dutch government in exile, on July 17, 1943, American bomber planes flew over Amsterdam with the intention of striking the Fokker aircraft factory. They completely missed their target and dropped bombs on a residential neighborhood, killing more than 150 civilians and destroying almost as many buildings. The victims of the debacle included eleven children who were singing at a local church when the bomb struck.

Italian Surrender

Two months after the Allies cleared the German and Italian armies from North Africa in May 1943, they invaded Sicily. This prompted the ousting of the Fascist Party, the arrest of Benito Mussolini, and the establishment of a new government under Marshal Pietro Badoglio. He signed an armistice with the Allies, who invaded the Italian mainland in early September. The Germans, meanwhile, formally occupied the part of Italy under their control, freed Mussolini, and put him in charge of the German client state known as the Repubblica Sociale Italiana (Italian Social Republic)—better known as the Republic of Salò, after the town where Mussolini lived in semi-forced residence.

Food Rationing

Before the German occupation of the Netherlands in May 1940, the Dutch recognized the threat of war and established a rationing system. Distribution cards were issued to Dutch residents, and as of October 1939, sugar could only be purchased with an official voucher. The Nazis understood that food was central to sustaining a healthy population and economy, and following the German invasion, Reichskommissar Arthur Seyss-Inquart established an office to oversee the Dutch food supply.

Rationing was quickly scaled up, and by June 1940, bread, flour, coffee, and tea were limited; butter, meat, cheese, and eggs were added to the voucher system by the end of the year. In April 1941, milk and potatoes were included on the list of restricted foods, which continued to grow over the course of the war. Approved individuals received permits to raise livestock, but for every pig slaughtered, one's meat coupons were withheld for more than one year.

Those in hiding had no access to the official rations; they had to rely on food bought on the black market. Resistance organizations attempted to provide aid to those in hiding by raiding the offices of authorities charged with running the food supply. In 1944, due to the number of voucher thefts and distribution card forgeries, the Nazis introduced a new edition of ration cards, hoping to prevent hiders from receiving food.

Resistance Organizations and Workers

Apart from the general workers' strike in February 1941, the German occupiers found the majority of Dutch citizens to be cooperative during the first three years of the occupation. This compliance made the work of a relatively small and dedicated number of Dutch citizens resisting the German occupation that much more significant—and risky. Opposition to the occupation came in many forms, through organized and spontaneous acts that included publishing illegal newspapers, espionage, assassinating key Dutch National Socialists, and concealing 28,000 Jewish and over 300,000 non-Jewish *onderduikers* (people in hiding)—though by the end of the war, 13,000 of the

Jewish *onderduikers* would be betrayed. Some 45,000 individuals, many of whom were Calvinists and Catholics, participated in the underground movement, although there is no exhaustive postwar inventory of participants or groups. Two of the largest organized resistance groups— the Landelijke Organisatie voor Hulp aan Onderduikers, or LO (National Organization for Assistance to the Hiders) and the Landelijke Knokploegen (National Action Groups)— were largely focused on assisting people in hiding. More than 10,000 Dutch resistance workers were killed during the war.

The Oranjehotel

Shortly after Germany occupied the Netherlands, the Sicherheitsdienst, or SD (Security Service), claimed a jail in the Dutch seaside town of Scheveningen to hold captive members of the resistance. The facility, officially the Polizeigefängnis Scheveningen (Scheveningen Police Prison), held an average of 1,200 to 1,500 prisoners and a total of 28,000 people between 1940 and 1945. The Dutch commonly referred to it as the Oranjehotel, referring both to the House of Orange—the Dutch royal dynasty—and the notion that a sojourn in the jail was a token of honor. Detention at the Oranjehotel was typically short term. Many prisoners were transferred to concentration camps, and 215 were sentenced to death in a summary court located in the jail and executed in the adjacent dunes. While some 734 prisoners died in the jail, the story that prisoners were shot to make space for newcomers is not supported by evidence.

D-Day

On June 6, 1944, more than 150,000 Allied troops, supported by 7,000 ships and boats and 11,000 aircraft, landed on the coast of Normandy in German-occupied France. The largest amphibian military operation ever undertaken succeeded in creating a beachhead that led, in 1944, to the liberation of France and, in 1945, in coordination with the Red Army's advance from the east, to the defeat of Germany.

The Battle for Brittany

After the Allied success in Normandy on D-Day, the Allies' offensive strategy was to push east toward Germany, while some American troops were sent west to secure the ports of Brittany in August 1944. With control of Brittany's harbors, the Allies expected to facilitate the delivery of supplies for the expeditionary force. Bitter fighting ensued in Saint-Malo and Brest, but the Germans surrendered after prolonged sieges.

V-2 Rocket Testing

The Germans developed two long-range, unmanned *Vergeltungswaffen* (vengeance weapons), the V-1 and V-2. The V-2 was a ballistic rocket that carried a 1,600-pound warhead designed by the German physicist Werner von Braun, and was first launched as part of a military operation on September 8, 1944. Its launch site was in the Dutch town of Wassenaar, its target London. Before the war's end, Germany launched more than 3,000 V-2s, primarily targeting Great Britain and Belgium. Technologically brilliant, the V-2 proved to be strategically useless. After the war, Von Braun was granted amnesty in exchange for advancing the United States' ballistic missile program.

The Liberation of Southern Holland

Operation Market Garden brought Allied soldiers to the southern Dutch province of Limburg on September 12, 1944. After the soldiers secured the region and proceeded with their mission to clear a pathway into Germany through the Netherlands, residents of Limburg were soon flying Dutch flags. The arrival of Allied soldiers marked the beginning of liberation for the Netherlands, even though Operation Market Garden did not succeed in creating a path for invading Germany, and much of the Netherlands remained under German occupation until April and May 1945.

Operation Market Garden

Operation Market Garden, September 17–25, 1944, was the Allies' risky plan to close in on the Germans. Paratroopers were to secure key bridges in the occupied Netherlands, with ground troops pushing northward to relieve these pockets of control, creating a pathway into northern Germany. Although the mission succeeded in liberating a portion of the southern Netherlands, it ultimately was a strategic failure due to bad weather and the surprise presence of SS Panzer Divisions near the final bridge, at Arnhem.

The Hunger Winter

In September 1944, the Dutch government in exile called on the employees of the Dutch Railways to strike in support of Operation Market Garden. After the defeat of the Allies at Arnhem, the strike continued, leading to a collapse of food supplies to the western Netherlands, which remained under German control. This resulted in the Hunger Winter. Shortages of fuel amplified the hardships. By February 1945, the official daily food ration provided just 350 calories, and widespread famine ultimately killed some 20,000 people.

The Battle of the Bulge

Hitler was bent on retaking ground lost to the Allies, and in late 1944, he set his sights on the dense forests and rugged hills in eastern Belgium. This region, the Ardennes, was only lightly held by American troops. On the morning of December 16, the German counteroffensive began driving toward Antwerp, thus cutting off major supply lines of the Allied Expeditionary Force and forcing the surrender of hundreds of thousands of soldiers. Using army units moved from the eastern front, the Germans pushed a large pocket into the Allied lines, which gave the operation its name: the Battle of the Bulge. The battle raged for a month in freezing temperatures and claimed 150,000 casualties. However, in January 1945, the Allies regained the military initiative and launched the final assault on the Reich.

The Liberation of the Netherlands

Although southern parts of the Netherlands were freed in September of 1944 during the largely unsuccessful Operation Market Garden, the Germans still held a vital crossing at the Rhine River, leaving the rest of the country in the war's final, desperate grip, suffering from famine and a bitterly cold winter. The First Canadian Army fought a prolonged battle against the Germans; in March 1945, they succeeded in driving the Germans out of the region between the Maas and Rhine Rivers. The Canadians continued their push to liberate the Netherlands and freed the cities of Amsterdam, Rotterdam, and The Hague. On May 5, Germany capitulated to Canada. Two days later, the Germans formally surrendered to the Allies, and World War II in Europe officially ended on May 8, 1945.

Operation Manna and Operation Chowhound

At the tail end of World War II in Europe, the Allies struck a deal with German authorities to allow humanitarian aid to reach millions of starving Dutch civilians. Great Britain began Operation Manna on April 29; the United States launched Operation Chowhound on May 1. Hundreds of low-flying Royal Air Force and US Air Force bombers dropped food packages at pre-established locations secured by Dutch volunteers. Food was distributed to the general population by means of the existing rationing system. These relief efforts delivered more than 11,000 tons of food to the starving Dutch.

The Fate of Dutch Jews

Fewer than 50,000 out of the 155,000 Dutch Jews and German Jewish refugees in the Netherlands were alive by May 1945. These included roughly 15,000 Jews who had survived in hiding, 3,000 Jews whose racial status was still under investigation, 1,000 Jews who were liberated from captivity in Westerbork and other places in the Netherlands, 7,800 Jews who survived because of their marriage to a non-Jewish partner, 5,500 Jews who were repatriated from the German camps, 2,000 Jews who returned from their places of refuge abroad, and more than 14,000 so-called Half Jews. Of the casualties, 99 percent were murdered outside of the Netherlands, in German-occupied Poland, or in Germany proper. Within the Netherlands, over 950 Jews died violent deaths: 500 at the hands of the Germans, and 452 as the result of suicide. With a fatality rate of 68 percent of the 155,000 combined Full and Half Jews as defined by the 1941 census, or 73 percent of the 140,000 Full Jews, Dutch Jewish losses were higher than average among European Jewry, which stood at 63 percent of the Jewish population overall.

Aliyah Bet and the SS *Exodus*

In 1922, the League of Nations gave Great Britain a Mandate for Palestine with the aim of "putting into effect the declaration originally made on November 2nd, 1917, by the Government of His Britannic Majesty, and adopted by the said Powers, in favor of the establishment in Palestine of a national home for the Jewish people, it being clearly understood that nothing should be done which might prejudice the civil and religious rights of existing non-Jewish communities in Palestine, or the rights and political status enjoyed by Jews in any other country." In consultation with the local Jewish Agency, British officials determined how many Jews were allowed to enter Mandatory Palestine each year based on the absorption capacity of the local economy. However, this proved more difficult than originally envisioned as a result of rising tensions and at times violent conflict between the Jewish and Arab inhabitants. In 1936—exactly at the time the need for a Jewish homeland became urgent—this system broke down when the Arab population began to revolt against the arrival of more Jews.

In 1939, the British government capitulated to Arab demands and limited Jewish immigration to 75,000 people over five years—effectively closing Palestine. Zionists responded by creating a program of illegal immigration called Aliyah Bet (Aliyah B) to distinguish it from the legal immigration known as Aliyah Aleph (Aliyah A). From 1939 to 1945, the Aliyah B program was modest in scope, but after the defeat of Nazi Germany there were thousands of Holocaust survivors who had nowhere to go. Between 1945 and May 1948, when Israel became an independent state, over 100,000 Jews packed in old ships tried to break the British blockade and reach Palestine. Over 50,000 were intercepted and interned by the British in camps in Cyprus or returned to Europe. Some 1,600 participants in the Aliyah B drowned. The most famous of the 142 maritime journeys to Palestine is the July 1947 voyage of the SS *Exodus*, a wreck of a ship carrying 4,500 Holocaust survivors. Violently intercepted by the British, it became a public relations disaster for the Mandatory power, hastening its decision to withdraw from Palestine as quickly as possible.

The Partition of Palestine and the State of Israel

After the end of World War II, Britain wished to exit the territory of Palestine and return the Mandate to the League of Nations' successor, the United Nations. On November 29, 1947, the United Nations voted to partition Palestine into two states: one Jewish, one Arab. In Palestine, the Jews accepted the UN decision, but the Arabs rejected it, as did Arabs outside of Palestine. On May 14, 1948, the last day of the Mandate, Jewish leaders in Tel Aviv proclaimed the state of Israel.

Indonesia

The Netherlands emerged from World War II hungry, traumatized, and poor. The Dutch soon faced another conflict with the uprising of the native population in the Dutch Indies. The Japanese occupation had nurtured an already existing independence movement, and when Japan capitulated in 1945, the movement's leaders exploited the power vacuum and declared an independent unitary republic: Indonesia. When Dutch government officials and army units returned from abroad, along with the Dutch colonial population from Japanese internment camps, they did not attempt

to reestablish the prewar status quo, but aimed for a political solution that acknowledged the Dutch as stakeholders in the region and also safeguarded the rights of the many minority populations. The result was a confused four-year period of negotiations and agreements alternating with military engagements. In 1949, both sides agreed on a formal transfer of sovereignty over the archipelago to a federative state, the United States of Indonesia, which was to remain linked to the Netherlands in a confederation modeled on the British Commonwealth. In 1950, the United States of Indonesia was dissolved into a unitary republic as previously proclaimed in 1945; in 1956, Indonesia withdrew from the confederation.

Why Were So Many Dutch Jews Murdered?

In 1965, on the twentieth anniversary of the liberation of the Netherlands, Jacob Presser's *Ondergang* (later published in Britain as *Ashes in the Wind* and in the United States as *The Destruction of the Dutch Jews*) appeared. The first full history of the Holocaust in the Netherlands quickly became a best seller. In an era that affirmed the virtue of civil disobedience, non-Jewish Netherlanders began to ask themselves uncomfortable questions about their passivity during the Holocaust. A generation later, historians began to investigate why the mortality rate of Jews in the Netherlands—a country without a tradition of antisemitism—was two times that in neighboring Belgium (where many Jews were foreigners) and three times that in France (which had a history of antisemitism), while almost all Danish Jews were saved.

Did the fact that Jews in the Netherlands felt secure before 1940 make them passive and naive? Or did the day-to-day efficiency of the Joodse Raad (Jewish Council) blind the Jews under its control to the catastrophic implications of its accommodation with the Germans? Did the pillar structure of Dutch society limit non-Jews' awareness of or compassion for their Jewish neighbors? Or was their failure to resist the Nazis' persecution of Dutch Jews rooted in the Dutch Calvinist culture of obedience to authority—or simply rooted in fear? Might a collaborating Dutch government, like the Vichy regime in France, have steered its own course in the matter of the Jews, providing a brake on German intentions? Should we credit the Germans' success in annihilating the Netherlands' Jewish population to the ideological commitment of Reichskommissar Arthur Seyss-Inquart and his immediate collaborators? Can we attribute it to the great number of Sicherheitspolizei (German security police) in the Netherlands, in comparison to that in France, Belgium, and Denmark? Or was it the unique combination of all of the above that made the loss of life so enormous?

Further Reading

History of the Netherlands
Blom, Johan Cornelis Hendrik, and Emiel Lamberts, eds.
History of the Low Countries
New York: Berghahn, 1999

Kennedy, James
A Concise History of the Netherlands
Cambridge, UK: Cambridge University Press, 2017

Jewish History
Baskin, Judith R., and Kenneth Seeskin, eds.
The Cambridge Guide to Jewish History, Religion, and Culture
Cambridge, UK: Cambridge University Press, 2010

Brenner, Michael
A Short History of the Jews
Translated by Jeremiah Riemer
Princeton, NJ: Princeton University Press, 2012

History of the Jews in the Netherlands before World War II
Blom, Johan Cornelis Hendrik, Renate G. Fuks-Mansfeld, and Ivo Schöffer, eds.
The History of the Jews in the Netherlands
Translated by Arnold Pomerans and Erica Pomerans
Oxford: Littmann Library of Jewish Civilization, 2002

Brasz, Chaya, and Yosef Kaplan
Dutch Jews as Perceived by Themselves and Others: Proceedings of the Eighth International Symposium on the History of the Jews in the Netherlands
Leiden: Brill, 2001

Israel, Jonathan, and Reinier Salverda, eds.
Dutch Jewry: Its History and Secular Culture (1500–2000)
Leiden: Brill, 2000

Antisemitism and Fascism
Laqueur, Walter
The Changing Face of Anti-Semitism: From Ancient Times to the Present Day
Oxford: Oxford University Press, 2008

Nirenberg, David
Anti-Judaism: The Western Tradition
New York: Norton, 2014

Snyder, Timothy
On Tyranny: Twenty Lessons from the Twentieth Century
New York: Tim Duggan, 2017

Wyman, David
The Abandonment of the Jews: America and the Holocaust
New York: Pantheon, 1984

Expulsion of the Jews and the Refugee Crisis
Dwork, Debórah, and Robert Jan van Pelt
Flight from the Reich: Refugee Jews, 1933–1946
New York: Norton, 2008

Moore, Bob
*Refugees from Nazi Germany
in the Netherlands, 1933–1940*
Dordrecht: Martinus Nijhoff, 1986

The Third Reich
Burleigh, Michael
The Third Reich: A New History
New York: Hill and Wang, 2001

Evans, Richard J.
The Third Reich in Power, 1933–1939
New York: Penguin, 2005

Mazower, Mark
Hitler's Empire: How the Nazis Ruled Europe
New York: Penguin, 2008

Shirer, William L.
The Rise and Fall of the Third Reich
New York: Simon & Schuster, 1960

The Holocaust
Cesarani, David
Final Solution: The Fate of the Jews, 1933–1949
New York: St. Martin's, 2016

Dawidowicz, Lucy
The War against the Jews: 1933–1945
New York: Bantam, 1986

Dwork, Debórah, and Robert Jan van Pelt
Holocaust: A History
New York: Norton, 2002

Rozett, Robert, and Shmuel Spector, eds.,
in association with Yad Vashem
"The Netherlands"
Encyclopedia of the Holocaust
Jerusalem: Jerusalem Publishing House, 2000

Snyder, Timothy
*Black Earth: The Holocaust as
History and Warning*
New York: Tim Duggan, 2016

The Holocaust in the Netherlands
Aalders, Gerard
*Nazi Looting: The Plunder of Dutch Jewry
during the Second World War*
Oxford: Berg, 2004

De Jong, Louis
Holland Fights the Nazis
London: Lindsay Drummond, 1941

De Jong, Louis, and Joseph W. F. Soppelman
*The Lion Rampant: The Story of Holland's
Resistance to the Nazis*
New York: Querido, 1943

Moore, Bob
*Victims and Survivors: The Nazi Persecution of the Jews
in the Netherlands, 1940–1945*
London: Arnold, 1997

Presser, Jacob
The Destruction of the Dutch Jews
Translated by Arnold Pomerans
New York: Dutton, 1969
BRITISH EDITION
Ashes in the Wind: The Destruction of Dutch Jewry
London: Souvenir Press, 1968

World War II
Beevor, Antony
The Second World War
London: Weidenfeld & Nicolson, 2012

Evans, Richard
*The Third Reich at War: How the Nazis Led Germany
from Conquest to Disaster*
London: Allen Lane, 2008

Goodwin, Doris Kearns
*No Ordinary Time: Franklin and Eleanor Roosevelt:
The Home Front in World War II*
New York: Simon & Schuster, 1995

World War II in the Netherlands
Amersfoort, Herman, and Piet Kamphuis, eds.
May 1940: The Battle for the Netherlands
Leiden: Brill, 2010

Badsey, Stephen
Arnhem 1944: Operation 'Market Garden'
Westport, CT: Praeger, 2004

De Jong, Louis
The Netherlands and Nazi Germany
Cambridge, MA: Harvard University Press, 1990

Hirschfeld, Gerhard
*Nazi Rule and Dutch Collaboration: The Netherlands
under German Occupation, 1940–1945*
Oxford: Berg, 1988

Van der Zee, Henri A.
The Hunger Winter: Occupied Holland, 1944–1945
Lincoln: University of Nebraska Press, 1998

Warmbrunn, Werner
The Dutch under German Occupation, 1940–1945
Stanford, CA: Stanford University Press, 1963

World War II in Poland
Kochanski, Halik
*The Eagle Unbowed: Poland and the Poles in the
Second World War*
Cambridge, MA: Harvard University Press, 2014

Concentration Camps

Aly, Götz, and Susanne Heim
Architects of Annihilation: Auschwitz and the
Logic of Destruction
Translated by Allan Blunden
London: Weidenfeld & Nicolson, 2002

Arad, Yitzhak
Belzec, Sobibor, Treblinka: The Operation Reinhard Death Camps
Bloomington: Indiana University Press, 1987

Blatman, Daniel
The Death Marches
Translated by Chaya Galai
Cambridge, MA: Harvard University Press, 2011

Boas, Jacob
Boulevard des Misères: The Story of Transit Camp Westerbork
Hamden, CT: Archon, 1985

De Jong, Louis
"The Netherlands and Auschwitz"
Yad Vashem Studies 7 (1968)

Dwork, Debórah, and Robert Jan van Pelt
Auschwitz: 1270 to the Present
New York: Norton, 1996

Richard Rashke
Escape from Sobibor
Boston: Houghton Mifflin, 1982

Schelvis, Jules
Sobibor: A History of a Nazi Death Camp
London: Bloomsbury Academic, 2014

Van Pelt, Robert Jan, Luis Ferreiro, and
Miriam Greenbaum, eds.
Auschwitz: Not Long Ago. Not Far Away.
New York: Abbeville, 2019

Wachsman, Nikolaus
KL: A History of the German Concentration Camps
New York: Farrar, Straus, and Giroux, 2015

Rescuers

Block, Gay, and Malka Drucker
Rescuers: Portraits of Moral Courage in the Holocaust
New York: Holmes & Meier, 1992

Flim, Bert-Jan
Saving the Children: History of the Organized Effort
to Rescue Jewish Children in the Netherlands, 1942–1945
Bethesda, MD: CDL, 2004

Paldiel, Mordecai
"The Netherlands"
The Path of the Righteous: Gentile Rescuers of Jews
during the Holocaust
Hoboken, NJ: KTAV, 1993

Wolf, Diane L.
Beyond Anne Frank: Hidden Children and Postwar
Families in Holland
Berkeley: University of California Press, 2007

Diaries and Memoirs

Frank, Anne
The Diary of Anne Frank: The Critical Edition
Edited by David Barnouw and Gerrold van der Stroom
Translated by Arnold Pomerans
New York: Doubleday, 1989

Frankl, Viktor E.
Man's Search for Meaning
Boston: Beacon, 1959

Ginz, Petr
The Diary of Petr Ginz, 1941–1942
Edited by Chava Pressburger
Translated by Elena Lappin
New York: Atlantic Monthly Press, 2004

Herzberg, Abel J.
Between Two Streams: A Diary from Bergen-Belsen
Translated by Jack Santcross
London: I. B. Tauris, 1997

Hillesum, Etty
Etty: The Letters and Diaries of Etty Hillesum, 1941–1943
Edited by Klaas A. D. Smelik
Translated by Arnold Pomerans
Grand Rapids, MI: William B. Eerdmans, 2002

Koker, David
At the Edge of the Abyss:
A Concentration Camp Diary, 1943–1944
Edited by Robert Jan van Pelt
Translated by Michiel Horn and John Irons
Evanston, IL: Northwestern University Press, 2012

Szpilman, Wladyslaw
The Pianist: The Extraordinary True Story
of One Man's Survival in Warsaw, 1939–1945
Translated by Anthea Bell
New York: Picador, 2000

Wiesel, Elie
Night
New York: Hill and Wang, 1960

Art from the Holocaust

Moreh-Rosenberg, Eliad, and Walter Smerling, eds.
Art from the Holocaust: 100 Works from the
Yad Vashem Collection
Cologne: Wienand Verlag GmbH, 2016

Salomon, Charlotte
Charlotte: Life or Theater?
New York: Viking, 1981

Volavkova, Hana, ed.
*I Never Saw Another Butterfly: Children's Drawings and Poems
from the Terezin Concentration Camp, 1942–1944*
New York: McGraw-Hill, 1964

Aftermath
Dwork, Déborah, and Robert Jan van Pelt
"German Persecution and Dutch Accommodation:
The Evolution of the Dutch National Consciousness
of the Judeocide"
The World Reacts to the Holocaust
Edited by David Wyman
Baltimore, MD: Johns Hopkins University Press, 1996

Hondius, Dienke
Return: Holocaust Survivors and Dutch Anti-Semitism
Westport, CT: Praeger, 2003

Lagrou, Pieter
*The Legacy of Nazi Occupation: Patriotic Memory
and National Recovery in Western Europe, 1945–1965*
Cambridge, UK: Cambridge University Press, 1999

Wyman, David S.
The World Reacts to the Holocaust
Baltimore, MD: Johns Hopkins University Press, 1996

Comparative Analysis of Mortality after the Holocaust
Blom, Johan Cornelis Hendrik
"The Persecution of the Jews in the Netherlands:
A Comparative Western European Perspective"
European History Quarterly 19 (1989)

Croes, Marnix
"The Holocaust in the Netherlands and the Rate
of Jewish Survival"
Holocaust and Genocide Studies 20, no. 3 (Winter 2006)

Griffioen, Pim, and Ron Zeller
"Anti-Jewish Policy and Organization of the
Deportations in France and the Netherlands, 1940–1944:
A Comparative Study"
Holocaust and Genocide Studies 20, no. 3 (Winter 2006)

Van Imhoff, Evert, Hanna van Solinge, and Bert-Jan Flim
"A Reconstruction of the Size and Composition of Jewish
Holocaust Survivors in the Netherlands, 1945"
Population Research and Policy Review 20 (2001)

Acknowledgments

My family exists because of those who saved them. With reverence and profound gratitude, I thank the Brillenburg Wurth, Dekkers, De Mars, Groeneveld, Heymann, Hos, Hunningher, Kuipers, Lafontaine, Leepel-Labotz, Miedema, Mierlo-Staring, Post, Van Dalen, Van der Leer, Van Gelder, Van Kampen, Van Vliet, Willemse, Wolf, Wouters-van der Lely, and Zoon families. Defying a horrific regime, these heroes offered hope and a means of survival—often to strangers. With deep respect, I also thank the resistance workers who helped hide and care for my family, but whose names I do not know.

The narrators of this book—Chaim and Fifi de Zoete, Erwin Geismar, Mirjam and David Geismar, Judith and Nathan Cohen, and Hadassah and Zigi Mandel—had the tenacity to resist, the strength and curiosity to move on, and the bravery to share their most personal and painful memories. For their stories and examples, I am filled with gratitude and admiration.

Nothing is possible without an idea. On the day that our families first met at the Breeplein Church in Rotterdam, where Kiene Brillenburg Wurth's grandparents hid mine, she said, "We should make a book." From that moment, my cousin Sharon Cohen-Strauss, my sister Warda Geismar, and I began to assemble our families' narratives, and the four of us (including Kiene) soon convened in New Haven to outline the project and create a plan. Sharon later proposed breaking up each person's larger story into fragments, "like a kaleidoscope," a suggestion that shaped the structure of *Invisible Years*. I am grateful to both Kiene and Sharon for the inspiration.

The words in this book would never have crystallized without the dedication and brilliance of four impressive women—Marjolijn de Jager, Jenny Magee, Kristin Swan, and Rani Arbo. Marjolijn translated some of the Dutch texts into English, beginning with my grandfather Chaim's seventy-page philosophical and theoretical letter, which many translators had turned down because of its complexity. Thanks to her incredible skill, Marjolijn's translation is true to Chaim's voice and makes his worthy ideas accessible to all. Although most of Chaim's letter is not included in this book, it was a critical source.

For a project as complex as this one, I would have been lost without the herculean efforts of Jenny Magee and Kristin Swan. Jenny researched and drafted the history briefs, locating the most reliable sources in a sea of conflicting dates and information and framing each brief as a short, engaging story. She next took on the developmental editing, reshaping and strengthening the narrative flow with remarkable sensitivity. Our regular meetings to deliberate the structure of the manuscript, for which there was no precedent, were a delightful and fulfilling creative collaboration. After a year, Jenny passed the baton to Kristin Swan, a highly skilled and meticulous editor who brought clarity to countless quandaries—editorial and beyond. I am indebted to Kristin for her tremendous commitment and indefatigable support. Her passionate devotion to this book and her acute awareness of its timeliness are greatly appreciated. I am so very lucky to have had not one, but two editors who truly understood this book's message and presentation.

The gifted musician and storyteller Rani Arbo helped shape the final version of my introduction. Heartfelt thanks to Rani for helping me speak with clarity.

I would particularly like to thank Robert Jan van Pelt for sharing his expertise on the German occupation of the Netherlands. In an extraordinary act of generosity, Robert Jan made contributions to this book that went far beyond my initial request to write a foreword, both reframing the chapter introductions and refining the history briefs. Robert Jan labored tirelessly and expeditiously to sharpen the historical framework for my family's story, and his thoughtful scholarship made this book considerably better.

I am especially indebted to my advisory board—Robert Bjornson, Brenda Danilowitz, Julie Fraenkel, Warda Geismar, Joelle Hoverson, Sara Jamshidi, Stephen Naron, Jae Rossman, and Jens Stenger—who believed in the project so fiercely and met regularly during the three-year period in which this book was developed. Their varied expertise, insights, and suggestions helped to make the book a reality. In addition to sharing sound advice during planning meetings, these individuals wrote letters on behalf of the project, made essential introductions, read and provided feedback on various drafts of the manuscript, took on production tasks, transcribed, translated, and researched.

I must also express my appreciation to fellow members of Girls Group, women working in independent creative occupations who meet monthly to share ideas and provide support: Warda Geismar, Joelle Hoverson, Janis Melone, and Denyse Schmidt. Their aesthetics are inspiring, their friendship and counsel a lifeline.

Thanks go to a number of gifted friends and colleagues who offered their expertise. Laura McPhee has been a champion of this book from the beginning, reading the manuscript, writing in support of the project, and introducing me to my agent. Laura told me, "Don't rush, savor the process"—a suggestion that I followed, perhaps to excess. Kenan Aktülün worked tirelessly to build the first *Invisible Years* website, with astute advice and guidance from Joelle Hoverson. Anne Sommer provided a final proofread with skill and efficiency, making valuable corrections before the book went to the printer. Jessica Holahan shared marketing wisdom, brainstormed ideas, and made helpful introductions. Julie Vance provided indispensable presentation direction. Nicola von Velsen gave early advice on how to get a book into the world.

My gratitude is also due to the following group of people for their generous assistance. Mordecai Paldiel, the former director of the Righteous Among the Nations Department at Yad Vashem, sent me the thirteen detailed reports that my grandfather Chaim wrote and submitted to Yad Vashem in honor of those who helped. I then had the privilege of meeting with Mordecai and was moved by his enthusiastic response. Thanks go to Helen Kauder, Patricia Klindienst, Donald Margulies, Mark Oppenheimer, and Michael Sittenfeld for offering ideas and thoughtful feedback; Jeanne Markel, Kathy Rosenbloom, and Chris and Esther Pullman for their excitement and for engaging their communities on behalf of *Invisible Years*; and Jo Ellen Ackerman and Lucinda Hitchcock for critiquing the design and making critical suggestions that made the book clearer and more approachable.

My mother Mirjam's last interview was conducted with great sensitivity by Marco Werman, the host of Public Radio International's *The World*, in 2015. It touched and informed many; I am so appreciative that this interview exists.

I could not have made this book if I hadn't learned from the very best. These design teachers provided concentrated direction and taught me how to see: Lawrence Bach, Dorothea and Armin Hoffman, Warren Lehrer, and especially the great Paul Rand. Alvin Eisenman, head of the graphic design program at the Yale School of Art from 1951 to 1990, perceptively suggested that I write my thesis on *Direction*, a magazine published from 1937 to 1945 as a vehicle for artists and writers to speak out against fascism and social injustice. My research on *Direction* was a catalyst for, and a bookend to, *Invisible Years*. The publication managers, editors, and production managers I work with in the museum publishing community have set a standard of excellence that informs the structure, text, and manufacture of *Invisible Years*. A special thank you to Mary Mayer, who awarded me my first book project and has been an ardent supporter ever since.

A number of colleagues contributed to the success of this project through their exceptional work. Dianne Woo's thorough proofreading was extremely valuable. High-quality photography by Christopher Gardner was critical in achieving exceptional reproductions. I am also thankful to Chris for making time for additional shots as new material was found, and for teaching me how to silhouette. The typeface designer Michael Abbink generously sent me the complete family of Kievit, which he named in homage to his Dutch heritage, suggesting that perhaps one day I might make use of it. Legible, quiet, and contemporary, Kievit fills the pages of this book. I particularly would like to thank the team at Conti Tipocolor for their dedicated efforts to bring this book to fruition with expert pre-press and printing skills—Roberto Conti, Laura Cuccoli, Alfredo Zanellato, and especially Marta Conti, who asked all the right questions and managed the project with sensitivity and professionalism.

Many people in the Netherlands shared their time, documents, and memories with me as I researched the book. Kiene Brillenburg Wurth kindly took us to her father Gert Brillenburg Wurth's house so we could borrow photographs of his parents, Gerrit and Gerda. Gert was a gracious host who enthusiastically recounted his recollections of our shared history. Anja Matser and

Henk den Haan teach schoolchildren and give talks and tours about the two families who were hidden in the Breeplein Church. I am grateful to them for their dedication and for welcoming my family, colleagues, and me when we visited. Thank you to Anja and Jaap van Gelderen for documenting the church's history. At the historical society in Gendt, Yvonne de Boer-Ravestein, Henk Klaasen, and Geert Visser provided a crucial photograph of Theo van Dalen and took us on an exuberant tour of Gendt. Jan Oonk shared his research on the Van Dalen and Cohen families. The Mierlo-Staring family, Zwi Goldberg, Barbara Stodel, and Peter van Zuilekom provided photographs and information. My conversations with Dieter Heymann were particularly special because he knew my grandfather Erwin; I am grateful to Dieter for all that I learned from him about my grandfather and about Dieter's mother, Erika, and also for sharing his photographs of Erika the courageous "tigress."

I am thankful for Hans (Chanan) Flörsheim's memoir, which describes the day my grandfather Erwin was taken by the Sicherheitsdienst, or SD (Security Service). Part of that passage is included in this book, adding crucial details to Erwin's narrative.

I would like to express my appreciation for three invaluable interviews that provided some of the source material for this book. Diane L. Wolf at the University of California, Davis, interviewed both of my parents, Mirjam and David Geismar. Mirjam also sat for an interview with the Survivors of the Shoah Visual History Foundation. And both gave interviews to the Fortunoff Video Archive for Holocaust Testimonies at Yale University in New Haven. Stephen Naron, the current director of the Fortunoff Video Archive, served on the advisory board for this book and has been a generous advocate in myriad ways, including making the introduction to Robert Jan van Pelt. My heartfelt thanks go to Stephen for his ongoing assistance and enthusiasm.

When my agent, Anne Edelstein, and later my publisher, David Godine, first learned about this unconventional book, both wanted to be involved without hesitation. Anne provided steadfast encouragement, offered wise advice on sculpting the manuscript, and guided the process with warmth and patience. I am grateful for her untiring efforts. David immediately understood both the significance of the narrative and the importance of the design to the book's content, and he recognized the value of high-quality production. I am honored that *Invisible Years* found a home on David R. Godine's fiftieth-anniversary list. Both Anne and David not only believed in the project but took risks for it that others would not. For this, I am deeply indebted.

At David R. Godine, Publisher, I would like to thank David Allender, managing director, for his dedication to making *Invisible Years* a success, and for his steadiness; Joshua Bodwell, managing editor, for his interest and excitement; and Ally Findley, editor and proofreader, for her able assistance. I thank Sue Berger Ramin for her efforts during her time at Godine. Publicist Lissa Warren, in collaboration with the team at Godine, offered invaluable advice and a smart approach to publicizing this book.

I would like to thank the Memorial Foundation for Jewish Culture for its generous support of this project and for its commitment to Jewish culture.

I treasure the bonds with family members strengthened through our close collaboration on this project.

My cousin Sharon worked on *Invisible Years* in multiple ways—researching, assembling, interviewing, and joining me in the Netherlands to pick up material and visit hiding addresses. Along with my appreciation for the many tasks Sharon assumed, I am grateful that she never doubted that this book would be made. Sharon's belief, encouragement, and friendship kept me going.

To Sharon's husband, Noam Strauss, who translated documents from Hebrew to English, thank you for challenging me by offering a different perspective on Israeli civics.

My cousin Hadassah Cohen-Lulav, expert on the elaborate Cohen family tree, repeatedly clarified relationships for me. I am thankful to Hadassah for introducing me to the poem "Could Have," by Wislawa Szymborska, about the role luck plays in survival, for always being the voice of reason, for cutting to the point when clarity was needed, and for the *Mission Impossible* theme music.

Chaja Polak, my first cousin once removed, writer, artist, friend, and role model, gave me the good advice that I had no choice but to devote myself to this book until it was finished and came to life. My most sincere thanks to Chaja for this. She also shared with me the important account of her experiences that appears in the pages of this book and connected me with distant relatives. I am particularly grateful to Chaja for tirelessly writing and speaking out about the painful truths of the Holocaust.

My aunt Judith, together with my mother and my uncle Zigi, generously contributed funds that made it possible to have Chaim's seventy-page letter professionally translated. Judith also provided extensive transcription and translation work; this book could not have been realized without a reliable Dutch-to-English translator always on call. I am inexpressibly grateful to her for answering my countless questions, for selflessly sharing the truth, for trusting me, and for believing in this project.

I am thankful to my sister Warda for offering help and at the same time letting me run with our shared family history to make this book my way. She has supported this project through extensive work on the archive. I am lucky to have a sister who is also a dear friend, who offers encouragement and advice and brings me tomato soup when I need it most.

I will remain forever grateful to Laurie Jarcho, Linda Bamfo-Adu, and Beatrice Agyemang Badu, who have taken such good care of our mother, Mirjam, for years. Doing a hard job and making it look effortless made it possible for me to focus on making this book. Their love, commitment, and generosity are a gift.

I am indebted to my parents, Mirjam and David, for their love, perseverance, and principles. Their drive to move forward and sense of personal responsibility offered my siblings and me a safe and secure life with opportunities they did not have. After enduring the horrific deaths of family members and friends, lost childhoods, and abandoned educations, my parents chose kindness, community service, and respect for all people.

In the process of making this book, I got to know my grandparents. I am inspired by their humanity, intellect, spirituality, and appreciation for beauty.

There are no words for the countless thanks that I owe to my husband, Robert Bjornson. Rob traveled with me from the beginning to visit the Breeplein Church, in the middle to conduct research in the Netherlands and Israel, and at the end to print this book in Italy. He translated my grandfather Erwin's memoir from German to English, patiently decoding the handwriting. He also tackled other German texts, including philosophical quotes in Chaim's letter and a variety of official documents. Rob is the one who discovered Erika Heymann, the woman who hid Erwin. Rob read and commented on the manuscript, the publishing contract, the marketing copy, and the legions of (often delicate) emails written to advance this project. He listened, advised, reassured, and talked through every detail of the manuscript and design and numerous logistical decisions and concerns. For years, he carried far more than his share of our partnership. Rob turned on the lights when I worked into the night and forgot to. He cooked. He cared for me. He waited. Thank you for being so incredibly supportive, for being my moral compass and my best friend. As we always say, everyone should have a Rob.

My daughter, Ana Geismar, was a teenager when this project started and a young woman at its completion. The advice I gave her, she now gives me. These are Ana's words of thanks that I now give back to her: "Thank you for always being there for me and loving me unconditionally. I would not be where I am today without all the love, laughter, and slight nudges in the right direction." Ana makes even the hardest days joyful. She keeps me going.

Finally, I would like to thank the readers of this book with these words from Elie Wiesel:

Anyone who listens to a witness becomes a witness, so those who hear us, those who read us, those who learn something from us, they will continue to bear witness for us. Until now, they're doing it with us. At a certain point in time, they will do it for all of us.

The witnesses in my family are my teachers and my inspiration. May they be yours, too.

DAPHNE GEISMAR

Elie Wiesel, video clip by Ainara Tiefenthäler, "Elie Wiesel Dies at 87," *The New York Times*, July 3, 2016.

Copyright

© 2020 by Daphne Geismar

The preparation and publication of this volume was supported by a grant from the Memorial Foundation for Jewish Culture.

Library of Congress Cataloging-in-Publication Data

Geismar, Daphne, 1961– author

Invisible Years: A Family's Collected Account of Separation and Survival during the Holocaust in the Netherlands

1st edition | Boston, Massachusetts: David R. Godine, 2020
Includes bibliographical references

LCCN 2019019477
ISBN 978-1-56792-659-0

Hardcover with illustrations throughout: alkaline paper

Jews—Netherlands—Biography | Geismar family | De Zoete family | Cohen family | Mandel family | Holocaust survivors—Netherlands—Biography | Holocaust, Jewish (1939–1945)—Netherlands | Netherlands—History—German occupation, 1940–1945

LCC DS135.N6 A1384 2020
DDC 940.53/180922492—DC23

LC record available at:
https://lccn.loc.gov/2019019477

Cover
Fifi & Chaim de Zoete with their daughters, Judith, Mirjam, and Hadassah, February 4, 1934

Back
Judith's book and Jewish Star, 1942

Endpapers
Paper liner from Mirjam's Holocaust drawer, the bottom drawer of a secretary desk that belonged to Erwin and Grete Geismar

Page 1
Erwin Geismar's memoir, page 1, July 21, 1943

Narrators: pages 6–15
Fifi & Chaim de Zoete with their daughters, Judith, Mirjam, and Hadassah, February 4, 1934

Hadassah, Mirjam, and Judith de Zoete, ca. 1939

Nathan Cohen, ca. late 1930s

David Geismar with his grandfather Max, May 28, 1939

Erwin Geismar with his wife, Grete, ca. 1930

Pages 190–91
Guests at the wedding of Hans Polak and Annetje Kupferschmidt-Polak, film still, November 15, 1939

This page
Front cover of Fifi's diary, June 20, 1945–1963

Design, typesetting, and production management
Daphne Geismar

Developmental editing
Jennifer Magee

Copyediting
Kristin Swan

Proofreading
Ally Findley
Anne Sommer
Dianne Woo

Photography
Christopher Gardner

Printing
Conti Tipocolor

Typeface
Kievit: a contemporary, humanistic face inspired by the classics, designed by Michael Abbink and Paul van der Laan

Image credits
Pages 110–11: Map originally published by the Edinburgh Geographical Institute, John Bartholomew & Son

Page 115: Courtesy of the Brillenburg Wurth family

Page 149: Courtesy of Henk Klaassen, Historische Kring Gente

Page 169: Courtesy of Dieter Heymann

Pages 190–91: Courtesy of Chaja Polak, and Ellen and Frank van Beenen

All other images are from the De Zoete / Cohen / Geismar family archive.

David R. Godine, Publisher
Fifteen Court Square, Suite 320
Boston, MA 02108-2536

1970 | 50 YEARS | 2020